D0433568

The Verdict

To Jim
Best wishes

Polly Toynbee

Also by Polly Toynbee and David Walker

Did Things Get Better?: An Audit of
Labour's Success and Failures (2001)

Better or Worse?: Has Labour Delivered? (2005)

Unjust Rewards: Ending the Greed
that is Bankrupting Britain (2008)

The Verdict

Did Labour Change Britain?

POLLY TOYNBEE AND
DAVID WALKER

GRANTA

Granta Publications, 12 Addison Avenue, London W11 4QR
First published in Great Britain by Granta Books, 2010

A CIP catalogue record for this book
is available from the British Library.

1 3 5 7 9 10 8 6 4 2

ISBN 978 1 84708 148 3

Printed and bound in Great Britain by
MPG Books Ltd, Bodmin, Cornwall

Contents

Part Three: Justice

Part Four: Home and Abroad

Introduction

A sudden quiet fell among the 2500 people rallying for Citizens UK at Central Hall, Westminster at the end of the 2010 election campaign. Fourteen-year-old Tia Sanchez stepped up to the lectern to tell Gordon Brown about her family's struggle to survive on the minimum wage. She talked of the difference a 'living wage' paying £2 more an hour would make to their lives: the English classes it would pay for, so her family could talk to her teachers, and not having to subsist on lentils by the end of each week. She broke down in tears thinking of her mother's working life: 'She could afford the Tube and I would see her for three hours more every day.' That her mother and grandmother were employed by the private firm contracted to clean the Chancellor of the Exchequer's own office in the Treasury was an irony not lost on the audience. Gordon Brown, who had occupied that office for a decade, responded with his best speech of a feeble campaign. With great passion he denounced poverty and injustice in biblical terms.

The moment illuminated Labour's love affair with outsourcing and 'flexibility', and their ambiguities over migration. The Sanchez family were Portuguese, EU citizens working in the UK. The episode also demonstrated Labour's resilience. The family's plight was why the Labour Party came into existence and this reminder of the persistence of social injustice showed their scope for renewal, even as electoral defeat loomed. It proved something else: politics matters. Laws, taxation and spending shape lives and livelihoods. Market forces can be malign and state action does improve things. Labour had already helped the Sanchez family by introducing the minimum wage; it was not enough, which was why the living-wage campaign got going. So the instance illustrates a theme of our book: to govern is inevitably to disappoint.

The 2010 campaign had no song, perhaps because Labour had few reasons to be cheerful. In the past, pollsters and brand directors had sifted through stacks of titles to find one with the right vibe. Though lacklustre, Labour's 2005 campaign echoed to U2's 'Beautiful Day'. The sound of 2001 had been 'Lifted' by Lighthouse Family and the euphoric hopes of 1997 soared with 'Things Can Only Get Better' by D:Ream.

D:Ream's keyboard player, Brian Cox, was a PhD student who, leaving music behind, became professor of physics at the University of Manchester. His life course, heralding Labour in 1997 through to his academic success, depended on the expansion of higher education and sustained extra spending on science during Labour's term. Professor Cox was now a television star presenting a BBC science programme, which Labour's generosity over licence-fee increases had helped make possible. Yet come 2010 he was not happy. Funding for big science was still not enough, Cox said, blaming Labour; he told the anti-Labour *Sunday Times* he would protest by voting Liberal Democrat.

Cox's complaint is government's permanent problem. There never can be enough, even when spending is rapidly rising. For most of us, most of the time, there is no 'bigger picture' beyond our particular concerns. Because expectations in 1997 were sky-high the Labour government was bound to fall short. Even so, where was the story it might have told Cox in rebuttal? Labour consistently failed at narrative, rarely weaving together what ministers were doing into a coherent account of their policies, strategy and limits.

Conventional wisdom despises the compromises of politics. But short of surrendering to authoritarians or technocrats, messiness is unavoidable. Politicians have to reconcile incompatible interests – such as the curiosity of particle physicists against nursery teachers. The hubbub and preening of the House of Commons eventually produce policy, and can make things better. John Dunn, the Cambridge political theorist, makes a general point about democracy but his conclusion also serves as Labour's epitaph: 'Government is neither aesthetically exhilarating nor spiritually inspiring; but it may nevertheless contribute immensely to enhancing human life.'

In May 1997 bright, enthusiastic MPs and ardent advisers took office intending to make a difference to the lives of their fellow citizens, especially those lacking money and opportunity. In this book, we assess whether they did, taking evidence from reports, statistics and evaluations – of which Labour commissioned a multitude. Our sources are noted at www.grantabooks.com/verdict. We also asked people. We collected their tales of the era: at a Brighton Jobcentre Plus, in the heart of Manchester's clubbing scene, in an eco-house in Woking and at a brand-new college in Middlesbrough. Some credited change to Labour, others failed to see a connection between distant Westminster and their here and now.

An Aston company director blamed Labour for disparaging manufacturing, yet welcomed Labour's attempts to rebuild his surrounding community in Birmingham. The 'embedded' police officer at Wright Robinson School in Gorton was sure her presence made a difference, but linked it to no political initiative or 'tough on crime' rhetoric. Lieutenant Pete Quentin, a reservist off to Afghanistan, knew very well his mission resulted from a grave government decision and it was one he – a Tory – heartily supported. In Braintree, Tracy Lindsell knew exactly which policies caused the Carousel children's centre to spring to life. But Andy Birk in his Rotherham butcher's shop blamed Labour directly and bitterly for decisions on local planning and car parks, which allowed Tesco to drain business from a dying town centre. And the fractious complaints of the Hatts of Sydenham were echoed in the newspapers, and Labour had to decide whether to listen or reject them.

Such snapshots remind us of the varied ways we attribute

praise and blame to the temporary holders of political power. Many are impervious to government. Historians such as David Kynaston, looking through diaries and other accounts of ordinary lives, find that even in such dramatic decades as the 1940s acquaintance with public affairs and political events was glancing, often slight or absent altogether. Ipsos MORI has a sobering graph that runs from 1988 that shows scarcely any change in our sense of well-being despite changes in ministers, parties and swings in collective fortune. Seventy per cent of people have always declared themselves content with their standard of living and 20 per cent – mainly the poorest – are permanently unhappy; the rest do not know. During the boom a few more registered satisfaction, a few less in recession; but the national state of mind has been remarkably stable. Politics, it seems, is weather. Like a sunny spell, it happens. In May 2010 a full third of registered voters did not put their cross on a ballot paper; add in the unregistered and it seems that a large fraction of British people are political bystanders.

Political passivity does not imply contentment; it may have to do with deprivation and inequality. Labour might have said: a fifth of people are unhappy because they are poor; more people would take part if they were better off. Published towards the end of Labour's time, *The Spirit Level* by Richard Wilkinson and Kate Pickett brought together international evidence to show that where wealth is distributed more equally not only are the poorest happier, but even the richest feel better. Here might have been a governing proposition.

But Labour were not entirely sure what they believed or, just as debilitating, whether what they believed was politically acceptable. Defeat in 1979 had left party heavyweights exhausted. In the 1980s Labourites fell into the trap of treating temporary political conditions as a permanent shift in sensibility, which the Tories exploited thanks to the strength of Margaret Thatcher's self-belief. By 1997 an over-anxious reading of opinion data led New Labour to fear that Thatcherism had entered the English soul. (Scotland, Wales and Northern Ireland were impervious.) In the 1990s Labour adopted a view of the world heavily influenced

Introduction

by Bill Clinton's political success in the US, even when it was contingent and peculiar to America. Labour's thinkers, Brown, Balls and Blairites such as Alan Milburn and Patricia Hewitt, capitulated. It is remarkable, in retrospect, how far the Labour government was in thrall to the zeitgeist of the mid-1990s. Labour politicians surrendered to the idea of unstoppable market forces and lopped off Labour's sense of political possibility. Their message was bleak: nothing can be done except within what global markets ordain.

Sometimes fatalism is appropriate. Labour were never going to transcend technology, culture, trade and social dynamics. Ageing, the growth in single-person households and the decline in the number of people in age groups prone to crime: such trends were beyond anything a transient Home Secretary could affect. The internet, mobile phones, pharmaceuticals, miniaturization, bio- and nano-technologies had their own worldwide momentum even if they also depended on government spending on research. Time and again in the chapters ahead, we are left wondering how much ministers understood of the country they governed and of global politics. Over Iraq or the banking collapse we have since become aware of the gaps in their knowledge, but how much did they think about the effectiveness of all the extra spending on health or consider the reliability of polling data on, say, attitudes towards tax? The former Downing Street insider Geoff Mulgan said governments underestimate what they can do in the long run and overestimate what they can do in the short run. Perhaps Labour ministers' trademark hyperbole stemmed from some unarticulated acknowledgement that their power was circumscribed: the less they felt they could do, the more they promised; but the more they promised, the more they risked disappointing. Blair and Brown were forever promising the greatest, the best, the first, the finest, 'a golden age', 'world-class' and 'world-beating' – certainly world-class braggadocio when modesty might have reaped more gratitude in the end.

Labour's first term was their most productive. It realized the minimum wage promised a century before by Keir Hardie and the commitment of former leader John Smith to devolve power within the UK. The Human Rights Act might have inaugurated a new pact between citizen and state. The windfall tax on excess profits to pay for the New Deal was a brilliant example of pragmatism or mild socialism, take your pick. With tax credits for pensioners and low-income families, the push on attainment in primary schools, the start of Sure Start for the under-fives, Labour appeared – were – a competent, moderately progressive government. But this was as good as it got. Even then, Labour were curiously unsure and hesitant, trimming their sails to every passing wind.

Still we had hopes. In *Did Things Get Better?* we argued that 'A second term would need new clarity of message. Without a far bolder stand on where the boundary between public good and private possession is to be placed, those great promises to abolish child poverty or make health and education the best and transport tolerable are likely to stay just that – promises.' In conversation Tony Blair liked to point out to us that Margaret Thatcher only invented Thatcherism in her second term. By implication Blairism would soon sharpen its ambiguous outlines. So it did, but not in ways that made Labour any more coherent. Our assessment of Labour in 2005 was overshadowed by Iraq. At home the second term was preoccupied by 'reform' and Labour's often manic efforts to outsource public services; what a waste of time and effort, viewed from the era of cuts. The 2005 election took place at the high-water mark of the great boom. Public spending gushed, private debt spiralled, house prices skyrocketed. With 'fewer children and pensioners living in dire hardship', we wrote in *Better or Worse?*, 'Blair's era was a better time to be British than for many decades'. That era came to a precipitate end as the crowds gathered outside Northern Rock in the autumn of 2007.

After the May 2010 election, Labour's leadership candidates all talked about listening more, as if defeat had put grommets in their ears. But not everyone has something to say. One of Labour's more irritating habits was to talk as if the populace writhed permanently in a state of civic excitation, ever eager to participate.

Introduction

Martin Pugh argues Labour have always had strong conservative elements in their make-up, reflecting a working-class culture that was patriotic, critical of social innovation, and often reactionary (*Speak for Britain: A New History of the Labour Party*, 2010). This strain showed in Labour's approach to crime and civil liberties – and their lack of imagination in foreign and military affairs. Labour were also fiscally conservative. Traumatized by defeat in 1992, and transfixed by focus groups of marginal voters in marginal seats, they had come to fear anything that looked like a tax increase. In three manifestos they repeatedly pledged never to raise income tax. That, we can now see, was a profound error, setting up an imbalance between revenue and spending that will dog the second decade of the century. It was a political mistake, too. *British Social Attitudes* (BSA), a creditable survey run yearly from 1984, showed Thatcherism had never persuaded the majority. Many regretted our society's unfairness and said the state's duty was to redress injustice. By 1998, 81 per cent said the gap between high and low incomes was too great and 53 per cent wanted an increase in tax for the better-off.

Attitudes to tax were mixed and they were malleable. Respondents to polls backed off the word 'redistribute' but they insisted on fairness. Their enthusiasm for spending on public services was high – and to that Labour responded well. Asked about taxing in order to spend more, an impressive 61 per cent said they wanted 'increased taxes and more spending on health, education and social benefits', with health at the top. But in the surveys voters faced two ways: not many cleanly and clearly assented to Scandinavian taxes to pay for the Scandinavian levels of services they demanded. They did not necessarily go to the American extreme, either.

Here surely was a persuadable public. The results in May 2010 suggested core 'progressive' support at 49 per cent, assuming the Liberal Democrat vote could be split and reallocated, and counting in the Nationalists and Greens. The exact figures are not the issue: what the voting demonstrated was potential for progressive policy, even at Labour's lowest ebb. Stan Greenberg, the veteran US pollster, concluded after the 2010 election that

British people were essentially social democratic in outlook and attitudes, strongly in favour of more financial regulation, not less, more government involvement not more free markets and preferred tax increases over cuts in public services.

So why, at high tide in 1997, were Labour so fearful and ready to suspect the worst of the public? Perhaps they lacked faith in their own legitimacy. Though the party won a Commons majority of 179, a higher proportion of voters had opted for John Major in 1992 than for Tony Blair in 1997. Fewer than three-quarters bothered to go out and mark a ballot paper at all, the lowest turnout in sixty-two years. Nervous to the point of paranoia, Labour came to power unsure whether the people wanted progressive government. But enough did. And their numbers grew when the 2008–9 crash and recession made many more British people suspect the ideological marketeers with their right-wing, roll-back-the-state recipes. Cameron's failure to break through with a clear majority was proof that Labour's statism was nearer to what the public wanted. The Blairites were wrong to assume a majority were individualist, aspirational and immune from worries about security or equity.

An all-too-plausible reason for Labour's fearfulness was the bias of the national press. Try governing calmly, let alone progressively, amid its catcalls, bullying and daily bile. Europhobic, Thatcher-adoring, tax-allergic, crime-neurotic, welfare-mean, liberal-bating, moral-prurient, feminist-detesting, punishment-addicted, foreigner-reviling, multicultural-contemptuous, state-paranoid and generosity-averse: this was the tone set by the *Daily Mail* and the Murdoch press, including *The Times* and especially the *Sunday Times*. Broadcasters' agendas were set by the press and bloggers followed their lead, often making reasoned argument inaudible above the clamour.

Those stumbling blearily out of Downing Street after Labour's defeat said their greatest release would be from the ever-present screens of 24-hour news, turned on in every office. A glance at a prime minister's appointments diary shows the weight of business. Ministers need to switch instantly from the epic to the minute, from the monumental to the factional. The civil service machine often amplifies tensions. Any fair verdict needs to allow for the adversities of public office.

A politician's fate can be pitiable. They do not necessarily know, nor are they necessarily known. On the Kennington Road in south-east London, ten minutes by delivery bike from Downing Street, is a curry house called Ghandis; Labour ministers and their officials used to patronize it during crises and late-night work sessions. In its window alongside the list of khormas and aloos sit framed photos of famous customers. Among them Geoff Hoon. Passing the window you blink, trying to recall the name, let alone the great offices of state he once held. When he was outed in March 2010 by journalists pretending to recruit to a lucrative public affairs consultancy his desperation was plain: 'me, I know people', he said.

Yet, expenses scandal included, the era's crook count is remarkably low. Although Tony and Cherie fell in love with lucre, and ex-ministers started to think they were worth £3000 a day as lobbyists, the disappointment with performance we register here is mitigated by the fact that so many ministers and MPs were honourable and willingly sacrificed private life and privacy for a public task.

In *The Verdict* we do not discuss internal conflicts in the Cabinet or Labour Party, nor ministers' psychology. Other books examine the feuds and animosities. Most Labour MPs assented to the government's policies. As Blair and Brown led, they followed, so we look away from the Westminster charivari.

Our judgement comes from unearthing what Labour did, not always the same as what they said they were doing. We have looked at the numbers, the facts on the ground and especially the way people's lives changed as a result of policies. We have relied on National Audit Office (NAO) reports, data compiled by the Office of National Statistics (ONS), the Treasury's record of Public Service Agreements, House of Commons select committee reports, and evaluations by the Institute for Fiscal Studies (IFS), the Centre for Economic Performance at the London School of Economics, the Centre for Markets and Public Organization at the University of Bristol, and work by Professors John Hills of the LSE, Stephen

Machin of University College, Danny Dorling of Sheffield and Michael Parkinson of Liverpool Universities; we owe a debt of gratitude to Ipsos MORI and especially its chief executive Ben Page. Conscious of the evidence, our job is to marry what Labour said it wanted to what people experienced. Here is the evidence of what happened, of the successes and failures, of the raw material from which to draw lessons and warnings. Judgement often rests on what happened to the money. Labour turned away from a national discussion about the cost of improving public services. They failed to raise enough tax to cover their own pledges, which increased the structural debt. The government never quite trusted the fiscal maturity of the British people, never accepted they knew they would only get what they paid for. Instead Blair and Brown seemed to believe their own rhetoric. With 'No return to boom and bust' they governed as if this was not just the end of ideology, but the end of economic history too: perpetual, unbroken growth would keep the bubble inflated for ever.

The legacy, compounded by the state's bail-out of the financial sector, was a hole in the public finances that let in successors who actively wanted to cut government down. The coalition government had the pretext it wanted, as analysts warned that the entirety of Labour's increments in public spending would have to be rewound, as if the years since 1997 had been a dream. The cuts make it all the more necessary to audit what Labour did, the ambitions realized and the targets missed – if only to record what is now being deconstructed and diminished. Canvassers despair of that deadly doorstep shrug: they're all the same and anyway what did the government ever do for us? Governments are not all the same. That is not hard to prove. The more searching question we ask in this book is: did Labour do well enough?

The Hatts' verdict

Here is a snapshot of the politicians' problem. Should they persuade the people? Or is it their lot to decide which of them to ignore in pursuit of doing the right thing, trusting that enough others will approve? There is no such thing as an 'ordinary family' to judge Labour's years in power, so we picked at random. In a country defined by retailing we called Sainsbury's and from lists of median-grade staff they plucked Barbara Hatt, as unknown to corporate HQ as she was to us. Her only qualification was that she was 'ordinary' in her pay; in 2010 she earned £24,000 a year, about £2000 more than the median for women earners.

Outgoing and gregarious, Barbara welcomed us to her family home in a quiet cul-de-sac in Sydenham, South London, not far from the Lewisham branch of Sainsbury's where she was customer services manager. The Hatts had moved here, upgrading from a two-bed flat in Herne Hill, just as Labour arrived in office. They owned a caravan in Rye in East Sussex for holidays. Better or worse for her and hers, how had the last thirteen years treated them? With a cheerful demeanour she poured tea, the sun streaming in through French windows opening onto a small garden. The scene was surely set for an optimistic, upbeat view.

Husband Brian Hatt was a self-employed roofer whose income fluctuated. Though it sank in the recession he was doing well enough to push the joint Hatt household income above the median. He worked with his father and his 24-year-old son Christopher in a business founded in 1954, three generations of Hatts working together. Christopher still lived at home, as did their youngest, twenty-year-old Catherine. She worked locally, at a financial services call centre handling requests for loans. Another daughter, Emma, worked as an assistant at a private nursing home in Rye, and was expecting a baby.

During the decade Barbara had moved up from the shop floor, having started as a checkout assistant. 'I said to myself, I'm better than this, I need something else. I was going to leave but they put me on the customer service desk, and I really liked that, so I stayed.' Of her job as customer services manager she said, 'I love it. I like meeting people, dealing with incidents, sorting things out.' Theft is common, and she dealt with a dozen cases a week, sending out banning letters to people caught stealing. 'Sometimes, if it's a homeless man eating a pasty and not paying, like I had last week, I'll pay for it out of my own pocket and send him on his way. If it's someone taking a whole load of Taste the Difference meat, that's another story. They do get angry when I ban them.'

She and Brian both had jobs they loved. Their children were in work, they had a fine house that had grown steeply in value. The decade had been good to them and they were weathering the recession. They could have adorned a Labour election poster.

But no, instead there was itchy discontent about safety in the streets, migrants and public services, combined with dismay at theft from her store. 'The NHS is worse, definitely worse,' she said. 'I've had asthma all my life and four years ago I seized up. I couldn't breathe and I was in King's hospital for three weeks. If you ask me, the care's not there any more, not like it used to be.' This was King's College Hospital, not far away in Denmark Hill, one of only thirty-seven hospitals to score 'excellent' on the Care Quality Commission's indicators of quality of service and finance – which only showed how regulators' ticks were no guarantee of patient satisfaction. Or perhaps that some patients are never satisfied.

Barbara went on. 'When I came back to outpatients I saw a doctor — didn't know me from Adam — hadn't bothered to read my notes. She told me I had a diagnosis of emphysema and she didn't even know I'd just been in hospital for it.' It was a standard grumble: impersonality and lost notes. 'The medication is very expensive, costing me £28 a month. I don't understand why diabetics get it free, but emphysema doesn't.'

As she was speaking she reached for her cigarettes, 'Do you mind?' she asked. No, but here was modern government's headache. What can and should the state do about unreasonable behaviour – people smoking, despite their emphysema, and still expecting care? Barbara's words were a typical response to Labour's years in power – a better hospital, yet more complaints, more doctors, but care quality allegedly falling.

How had her children found their schools? 'Good, really good. I can't speak too highly, especially Cator Park School for girls.' In 2010 Cator Park was garlanded among the most improved schools in the country and the head invited to a Downing Street reception. 'Such chances and opportunities. My eldest went to Mexico for a month with the school, to look after orphans. She said it was the most life-changing experience she ever had. My youngest went to Russia, to stay with a Russian family and she says she'll never forget it, all her life.'

That sounds very positive, but Barbara felt unsafe in her area. 'I won't go out at night. I always fetched and carried the children every evening when they were teenagers, never let them out alone. I think crime has definitely got worse.' Have they actually been victims? 'No. But you don't feel safe because you never see the police out on the beat, not once. I don't think I've seen a community support officer ever round here.' Had there been any crime, any break-ins in their street of around eighty houses? 'No, none at all, not in all the years we've lived here.'

Here was Labour's crime problem – unease and fear, despite record numbers of police and a record drop in crime. However many police were hired, it was never going to be enough to override a nagging sense of insecurity.

The Hatts had a bleak outlook. 'This country's been dragged down. It's not a country I can be proud of any more. It's very hard for young people these days, trying to make it on their own. They need our help to get started, house prices as they are.' Here again, Barbara and Brian had done well in the long boom – but the rise in the price of their house made house purchase too expensive for their own children. 'My Emma is on the housing list in Hastings now she's having a baby, but she's only band D, no chance. But my husband's nephew's girlfriend is pregnant and she tells us, "They've given me a halfway house and then I'll have a flat when I have the baby", because she's seventeen. Well, my Catherine said, "That's another one I've got to pay for!" It's so wrong. I'm very disillusioned. I can't bear to read the paper any more.'

Perhaps Barbara was programmed to complain. She relied on the *Daily Mail*. 'I read the other day about an African woman having a baby here, and they paid for her to go home. Is that right? Immigrants have taken the houses and the jobs that should be for our children. They come over here and use our services.

Do you know, we were coming back from holiday in Turkey and in the airport this Indian lady searched my things. "Are you British?" she asked. Now that really got my back up.'

But in Sainsbury's she must have worked with different races? 'Oh yes, and I get on very well with Chinese, Indians and Africans. I like them, but I still don't think they should be here. Our country should be for our people. It's not our country any more.' What proportion of people in Britain did she think were foreign-born? She asserted 40 per cent – four times the true figure. But that exaggeration is common, perhaps to do with the suddenness of migration during the boom years. It's too simple to say people are prejudiced – or 'bigoted', the word Gordon Brown used in the election when he thought his mike was off. When we asked which charity the Hatts supported, the answer was sickle cell anaemia. Did Barbara know that was a disease unique to black people? 'Oh yes', the decision to contribute was 'for the children'.

Barbara Hatt epitomized the times. Personally prosperous, she acknowledged improvement, the better schools and hospitals. But she was also disturbed by social and ethnic change, exaggerating them, and relying on media misinformation. The Hatts were not about to vote Labour: in fact, they and their parents had always been traditional working-class Conservatives.

In our democracy, politicians are told to listen, and they do, avidly, anxiously, through polling and focus groups. But what if the people being listened to are wrong-headed, under-informed or even deaf? During the Labour years many judged the economy and society around them – and the government – in a fog of fear and misapprehension. Do we blame Labour, or commiserate?

PART ONE

Did Things Get Better?

CHAPTER 1

Better educated?

'Education, education, education' was the mantra. Labour adapted Tory reforms and pumped money in, doubling cash spending on education between 1997 and 2009, a real-terms increase of three-quarters. Unlike their predecessors, ministers believed passionately and positively in better schools for all. Schools would fill productivity gaps, equalize opportunities, step up social mobility and cut anti-social behaviour. What a weight to carry. Labour legislated, set a mass of targets, hired teachers and assistants and, for the four years from 1997, imposed on schools the fierce will of a determined minister, David Blunkett. It worked, more or less. Primary education improved. But for secondary schools, Blair's obsessions with choice and faith led, from 2001, to a relentless churn of policies. How schools were organized mattered more to Labour than what they did. Alongside, in their different ways, further and higher education blossomed. So education was, in the main, a Labour success. The political benefits were slim, however, because onerous targets and incessant interventions lost the support of teachers. Labour did not 'de-professionalize' – look at the way head teachers' status and salaries were boosted – but the charge stuck. Teachers and lecturers were grumpily discontent and their disaffection with Labour leached out, discolouring a deservedly positive perceptions of those shiny new whiteboards.

*

Did Things Get Better?

In the playground of Oakthorpe primary, the headmaster's expansive gesture conjured for us the comings and goings he had witnessed at the Enfield school over thirty-two years. George Cumner-Price became deputy head in 1978 and survived fourteen education secretaries, giving him a cool perspective on the fads, schemes and ideologies passing in and out of the school gates. His report card on the era carries clout.

Spending drought in the later Tory years had left schools scuffed and shabby. Inventories listed leaking roofs and outside lavatories; children shared ragged textbooks amid a dinginess that said neither children nor their teachers had value. After thirteen years of Labour much was better in Enfield, Cumner-Price told us. A tide of new money had washed through his school. Across England, primary school spending on each pupil rose from £2210 in 1997–8 to £3580 by 2007–8 in real terms, an increase of a third. The head showed off a fine new building for his top year, with its own library and common room where the oldest children gained confidence before moving on to secondary school. Labour renovated. The primary school where we voted in the 2010 election was almost unrecognizable from the 1990s. Buildings had sprung up, among them a new nursery; the playground had been relaid. Outside Oakthorpe an electronic noticeboard told parents and children what was happening day by day and in the week ahead, and the school kept in touch with parents by text message.

But new buildings, equipment and desks were the easier bit. Schools reflect the society around them. Lately, Oakthorpe's intake has become more difficult. One in six pupils qualify for free school meals, about average for Enfield. In recent years the borough became polyglot: half the children do not speak English as a first language and at any one time a tenth are at an early stage of learning it. More children have severe physical and other problems, which a decade ago would have sealed them into the apartheid of special schools. The jury is out on integration versus separation. What Cumner-Price knew was that he never had to deal with so many asthma pumps before or with autism, a condition the incidence – or the awareness – of which had grown.

Cumner-Price treasured his teaching assistants, one for each class, a Labour-era innovation. Summing up in the *Times Educational Supplement* in 2010, another head, Geoff Barton of King Edward VI School, Bury St Edmunds, judged 'one of Labour's greatest achievements' to be 'transforming the landscape of who works in schools: teaching assistants, behaviour managers, learning mentors. There is an accomplished army of adults other than teachers whose job is to help pupils to learn, and they make a huge impact.' This was borne out by a study for the Training and Development Agency for Schools that found schools with fewer assistants did less well than those with a 'high density'. At Oakthorpe, Cumner-Price did not hesitate to declare teaching quality immeasurably better. His formula could start a maths lesson. Quality teachers + extra numbers = better results. Under the Tories he had gained control of his school budget; in 2009–10 it was £2.6 million a year for 500 children, with an unprecedented 120 staff. He chose to spend most on keeping his youngest classes small. Now every child started learning some German and had a chance at playing either clarinet or saxophone.

Due to retire in 2011, he registered the Tories' national curriculum as an improvement on the looser 'independent learning' of the 1970s, but the big changes were Blunkett's. Labour's most radical move was a prescribed hour each day dedicated to reading and, from 1999, a compulsory daily maths lesson. They had an almost immediate impact on results. Every Child Counts strove for more bang for the extra spending on primary maths, and the NAO registered its 'positive impact'.

The emphasis on monitoring and targets stemmed from Labour's need to prove extra money was buying progress. Such spending was by no means excessive. Under Labour the UK climbed to just above the OECD average and primary class sizes were still relatively high compared with Germany, France, even the US. Ministers wanted evidence, and had many parents on their side in insisting on Standard Assessment Tests (Sats).

Cumner-Price and his teachers supported Sats for eleven-year-olds. 'They focus the mind, they give us something to work towards. They are externally examined, so we value them as proof of all we have done.' But did Labour push too far on testing and directed learning? Ministers failed to see that their mistrust of the professionals, manifest in the great apparatus of assessments and targets, itself bred mistrust. But teachers also welcomed the new directedness. Cumner-Price considered it an advance that from 2003, lessons had to start with a statement on the board declaring exactly what the learning objective for that session was.

Labour often sounded dogmatic, even when the evidence did not say conclusively 'what works', in setting, school organization or pedagogy. In the classroom you had to rely on the practical wisdom of the teacher, but Labour – Blair especially – were suspicious of the variability of performance that would result if the professionals had more autonomy. That tension between professionalism, skill and insistence on external controls was perhaps not resolvable.

Within days of taking power, Blunkett named and shamed eighteen schools. Putting schools under 'special measures', a regime of close supervision by Ofsted and teaching support, was his dread instrument for under-performers. Three years into Labour's tenure 396 schools, around 2 per cent, were still failing and studies showed some schools slipped back once out of special measures, weighed down by catchment, culture and poor teachers. Labour's laudable determination to reach down into schools and secure children's well-being – the same thrust that lay behind the white paper *Every Child Matters* – often toppled into excess. The *Guardian* (11 December 2009) reported Ofsted demanding that a school carry out a risk assessment on one head teacher's West Highland terrier because of risks to 'the health and safety of the children owing to the presence of the dog'. But then Ofsted itself complained, in February 2010, that the effort to raise standards had been undermined by too many government initiatives, a superfluity of strategies, overloading teachers with commands on the curriculum and on how to teach.

In 2009 a group of academics led by Professor Robin Alexander of Cambridge University published a sweeping review of primary education, which in its florid language, absurdly critical of the government, showed the depth of the education profession's disaffection. Yet even it pronounced primary schools fundamentally sound. Under social pressure they were 'in good heart'. Labour could claim to have refurbished and made them more effective educational institutions. But that is only half the verdict. Labour could probably have done as much without their frantic busyness and the barrage of edicts and interventions.

The *Guardian* picked Oakfield more or less at random in 2001 for its four-year study of public services in Enfield: it was happy, flourishing and over-subscribed. Its eleven-year-olds scored 287 out of 300 on the Sats, compared with an England average that had been inching up each year and in 2008 stood at 248. Oakthorpe is a good school, in the top quartile of England's 15,000 primaries. But 900 other primaries still saw most of their pupils leaving in the summer of 2009 without being able to write a proper sentence using commas or tackle basic arithmetic.

Attainment increased markedly between 1998 and 2000, but later progress was limited. Results in Labour's last summer were disappointing: the number reaching the standard result for their age group in English was down one point to 80 per cent, ending the upwards trend of the previous fifteen years. Maths results were unchanged at 78 per cent and science at 88 per cent. 'Secure in the basics' was a phrase ministers used, pointing to how many more primary pupils were leaving in that benign state. But Labour had pumped up expectation, misunderstanding causal complexities and timescales and neglecting the strong effect of social class. By 2010 so much more needed to be done to strengthen the weaker schools and to haul poorer pupils past the milestones of standard performance. A fifth of England's children were still leaving primary school neither literate nor numerate enough to get to grips with secondary education, on track to end eleven years of compulsory education with no qualifications.

Oakthorpe's eleven-year-olds scattered to secondary schools across the borough, Cumner-Price fearing for his charges' welfare in their thronging corridors and playgrounds. 'A part of me,' he said plaintively, 'wishes we could just keep them, and go on up the age range right here in a small and familiar place.' Similarly, Labour's policies for secondary education were scatter-gun in comparison. Was their priority improving or replacing the comprehensives? Where was the evidence that setting up new quasi-autonomous schools did anything for their standards – unless they were selective in their intake? Ministers' tense and unremitting focus on results gave the schools focus but at the price of a twenty-first-century version of rote learning.

Not many Oakthorpe pupils transferred at eleven to Lea Valley High in the east of Enfield: it was in a different part of the borough and, in schooling, geography is paramount. We went to it as a case study in 'transformation'; many of Labour's devices for improving secondary education were on display there. When Janet Cullen arrived as head in 1995 from a comprehensive in Chorleywood the school was called, less appealingly, Bullsmoor – and its nearest railway station is still Turkey Street. It was a 'low aspiration school where the staff didn't believe in the pupils', Cullen says, a secondary modern in all but name, with only 13 per cent of its sixteen-year-olds getting five good GCSEs. Rolls were falling, with 640 racketing around in a school built for 1000, and although only twenty years old, its buildings were decaying. 'To change a school's culture is like turning a juggernaut.' It took time and money, which is what Labour provided. 'Only now I feel change in the last few years is so embedded that it will never slip back,' Cullen told us.

In 2002 Lea Valley High became a specialist sports school, since when it has built a spectacular gym and pitches. With irony, since she had no personal interest in sport, Cullen says the new ethos pulled people together, crossed language and cultural barriers, made leaders and raised self-esteem. Specialism was a gimmick, adapted from a Tory idea. At first schools could select a tenth of their pupils for 'aptitude' in languages, arts and business studies, and by 2010 most secondaries were specialist in something. The first specialist schools had attracted alert parents, improving their intake and results. But in 2004 Labour did away with selection, which in fact only 100 schools had ever used.

Certainly Lea Valley High's specialism had no impact on its intake. Half the pupils were on free school meals, and they spoke between them sixty-five languages. They included both the children of diplomats from war-torn Somalia or Iran, who benefit from strong encouragement from parents, and the children of poor rural foreign families not literate even in their own language. Migration into the eastern part of Enfield was big and fast, yet far from unusual. It was a tiny miracle that the local authority coped so well and it is puzzling how little impact this social transformation had on borough politics.

In theory Oakthorpe's eleven-year-olds could choose the borough's surviving state-maintained grammar school. Or rather, it might choose them, if they passed its tests. English secondary education remained partially selective and the survival of the grammars proved how confused the government was. When Blunkett had famously said 'read my lips, no selection by examination or interview', he seemed to be about to kill off the grammars that remained in Kent, Buckinghamshire, the Wirral and Enfield. But their middle-classness was shown by the fact that only 2.7 per cent of grammar pupils were on free school meals, compared with 17 per cent across all English schools. Their parents' wrath was too much for Blunkett. His lips had been misread.

Labour did, as promised, abolish assisted places in private schools, a Tory scheme paying private schools for the privilege of cherry-picking high-fliers from local primaries. That, however, was as far as it looked likely to go in tackling private education. Labour thrust this hot potato into the lap of the Charity Commission, after new charity law questioned why tax breaks should pay to educate the children of the best-off. Research by Professor Steven Machin of University College London showed how in Labour's last year, ex-public schoolboys were earning 8 per cent more on average than contemporaries with everything else in common in class and background except schooling. After making desultory offers to open their sports fields to oiks a few days a year, the public schools successfully bullied the Charity Commission into postponing the date at which it had threatened to punish them for failing to prove how 'charitable' they were. Public school heads even started to undermine the qualifications on offer in state schools. The head-master of Harrow, Barnaby Lenon, inveighed against the quality of GCSEs. 'Let us not deceive our children, and especially children from poorer homes, with worthless qualifications,' he said with breathtaking condescension. In the years to 2008, state school spending on each pupil had increased faster than in private schools. Even so, it rose only from 50 per cent of what private schools spent in 1997–8 to 58 per cent in 2006–7. In his 2006 budget, Brown promised to raise state school spending per pupil to the level in private schools. That might have been trans-formative – research had concluded that spending had a 'positive and significant effect' on all tests – but it was a promise Labour came nowhere near realizing.

The government puzzled over how to separate children from the often suffocating constraints of home and background yet recognize the natural right of parents to push their offspring. Equality vied with choice. Blair championed the latter; his press secretary, Alastair Campbell, too avidly reading the right-wing press, made a snide remark about ending 'bog-standard com-prehensives'. Odd schemes followed. 'Gifted and talented' was a way for Labour to signal belief in excellence and the need to put sheep and goats into different pens. Head teachers should pick their brightest children and give them extra help or cultural trips – which often meant middle-class pupils getting more of what their families were already giving them. But at the same time the government judged schools on their attainment rates and how many failing children they pushed over the exam hurdles.

Academies and 'faith' schools were examples of how Labour tried to straddle choice and equality. Behind the academies was a fierce desire to raise ambitions in the poorest urban areas and a conviction that state schools were letting children down. But instead of mending them, Labour hared after something new, a signature Blair touch, something for businessmen to run. In exchange for £2 million, companies won control over academies' governing bodies, curriculum and selection of heads. Out of the

woodwork came a car dealer with extreme evangelical creation-
ist views and assorted philanthropists with little experience of
education at all.

Academies were comprehensive and were intended to be an
extra in poor areas. A London borough such as Southwark, with
black, religious parents, became a happy hunting ground for
Christian academy-builders. Lord Harris of Peckham, a carpet
store magnate and a prominent backer of the Tory Party, became
a serial founder of academies across South London. But business
had neither the people nor the social commitment to fulfil
Labour's fantasy. Some sponsors even failed to put up the £2 million; others abused the lax accounting rules. Labour soon had to
dilute their own idea and allow councils, universities and educational institutions to sponsor academies. By 2010, over 300
academies had opened, with a further 100 in construction, each
costing far more than ordinary rebuilt schools.

How good they were depended on catchment. At Lea Valley
High, Janet Cullen's response was dismay. 'Three! We have three
academies locally now,' she protested. 'They can pay their teachers more, competing with us. The religious academy near by
said they would work closely with us, but they haven't.' Schools
cannot escape their ecology. Praising a grammar school in Kent
for its marvellous results is naive; it picks students who are going
to perform better by definition. The only relevant picture is
county-wide, embracing the secondary moderns. And Kent's overall performance remained indifferent.

Labour wanted to believe that the philanthropists injected
adrenalin into the academies. In 2009 education minister Jim
Knight said bluntly, 'they work'. Yes, they raised the number of
pupils getting five good GCSEs at a faster rate. Ofsted scored
leadership and governance as good or outstanding in nine out of
ten academies compared with six out of ten schools nationally.
Tales of transformation were rife. When Kathy August became
head of Ducie High School it was 'like a badly run youth club in
the late 1960s'. In 2005 it became Manchester Academy under
the United Church Schools Trust, an Anglican charity running
private schools. Zero tolerance of bad behaviour and a new

building helped 60 per cent of pupils get five GCSEs and 39 per cent GCSEs at grades A–C.

But a go-ahead highly paid leader and sparkling new buildings would probably do the trick anywhere. Researchers commissioned by the Sutton Trust found the proportion of poor children enrolled in academies falling over time, implying surrounding schools were taking them in higher numbers. 'Rises in achievement have coincided with a decline in the proportion of disadvantaged pupils in academies,' they said. The NAO gave academies six out of ten, hedging its bets (rightly) by saying it was too early to pronounce; it noted lack of collaboration between academies and neighbouring schools. No miracle cure, then. Some 26 out of 36 academies that had been open for at least four years in 2007 still did not meet the national target of 30 per cent with five good GCSEs including English and maths. The Institute of Education wondered whether academies were simply attracting better heads: they were paid between £18,000 and £32,000 more on average.

Growth in Asian numbers created pressure to add Hindu and Islamic schools to the established Anglican and Roman Catholic (and a handful of Jewish) schools, even though after 9/11 separate schools looked like a contradiction of the government's own policies for cohesion and security. Another Labour dilemma was diversity versus equality. Diversity won, Labour feeling especially tender about demands for their own schools from Muslims, who usually voted Labour.

Blunkett famously wished he could 'bottle the magic' of faith and spread it to other schools. The evidence debunked the magic; it was simply selection. Anglican primaries attracted middle-class parents, and what was amazing was their sudden appearance in the pews, hunkering down on hassocks to prove their children's fitness for admission. Four Muslim schools were among Labour's new faith cohort and, like the others, they said they were selecting on religious adherence but in fact filtered children by background. Faith schools screened out the chaotic families, whose children would then congregate disproportionately in neighbouring schools. A joint study by the London School of

Economics and the Institute of Education in 2009 found no area-wide improvement in attainment in places with faith schools. Yes, they got better exam results, but only because pupils had been 'sorted'.

When Lea Valley High started in 1996, 13 per cent got five A–C GCSEs. Now 56 per cent reached that target, a remarkable achievement. Overall, educational improvement at age sixteen was 'massive', according to an evaluation by the London School of Economics. Exam results are what count – for pupils, parents, schools and education ministers alike. Pass rates at GCSE rose steadily: in 1997, 45.1 per cent achieved five A–C grade GCSEs and 67.1 per cent in 2009. Labour tightened the definition of failing: in no school should less than 30 per cent of the age group get five A–C GCSEs, including maths and English. Half fell below the bar in 1997; in 2009 only a tenth. At Lea Valley High 38 per cent got there, respectably above the official minimum.

Glass half full or half empty? Half of all pupils now left with five good GCSEs. But in almost 1000 secondary schools, one in three, less than half, made the expected progress in English and maths between the ages of eleven and sixteen. Ministers noted proudly that average school performance in 1997 had become the bottom marker by 2009 – not bad. Progress was most marked in poor areas, especially in London. Critics alleged inflation of grades and machinations by head teachers, encouraging pupils into easier subjects. Tim Oates, director of assessment at the Cambridge University exams board, denounced 'faddish' changes that made it impossible to compare standards; he alleged examiners were giving the benefit of the doubt and results were better because students had access to past papers. Such claims are hard to assess. Overall, achievement reached around the OECD average for sixteen-year-olds, according to the Programme for International Student Assessment, but we cannot say whether educational quality improved over time.

Janet Cullen, like many heads, had no doubts. In 1995 the school had 38 staff for 640 students, but now it has 150 teachers for a rising roll of 1200 pupils. 'The calibre of teachers is much higher. The expectation of teachers is higher and so is their expectation of their students,' the head said. She praised the Teach First programme that each year assigned to her four young teachers from top universities, who pledged to stay for two years before choosing a career.

Since 1997 the total number of teachers in England grew by 32,000; schools had 100,000 more teaching assistants and 70,000 more support staff. Schools were now recruiting 37,000 graduates a year into the profession, a hefty slice of the output from universities. And schools were filling recruitment quotas even in scarce specialities such as maths and science – even before the recession. Graham Holly of the Training and Development Agency for Schools (a Labour-era quango) remarked, '[C]ontrast it with thirteen years ago, we were in crisis. There were four-day weeks in some schools because there weren't enough teachers to stand in front of a classroom.' Some were unconvinced. Professor Alan Smithers of the University of Buckingham found a third of science teachers had no more than two A levels when over three-quarters of history teachers had a first-class degree or a 2.1.

Average teacher salaries increased by £5000 a year, up 17 per cent in real terms between 1997 and 2007, with head teachers getting a 32 per cent rise and newly qualified teachers 13 per cent. Starting pay rose from £14,280 in 1997 to £20,627 in 2009. Conditions improved too. In January 2003 the government launched a 'concerted attack on unnecessary paperwork and bureaucracy', which cut teachers' administrative duties and increased their 'non-contact' time outside the classroom. Full-time support staff in English schools rose from 133,500 to 322,500, half of them teaching assistants. The same period saw school technicians nearly double in number.

Teaching became a popular career. Good graduates listed it in their top job choices in the boom years, not just as a refuge after the bust. It had sunk well down the table of choices in the 1980s and 1990s, but after 2000 was consistently in the top two or three. The Institute for Education reckoned recruitment advertising campaigns were a great success. Teaching gained in glamour and respect: Labour succeeded in making it cool. Paradoxically, in the light of teachers' criticisms of targets and testing, Labour made an effort to improve their professional status in 2000 by creating the General Teaching Council, which gave them a role in regulating admissions to their own ranks.

Pupil absences dropped; with government encouragement, more schools insisted on uniforms. Yet something went awry. Perhaps teaching was just more difficult. The unions complained bitterly about indiscipline and assault, and the media revelled in stories about cyber-bullying by internet and phone, both among children and of teachers by children. The police became a permanent presence in many schools. At Lea Valley High, as elsewhere in Enfield, a Safer Schools Officer patrolled every afternoon. Even minor acts of violence, sexual harassment and playground bullying were immediately reported. Cullen noted: 'Children know that their complaints are taken seriously and action will be taken.'

School loomed larger in the lives of pupils. By 2009, 17,000 were offering after-hours homework clubs to help children who found studying difficult in noisy, cramped homes. Sport, art, music and drama classes expanded, offering more of the extras that middle-class children took for granted.

If brighter classrooms and open, airy halls improve school attainment, Labour left a mark. Lea Valley School was completely rebuilt in 2004 under the Private Finance Initiative (PFI). The scheme had drawbacks, the head said, but even so it was better than slow and disruptive refurbishment. 'It's a fantastic building and the PFI company do keep it up very well.' But the cost was high: she had to hand over £1 million a year to the contractors and could not get a new toilet roll without presenting a chit at the corporate help desk. School meals were bad, and there was nothing she could do about it, whatever Jamie Oliver recommended.

Schools had Hobson's choice: in the early years Labour insisted PFI was the only way to demolish or remodel decrepit buildings. In 2004 the government launched Building Schools for the Future, promising that all 3500 secondary schools in England would be rebuilt or refurbished by 2020. The plan was to rebuild half the schools, remodel a third and refurbish the rest, some with PFI, others financed by conventional borrowing. But it took time to start building and only a fraction were built or begun before the Tory–Lib Dem government pulled the plug in summer 2010.

Nonetheless, by 2008 capital investment was running at eight times the 1997 level of £1 billion. In total 3000 schools were made over or rebuilt, with modern classrooms, sports facilities and kitchens. The new schools were both magnificent and innovative and sometimes disappointingly bog-standard in design. Lea Valley High had been transformed, inside and out. Janet Cullen said an old Bullsmoor pupil would scarcely recognize the place, especially how lessons were taught. 'There are interactive white boards in every class, most lessons are done with power point and video clips, lessons with IT that parents can access and pupils can look at again. The pupils do still take notes, but it's all there for them to look at again any time.'

In retrospect, Labour were educational idealists. Schools, they believed, are potent, so they advocated more hours, and extending the school day to include pre- and after-school clubs. A previous Labour government had tortured itself over its failed pledge to raise the school-leaving age to sixteen – promised in 1964 but not realized till 1972 by that well-known progressive Margaret Thatcher. Almost as an afterthought this Labour government decreed that all would stay on in some form of education to the age of seventeen by 2013 and to eighteen from 2015. It casually introduced a 'September Guarantee', so that by the end of that autumn month every sixteen-year-old school leaver would have 'a suitable place in learning' or training; it was extended to seventeen-year-olds as an anti-recession measure in 2008, giving another chance to those who had enrolled on one-year courses, or who had left a course or job.

The archipelago of courses and institutions under the name 'further education' is scattered. To the many with their sights on university it is largely unknown territory. In a disjointed way Labour nurtured this sector, spending more, expanding the colleges' remedial work and busying themselves over FE qualifications. But because of the sector's diversity, evaluating the effectiveness of Labour's FE policies is harder than for schools. Labour's target of 80 per cent of 16–18-year-olds in learning of one kind or another was hit in 2004. But with what effects on productivity or students' life chances?

Because Labour believed passionately that more education should be an instrument of social progress, they paid students. After a successful trial in poor areas, maintenance allowances for children of families with low incomes were introduced. On a sliding scale students could claim between £10 and £30 a week if they stayed on at college or school. In Sheffield the low-income ward of Manor Castle had a staying-on rate in 2005 of 51.5 per cent of sixteen-year-olds, against 95.4 per cent in better-off Broomhill. By 2007, most wards had seen an increase in the rates, with 14.5 per cent more sixteen-year-olds remaining at school.

But Labour could not decide what students should do in these 'transitional' sixteen-to-nineteen years. They created the giant Learning and Skills Council to pass funds to further education colleges and school sixth forms, to lower the barriers between different institutions and qualifications. Exams that propelled students into higher education still dominated. The government commissioned a review from the ex-chief inspector of education, Mike Tomlinson. He applauded improvement in GCSEs, but repeated the findings of earlier inquiries: schools and colleges did not offer enough courses and exams after sixteen, especially when the jobs market was hard to read. The government quailed. Tomlinson's proposals would mean absorbing A level into a 'comprehensive scheme'. Academic and vocational qualifications were supposed to be equivalent but sixteen-to-nineteen qualifications mirrored the old 'binary' divide in higher education between the polytechnics and universities. Labour were unsure, but reached into the schools to put some fourteen-year-olds on a path leading to more practical courses – the foundation learning tier. Most striking was the revival of apprenticeships, which increased from 75,000 in 1997 to 225,000 in 2007–8. The promise was that every qualified sixteen-year-old would be guaranteed an apprenticeship – and those that fell below standard promised a foundation course to catch up.

Labour promoted National Vocational Qualifications (NVQs). Practical and work-based, in subjects such as construction, childcare or retail, they included numeracy and literacy grades. In health and social care the NVQ Two (equivalent to GCSE) became a compulsory minimum. To encourage as many people as possible to acquire basic skills, training was made free up to NVQ Two. But employers complained. Sir Terry Leahy of Tesco said his new cashiers could not do basic sums. Others claimed skills shortages forced them to employ staff from abroad. Why did they not do more themselves? – the TUC said only four out of ten firms offered staff training. The government, anxious to please the employers, kept inviting them to join training bodies and even created new sector skills councils to accommodate them, but too many companies ducked out. The University of Buckingham's Alan Smithers, no friend of Labour, told employers to stop complaining, devise the qualifications they thought suitable, recruit on them and then pay people for having them.

Tomlinson's grand scheme rejected, Labour tinkered. Their AS levels for seventeen-year-olds, in between GCSEs and A levels, became just another exam. Very few stayed on to take it who were not doing A levels anyway. The other residual from Tomlinson was the Diploma, aimed at bringing the practical and academic together in a new fourteen-to-nineteen curriculum that would offer grading right up to university entry. Integrating diploma courses with existing vocational courses and GCSEs demanded rare collaboration between schools, councils, employers and colleges. Whether it had started was unclear by the time Labour lost power.

Costing £4 billion a year, 429 FE colleges offered over 12,000 different qualifications. Labour increased spending from £3900 for each FE student in England to £5470 (in constant 2007–8 prices). At the same time student funding in higher education declined from £5680 to £4220 – though university students qualified for grants and loans as well. The OECD said in 2005 the UK spent more on each student than France and Germany, but half the American figure. In some areas, FE colleges became major local employers, some seeking to offer degrees and eventually gaining university status. But how vocational should colleges be, how far should course fees cover learning for pleasure: music, arts, languages? Not far from Lea Valley High on Bullsmoor Lane in Enfield is Capel Manor College, offering courses in garden design, horticulture, floristry and 'balloon artistry', popular with people seeking a career change, according to principal Steve Dowbiggin. He complained that standardizing vocational qualifications risked squeezing out part-time and short courses on the boundary between vocation and leisure pursuit. Labour often managed to appear both obsessed by the needs of employers and fuzzy about what should be the appropriate division between private cost and public benefit.

For young people at risk of dropping out, Labour started a centrally run careers and advice service called Connexions. It had a budget of £450 million a year to advise 13–19-year-olds, together with those up to twenty-five with learning difficulties and disabilities – a sum double that of the local careers services it replaced. But the size of Connexions' principal target group, the Neets (Not in Education, Employment or Training), proved a stubborn statistic, even as young people moved in and out of the status.

Labour had a plan to improve the literacy and numeracy of people of working age. Participation in adult learning went up, but by 2010, 22 per cent of UK adults were still thought to have the lowest level of job skills, against 17 per cent in comparable European countries. Participation in training was relatively high, but British courses were often shorter. By 2010 auditors found 2.25 million adults on course to realize the target for improving their basic skills, though their literacy had proved easier to push up than their numeracy. But the headline figure for adults with 'poor levels of literacy' remained about 17 million; perhaps not being able fully to grasp written material helped explain why a third of electors took no part in the 2010 election. Between 2001 and 2004, spending on English for Speakers of Other Languages courses tripled to almost £300 million a year, though demand continued to outrun supply.

Did Things Get Better?

In the 1997 election Labour had boasted of a University for Industry that would equip the seven million without basic literacy and numeracy. In the event, there was to be no Blair repeat of Harold Wilson's great legacy – the Open University. Under the brand name 'learndirect', the new organization offered online courses with an emphasis on flexibility, (cheaper) home learning and 'bite-sized chunks'.

Labour invented individual learning accounts to subsidize courses for those lacking skills and qualifications. They uncovered a tremendous appetite for self-improvement – and criminality. Take-up, from September 2000, exceeded Whitehall expectations. As 2.6 million accounts opened, spending pushed to £273 million against a £200 million budget. Inadequately planned and introduced too quickly, the NAO complained, the learning accounts lacked a business model and civil servants had no way of guaranteeing the quality of courses. Bogus colleges with phantom students committed widespread fraud and the government shut the scheme down abruptly. Here was a good idea badly handled, ministers overreaching themselves and the administrative system incapable. No heads rolled.

At every level in education, Labour stood for more. Only in higher education, where 'more means worse' elitist impulses still had resonance, did this instinct to expand provoke a backlash. Here, in deference to the cultural consensus that more studying and learning were both good and necessary, antagonism to expansion was often dressed up as complaint about financing. These years saw remarkable growth. Visiting a campus or the university quarters of cities such as Leeds, Hull, Preston or Bristol, you dodged building works as the cranes swung above. Universities UK, in a February 2010 briefing paper, acknowledged 'heavy investment in the infrastructure supporting teaching (lecture theatres, libraries, IT, social learning spaces) and support services (careers, student unions, academic study support)'.

In the ten years after 1997, undergraduate and postgraduate numbers together rose from 1.8 million to 2.4 million, of whom 1.6 million were 'mature', aged over twenty-one. The UK student

34

population had been rising fast since the Tories rebadged polytechnics as universities in 1992 and encouraged more applicants,
who came, because graduates earned a lifetime premium for their
degrees. Blair, in the manner of his unprepared and uncosted
declaration on child poverty, committed the government to a
target of half the 18–30-year group going to university. (On an
elastic definition of higher education, it got to 45 per cent by
2009.) This was one of those Labour back-of-the-envelope targets but intuitively it sounded right. Higher education was weft
and woof in the fabric of modernity; *British Social Attitudes* consistently found holders of degrees were more progressive, liberal
and tolerant.

The Tories had expanded on the cheap. State support fell
from £9000 a head in 1989 to £6000 when Labour took office.
Whichever party had won in 1997, it would have faced the tide
of demand for higher education on limited funds. The new government had to choose between further degradation in the
amount of support, apportioning more of the education budget
to universities, or new income from fees. Vice-chancellors produced
a suspiciously neat number in claiming the higher education
budget produced a 300 per cent return to GDP. Was it really
such good value, compared with early years and primary
schools, or apprenticeships and technological reskilling? Universities, for all their reputation as hotbeds of radical thought,
resisted the reform necessitated by the arrival of students in
their millions. They moaned that they could not make out the
thin clear stream of excellence in the turbid waters of mass
A level accomplishment. The professors' fate was that large
scale higher education would bring a different, less comfortable
experience for students and their teachers. For a start, university academics would have to do more teaching, and few had
any teaching qualification. At a conference we heard a lecturer at
the University of Lincoln openly say: 'I have absolutely no
training as an educator, none as an administrator, no training
whatsoever.' Yet Lincoln, a new foundation, was mainly an institution for teaching students rather than conducting high-level
research.

Labour ducked such questions, already frightened by the accusation they were interfering with precious academic autonomy. Ministers hardly dared ask whether, for example, students might learn more quickly on intensive and less costly two-year courses – though some places, such as Staffordshire University, got on with it. Or whether students could take much longer than the traditional three years by studying and working part time and living more cheaply at home; Labour neglected support for part-timers. Reform would cut the expensive annual trek of hundreds of thousands of undergraduates criss-crossing the country to stay in purpose-built accommodation miles from their parents' homes. But the 'cultural' attractions of higher education as a rite of passage and a three-year extension of youth remained too strong to challenge. Labour pumped money into student support (£2.5 billion a year in 2010), at a higher rate than other countries.

The universities hesitated over whether world-class research and effective undergraduate teaching nestled comfortably together in the same plate-glass or even ivy-clad institutions. Labour ministers were clumsy, often crudely utilitarian in tone, as if they thought colleges merely the handmaids of commerce. Universities were as obtuse, proclaiming in the same breath their virtuous autonomy while demanding ever higher subsidy – and studiously avoiding responsibility for the rest of education. They proved reluctant partners in the secondary academies, and their own exam boards could sound reactionary. One result of allowing universities to charge higher fees was jet-setting vice-chancellors, off to seek foreign students who would pay more than home-grown ones. They talked up higher education as an 'export' without coming clean on the subsidy required. Where was the social justice in British taxpayers contributing to the education of well-off young Chinese?

Universities' own standards deserved scrutiny, but vice-chancellors covered their tracks. In 2009 a record one in seven students earned first-class degrees and half of them 2.1s. Publicly, vice-chancellors protested that a degree from Bath Spa University was the same as one from the University of Bath. They were not equivalent but ministers chose not to unlock this secret garden. Universities used their freedom to expand, and managers' jobs rose three times as fast as those of academics from 2003 – but the 10 per cent increase in professors and lecturers over the same years was also remarkable. Universities were efficient in the sense that around four-fifths of those who enrolled as undergraduates got degrees, a good figure compared with other countries where the drop-out rate was high. The government chief scientist David King noted in a paper in *Nature* that the UK's share of world scientific publications was disproportionately high. With only 1 per cent of the world population, the UK produced 9 per cent of all scientific papers and received 12 per cent of citations. Still, the elite universities were growing restive. They, and the science establishment at large, talked a version of intellectual mercantilism, warning 'the UK would fall behind' unless research were concentrated behind their high walls. The other universities protested at the idea they should become humdrum teachers, not researchers – and the matter remained unresolved.

These years might have been a time of celebration and confidence – UK universities were doing well – but instead money hung over them like a pall. Blunkett brought in £1000-a-year tuition charges in 1998, abolishing means-tested maintenance grants, replacing them with cheap student loans repaid through income tax. Only 50 per cent of undergraduates paid the full fee. Blair and Brown fought over the timing of the tuition payment: whether upfront, paid for by a loan, or later by a life-long graduate tax. Financially, it did not make much difference. An upfront payment did not seem to deter students. A natural experiment unfolded as Scotland went down one path (free now, pay later), while England and Wales tried the other. When permitted fees rose to £3000, a more realistic contribution to costs, Labour had another internal row and as a result introduced more generous non-repayable maintenance grants, means-tested but available to about a third of all students. Taken together, the grants and the low-interest loans, repayable only when a former student's income rose above £15,000 a year, allowed even the poorest to enrol.

Did Things Get Better?

One in eight 18–19-year-olds from the poorest homes went to university in the mid 1990s; by 2010 it was one in five. The Higher Education Funding Council for England took this as evidence that tuition fees had not deterred poor students. True, only 4 per cent of children who received free school meals at the age of fifteen went on to university, compared with 33 per cent of other children. But growing numbers were 'the greatest social achievement of the 1997 Labour government', according to Professor Danny Dorling of Sheffield University. This had been all the easier, he added, because the whole education system expanded, and the middle class had given nothing up. Of course, access to university was not an admission ticket to the groves of academe. A Sheffield study showed how young people from the better-off half of Hallam were more likely to attend older universities while the less well-off were more likely to attend an ex-polytechnic.

Brown, in a fit of political assertiveness, had said Oxford's rejection of Laura Spence, a young woman with top A levels from a Tyneside comprehensive, was an 'absolute scandal'. Labour blustered, and told elite universities to open their hallowed gates and seek out comprehensive candidates. An Exeter University study found private schools had tightened their grip on places in the top ten universities between 2004 and 2007. Although they educated 7 per cent of British children, they gained one out of four places at top universities.

Yet Labour had, semi-consciously, addressed the largest of inequalities. Without announcement, they upturned the hierarchy of education spending. The Institute for Fiscal Studies reported: 'We have seen a clear shift in funding priorities towards younger children, with the UK becoming one of the developed world's biggest spenders on early years programmes. This shift in emphasis continues higher up the education system: public spending on school-age children has caught up with (and is set to overtake) spending on college and university students.' Extra funding for primary schools had pushed through into improved attainment at GCSE and now – it seemed – higher education was showing the results.

This was all the more noteworthy since Labour had not, despite Blair's 'education, education, education' mantra, increased spending that much, certainly not compared with health. Total education spending went up by 1 per cent of GDP, to 5.8 per cent in 2008, a fraction above the average for OECD countries. Using international comparisons to compensate for the possibility of 'grade inflation' at home, the Centre for Economic Performance showed England moving up a few places in the OECD league table. As for the extra money, it found 'modest effects but large enough to be cost effective, especially for pupils from poor homes'.

Whether the UK economy became more productive as a result of extra education spending was hard to gauge. But even those who deplored Labour as utilitarians and philistines could not deny the likelihood that educational expansion would bring cultural betterment. Parents and students were in general proud and pleased with what the Labour years offered.

Labour shared the Tory suspicion of the educational competence of councils. But how the schools were to be run and to whom they should account remained questions to which Labour could offer no definitive answers, allowing the Tories to campaign in 2010 with 'parent power' as their solution.

More teachers queuing up at the coffee machine in the staffroom did not automatically improve schooling. Labour had to contend with the dismaying finding by ONS that productivity in education fell – by as much as 1 per cent a year. This was, the statisticians admitted, a crude combination of teachers' pay and capital costs on one side measured against exam performance on the other. Ministers rightly riposted that schools 'produce' much more than exam results, but lacked reliable measures of what else schools do.

Despite the introduction of national literacy and numeracy strategies, improvements in results were slower than the government would have liked, as missed national targets attested. International comparisons suggest England's pupils now perform about as well as their peers in the rest of the developed world, providing little cause for panic, but also faint cause for celebration.

More children stayed on longer and learnt more under Labour. But successive ministers were defeated by the same hard old truths about British society. Schools reflect the society around them far more than they alone can ever hope to change it. In an unequal society, schools are fated to reproduce the maldistribution of life chances. Still, there were the first small green shoots of progress. Paul Gregg and other researchers at Bristol University, comparing the GCSE results of children born in 1970 with those born in 1990 who started school just about when Labour took office, found a weakening of the link between a student's results and their social class. It was only a glimmer, but it might mean that any future government wanting to maximize opportunity will also have to follow Labour's approach.

Middlesbrough College's verdict

Its tiled facade shimmers in the cold winter sun, rising up from the old Middlesbrough docks, until recently desolate waste ground. This architectural wonder is a college, giving silver and bronze form to the conclusion of the Institute for Fiscal Studies that education was by 2010 'broader in scope and richer in resources than when Labour came to power'. From his office in the new building, principal John Hogg looked down to the water below, hands deep in the pockets of a tailored green tweed suit. A decade or so ago this backwater of the Tees used to catch fire spontaneously because of chemical industry pollution. 'Now seals swim in and catch salmon. Yes, salmon. Amazing, isn't it?'

Middlesbrough College opened in 2008, incorporating sixth form, further and higher education, adult courses, apprenticeships and just about anything else students and area employers ask for. Next door, work was progressing on a huge Anish Kapoor sculpture of hoops and wires, destined to be a Teesside landmark, a structure to make Meccano makers drool, not far from the transporter bridge that carries 200 people a time across the river towards Hartlepool in a gondola. Teesside used to be an unemployment black spot. People left and those left behind were dispirited: it was not altogether the schools' fault Middlesbrough had such low results at GCSE.

Principal Hogg, a seventeen-year veteran of the college and principal since 2000, was a local character held in warm affection by his 3500 students. He pushed through this £70 million spectacular, liquidating 'four horrible campuses'. FE used to be Cinderella in the educational kitchen; no one talked much about it because the chattering classes' children did not go there. Yet colleges such as this taught nearly five million full- and part-time students a year, people of all ages finding their first, second or third chances in life. FE is the British class divide on parade. 'I'm here to turn out technicians,' Hogg said. 'Every time I turn on a light switch or a tap I don't know how they work, haven't a clue but it is a miracle and it's done by people trained here. But of course there's no parity of esteem.' Some were doing A levels, some National Diplomas and, with enough points, went on to Teesside University to study everything from hospitality and tourism to electrical engineering. Others struggled through a foundation course in Skills for Life, which rescued the unemployable by making them basically literate.

In the lift young students clutched yellow forms. 'Couldn't do without those,' Hogg noted. They were for the Educational Maintenance Allowance paying the poorest £35 a week to stay on after sixteen. Did students know Labour brought these in? No. Half the under-nineteens at the college get the allowances, most of them poor enough to draw the full sum.

The Street runs through the building, a wide, bright corridor, plate glass on either side, showing the inside workings of a hairdressing salon, a travel agency, a yoga class, all courses open to view as well as thriving student-run businesses. High above in a tulip-shaped pod is an internet cafe open to all. Students are lent laptops too. 'They can't function in the modern world without a mobile phone and a laptop,' the principal said. True, but society outside is riven between the have-broadband and have-nots.

Students gathered for lunch. Kaley, sixteen, pale powdered face and long black hair, had taken a wrong course. 'I went to art college to do fashion design, but it wasn't what I expected, too much research and stuff, not enough making clothes. But my auntie works here in the college in admin and she said I should come here. I'm doing health and social care, learning how the body works, with a bit of science too.' Does she like it? 'No, I hate the placement one day a week in a care home. They make me clean out the budgie cages, and I'm allergic to birds.' Will she stick it out? 'Oh yes, definitely. I'll do this course, and then I'll go for an A level in English and in art after, and get enough points to go to Uni. I'll definitely stay at it now, whether I like it or not.' She looked as though she would.

Anthony, staring at his shoes, talked in a monotone, a quick-fire mumble: 'I did try to get a job. I put a load of CVs into shops, but nothing. I looked in the computer at the job centre, but there was nothing, really. I just stayed home.' Connexions, the careers and advice service, suggested a sports course here might interest him. The college held taster days for the Neets (Not in Education, Employment or Training), to sample activities that might lure them in. With Anthony it worked. He ought to get an NVQ One in sport and recreation, then an NVQ Two. Then? 'Work in a gym, I hope.' His tutors wanted to teach him how to fill in forms, use a computer, how to speak, go to interviews, shake people by the hand and look them in the eye. 'It's not the bits of paper qual-ifications that count,' one said. 'It's the soft skills that make someone employable.'

Lee was glum either by nature or because of long family expe-rience. At eighteen, he had been out of school many months, failing to find work. Now he was doing an NVQ Two in plumb-ing. 'I'd like an apprenticeship after, but there are none. I've tried.' Where did he think he would be in a year? 'On the dole, I expect.' Under the Young Person's Guarantee, rolling out in 2010, the government promised all qualified young people an apprenticeship. Had he heard of that? 'No, never.' Middles-brough College enrolled students who, in 2010, had never been outside a one-mile radius of their home; some had never seen the sea, only a few miles away.

The college offered IT courses for teenage mums, food hygiene for caterers, horticulture, retail, certificates in the handling of medicines for care assistants and high-end electrical engineering. 'We do badly on A levels,' Hogg admitted, 'but 20 per cent above average in our vocational results.' Students who succeeded tended to leave the area. 'Middlesbrough exports its qualified students by the thousand. I meet them all the time. I was in Waterloo station the other day and this old student dashed up to me and shook my hand. "Mr Hogg," he said, "I'm working for Marco Pierre White." Amazing. He'd done catering with us, and just walked in there and asked for a job, he had that self-confidence. They tested him then and there and he cooked so well they took him on. I keep meeting people like that – and, well, it makes my day.'

Labour had made a difference. 'They made us feel we mattered. Maybe it started with Blunkett and the kind of education he'd had. He understood about second chances from his dreadful education.' Money followed, a chance to grow and offer a wider variety of courses to more people. Hogg spoke of the confusion caused by Labour's diplomas; schools were supposed to offer this new vocational strand equivalent to A levels, but it had failed to take off. 'They should have given that to us – but of course schools didn't want to lose students. We should be able to offer everything vocational to fourteen-year-olds to stop them dropping out of school. I've seen kids on construction diplomas in schools who have never touched a brick because they haven't the facilities.'

What else? 'There is a climate of fear about targets. That makes a lot of colleges risk-averse, avoiding anyone who might depress their success rate. I don't do that, I take anyone and everyone. I even take 250 extra students I'm not funded for rather than turn anyone away. That's why we get an outstanding for social inclusion from Ofsted, but unsatisfactory for A levels.' John Hogg was retiring in 2010, leaving a neglected sector in better shape than before 1997.

CHAPTER 2

Healthier?

On the eve of the 1997 general election Labour made a last-minute pitch, telling voters they had 'twenty-four hours to save the NHS'. Labour took their victory as a mandate to spend, which – after a three-year delay – they did by 7 per cent a year more in real terms in the decade to 2010. Labour left the NHS in better health: it ran faster, smoother, more efficiently, its formerly shabby face scrubbed up, regaining self-confidence. Waiting times for elective surgery were the touchstone. Labour redeemed their pledge to cut them and a close observer, Nick Timmins of the *Financial Times,* said that, except for orthopaedics and a few hundred patients waiting for neurosurgery, where the shortage of surgeons was worldwide, no one in England need wait more than eighteen weeks from first seeing their GP to having their operation. Another sign of Labour's accomplishment was political. Before the 2010 election, the Tories had made profuse promises on NHS spending. The election of Barack Obama and the Democrats' struggle to give US healthcare the inclusiveness of the NHS showed the world swinging towards the European not the American way. Labour came to an honest bargain with people who told pollsters they wanted more and better healthcare. The 2001 increase in National Insurance pegged explicitly to increased health spending said: better services cost more. The increase was popular.

NHS spending was a Labour triumph, but with it came a

fixation on the minutiae of healthcare, not just organizations and management, but operations, clinical practice and recovery rates. As in schooling, Labour ministers sitting in Whitehall could not stop themselves tinkering. Plans, reforms, edicts and reorganizations spewed out. In Scotland and Wales their absence showed how little Labour meddling mattered to patients. What mattered was more money.

'No one could justifiably deny the past decade has seen an improvement in quality in the NHS,' concluded disinterested foreign observers in a 2009 Nuffield Trust study. British healthcare did well by international comparison, and not just with the hugely expensive and unfair American scheme. The IMF, no friend of 'socialized medicine', wished the Chinese would adopt something similar to the NHS.

But the Nuffield judgement was qualified. Dentistry and services for dementia were still relatively neglected. As for value for money, 'given the generous increase in resources dedicated to healthcare there are many who question whether progress has been as marked, as rapid, or as predictable as might have been expected'. Blame for that rests, in part, on the endless 'reforms' perpetrated by Blair and Labour's market enthusiasts, among them Alan Milburn, Patricia Hewitt and John Reid. They spent so much time and goodwill chopping and churning, refusing to admit a redoubtable truth. The NHS, big, baggy and shot through with anomalies, worked pretty well. What the anorexic patient they inherited in 1997 needed most was fattening up. Force-feeding was the wrong therapy: the NHS probably got too much extra, too fast, according to Lord Norman Warner, the former social services chief who became a Labour minister.

A lot of British people were in a not dissimilar position, eating and drinking too much. A shelf-full of reports said that unless people lived healthier lives, they would harm themselves and impose mounting costs on the NHS. But government action on eating, drinking and exercise was criticized as 'nannying' and Labour rebuttals were half-hearted. They ducked dealing with the food and drink manufacturers, let alone the social inequalities that were at the root of much obesity. How do you tell consumers what is good for them, when choice is paramount and 'my rights' extend to behaviour that is self-evidently unhealthy? Remember Barbara Hatt of Sydenham, complaining about her emphysema treatment then lighting up another cigarette.

Nonetheless, after thirteen years the UK was in better health, even if the exact part played by government policies was debatable. The death rate fell by 17 per cent. Life expectancy continued its remarkable ascent. For every 100,000 of those aged under seventy-five, circulatory disease accounted for 129 deaths in 1998, but only 74 in 2007, exceeding the target Labour set themselves. Wonder drugs, such as statins, played their part, but how people ate, drank and exercised was critical.

Labour set myriad targets, even one for fewer suicides. (They dropped, but by less than the 20 per cent target; in fact, the government made assisted suicide slightly easier, at least for those with terminal conditions.) Smoking was suicide of a kind and Labour accelerated the downward trend in adult smoking. The NHS helped 2.4 million people to quit in the decade to 2009. Despite its flirtation with Bernie Ecclestone, the Formula One boss, the government banned tobacco promotions in 2002, following an EU directive; and cigarette packets became even more admonitory. But ministers hesitated before banning smoking in public places in 2007. They only dared after drinkers' cities – such as Liverpool in 2004, followed by Dublin – took the lead. Cancer Research UK said that after the ban people gave up smoking four times faster than before.

Food was trickier. Six out of ten adults were overweight (compared with one in three in France) and obesity cost the NHS an extra £4.2 billion a year through liver and heart disease, cancer and diabetes. In 1995, 24 per cent of children aged two to fifteen were clinically obese and overweight, and 30 per cent in 2007. Commendably, ministers studied the problems, and planned their campaigns, but they also over-promised and proved reluctant to confront commercial interests. Obesity was tackled first in Health Action Zones, their boundaries drawn around poorer areas. But they were abandoned in 2003 and Professor Ken Judge assessed them to be 'implemented too hastily, too poorly resourced and provided with insufficient support and clear direction to make a contribution to reducing health inequalities in the time they were given'.

The order went out that across England schoolchildren were to play a minimum amount of sport. This worked. Fewer than one in four state schoolchildren were doing two hours of PE a week in 1997 but, with £2.4 billion extra injected into school sport since 2003, by 2010 more than nine in ten were doing the stipulated PE. Next, fruit. The 2000 NHS Plan ordered a free daily piece for two million 4–6-year-olds. Poor areas got the apples and oranges first; Scottish schools took up fruit as well. By 2009, 440 million pieces of fruit or portions of vegetables were being given to over two million children in 16,000 English schools each year. But their dietary value depended on what children consumed at home; fruit had a beneficial effect but children reverted to old habits once they were too old to qualify.

Jamie Oliver, superstar chef, discovered school food ingredients cost only 37p for each child. For the cameras he dangled obscene turkey twizzlers and an embarrassed government promised £280 million more for meals with, as ever, a new advisory quango, the School Food Trust. For Mike Baker, the education writer, it was suddenly hard to believe there had been so little fuss when the Tories abolished school meal nutritional requirements in the 1980s. Why had parents been so quiescent? The answer came in an onscreen moment of revelation as parents at Rawmarsh School in Rotherham pushed chips from Chubby's burger bar through the school fence. (It was all slightly stagy but the clip's popularity on YouTube instantly made the episode seem typical.) Labour MPs, drawing their votes from such places, feared headlines about a 'war on chips' and compromised by insisting schools make healthy alternatives available.

Labour, keen to improve diets, faced the horrible complexity of people's lives and the intractability of their attitudes towards food, exercise and health. To change them the government needed focus, persistence and coherence, simultaneously encouraging breastfeeding in Sure Start centres, promoting sports in schools, making urban cycling and walking easier, and driving to school harder. Labour also needed to sort out their own thinking about 'choice' and personalization; it made no sense to extol consumer sovereignty one minute and condemn what was in the shopping basket the next. But public health budgets rose and the Department of Health campaigned. Sport England cashed in with over £700 million 'to build a world class community sport infrastructure to sustain and increase participation in sport and allow everyone the chance to develop their sporting talents', the report *Healthy Weight, Healthy Lives* said in January 2008. New targets included getting each person in England to walk at least a thousand more steps a day by 2012.

Awareness grew. The *Clithero Advertiser & Times* (11 March 2010) gave local restaurant owner Paul Heathcote a plug for his new healthy menu at the Olive Press restaurant in York Street – where he was talking about 'balanced choices' and replacing fizzy drinks. However, a survey by the Food Standards Agency found consumption of dietary fat had not changed much in the decade to 2010 and saturated fat, the evil genius in heart disease, was still 20 per cent above target. Only a third of adults and one in seven teenagers were eating five portions of fruit and veg a day. Cornish mackerel would escape extinction: few ate the recommended one weekly portion of oily fish a week. As for Labour's ambitions to stir up a nation of couch potatoes, only 39 per cent of men and 29 per cent of women met the Chief Medical Officer's minimum recommendations for physical activity in adults in 2008.

But just as ministers were glumly contemplating failure, in November 2009 the National Heart Forum said rates of growth in child obesity were starting to slow. The head of nutrition at the Medical Research Council noted 'a shift in public awareness and attitude, coupled with concrete local initiatives to support healthier eating and more physical activity for children'.

The government resisted calls for compulsory food labelling with traffic-light signals alerting shoppers to high salt, sugar and fat content: the supermarkets were far more effective lobbyists than health researchers and Labour lacked the conviction to bang the drum for regulation. Not until 2007 did the law stop junk-food advertising on children's television. By 2010 only 15 per cent of drinks carried the message agreed under a voluntary protocol between the industry and government in 2007. Radical measures, such as a tax on sugar in soft drinks, a ban on advertising high-fat food and cigarette-style warning labels on food packaging, were never likely. Healthy eating demanded a recalibration of how state and business affected society and behaviour, and a rethink of the political identity Labour had assumed.

Labour tried not to think about causes and focused instead on symptoms. Health and education were the chosen instruments to lessen the effects of inequalities; the brute facts of low income were ignored. But teenage pregnancy confirmed you could not extract 'health' from its social context: the households in which young women became pregnant were poor ones. The younger the mother, the worse her and her children's life chances and the more likely both would later need healthcare. As with obesity, Labour set themselves a near-impossible target – to cut the conception rate for under-18s in half by 2010. It missed by a mile; teenage pregnancy fell by a tenth by 2008.

Everyone was living longer – good news. But the gap in life expectancy between men in poorest areas and the average grew by 2 per cent. For women the gap was worse: it widened by 11 per cent from 1997. Death rates remained lowest in the better-off South East, worst in the North West. Working-class men were reluctant to go for checks; the middle classes responded fastest to health messages, so benefited most from awareness campaigns. Fewer from poorer households died of cancer but fewer among the better-off, too, so the gap remained.

All classes drank more. Average consumption had risen from 3.5 litres of pure alcohol a head in 1947 to 9.5 in 2010. Health suffered: in England, hospital admissions caused by alcohol grew by nearly two-thirds between 2002 and 2008 and UK deaths from alcohol doubled in the fifteen years to 2006. (The problem was not uniquely British, as shown by the big rise in young Germans treated in hospital for drink.) The Commons health committee demanded that supermarkets and public services charge a minimum price for each unit of alcohol. The Chief Medical Officer backed the proposal, as did the Scottish Nationalist government in Edinburgh, but Labour demurred. They seemed to have become not just the brewers' (and supermarkets') party like the Tory Party of old, but the party party. Urban regeneration in Manchester, Newcastle upon Tyne and elsewhere depended on drink. The government could not reject this inner-city reviver whatever the public health benefits, and Labour MPs demanded to know why the poor should pay more for their pleasures. The party went on.

Drink was an example of an inconvenient truth. The NHS was Elastoplast for social and behavioural problems. Hospitals were warehouses. Nearly three-quarters of NHS money and care went on long-term conditions from which patients did not get better. Patients with long-term conditions occupied a third of hospital beds; home, GP and community nursing would have been a better formula for both patient and budget. A 'health' government would have cut hospitals and expanded home and community care, but ministers were reluctant to invite riotous campaigns to keep open inefficient, expensive and much-loved hospitals. They had not helped themselves when in opposition they had shamelessly attacked the Tories over closures, and they came to power promising to save every hospital under threat, including the redundant St Bartholomew's in the City of London; the Tories repeated the error in 2010 with what sounded like a promise never to close a single unit.

Yet it is all too easy to prescribe calm and considered policy-making when ministers' lives were made nasty and short thanks to the brutish hysteria of the media. Labour's attachment to Tory spending plans intensified the pressures during their first three years. As Mrs Thatcher had found, the NHS is a smouldering volcano. Neglect it for too long, Vesuvius explodes and political lava flows. The year Labour took over, the NHS budget increased by zero per cent. People were going blind because hospitals delayed their cataract treatments. The median waiting time for a cataract repair operation in 1998 was over 200 days (it was a quarter of that, ten years on). A fifth of lung cancers became inoperable as patients waited for surgery. Mavis Skeet led the news for days; this poor woman suffering from throat cancer had her operation cancelled four times in five weeks. The Millennium winter of 1999 saw a classic crisis, a flu outbreak filling beds.

This might have been a pivotal moment, the occasion for mature debate about costs and revenues. You get what you pay for. A better-provisioned NHS would cost money: higher tax, charges or a new stream of revenue dedicated to healthcare. Instead, with Blair–Brown antagonism sharp, the government panicked. In January 2000, rather than waiting for his chancellor's July spending review, Blair headed for the sofa on *Breakfast with Frost*. He blithely announced that UK healthcare spending would rise to match the EU average, which entailed an increase of at least another 2 per cent of growing GDP.

Did Labour overreact, sacrificing a measured approach to spending for the sake of a soundbite? Soon the NHS was consuming nearly £1 of every £5 of public spending. Since its creation, NHS spending had grown each year by 4 per cent in real terms; Labour upped this to 7 per cent. The result was that from 2000 the NHS enjoyed a record decade and spending doubled in real terms, pushing it to 9.3 per cent of GDP in 2010–11, close enough to the EU average to redeem Blair's promise. (At the same time health commitments were rising elsewhere. For comparison, between 1997 and 2005, the UK increased health spending per capita by 79 per cent, compared with 38 per cent in Germany and 53 per cent in France.)

NHS staff grew by 26 per cent from 1997, 272,000 more in a decade. Of these, 161,500 were clinical professionals. Labour employed 89,000 more nurses and 44,000 more doctors, attracting them in with much better pay. Of the £43 billion increase in spending from 2002 to 2007, pay and price inflation accounted for £20 billion, or nearly half.

Labour made a grand bargain with the NHS unions called Agenda for Change, revising grades to pay nursing and non-clinical staff for extra training and responsibilities; nurses could move up pay scales while staying on the wards. Nurses' scales that in 1997 ran from £12,000 to £26,000 improved by 2007 to run from £19,000 to £90,000. At first appalled at the cost, £28 billion payable from December 2004, managers eventually favoured the reform, saying it encouraged staff and pushed them to acquire skills. An evaluation by the King's Fund said change was rushed: transferring staff to the new scales became an end in itself rather than a way of treating patients quicker and better.

For consultants, the British Medical Association pulled off a coup in 2003. The government wanted managers to take control of senior doctors' working hours. Since the birth of the NHS, consultants had leeway for private practice or the golf course. Now they had to work forty-eight hours and offer any extra time to the NHS first. But the Department of Health miscalculated. The NAO said damningly that 'it did not collect sufficiently robust evidence on the numbers of hours worked by consultants' before agreeing the new contract. Many had in fact been doing overtime, only now they were paid. Pay increased by 25 per cent over the next three years, costing an extra £725 million – money that bought the same number of working hours or fewer. By 2006 consultants were on an average of £110,000, for working just over fifty hours a week.

The Office for National Statistics (ONS) said increases in staff numbers and pay were not matched by increased output, so NHS productivity fell over the decade to 2008. But these measurements are strongly disputed: other studies said that from 2004, care improvements, reduced reliance on temporary staff and higher throughput of patients turned the productivity tide – helped by higher-quality finance managers.

The new money bought physical transformation, immediately visible to patients and relatives coming through those new glass atriums, though they might moan about higher car park charges. Capital spending rose from £1.1 billion to £5.5 billion over the decade to 2007–8. That built 100 hospitals, pushing the average age of NHS buildings down dramatically: in 1997 half were

Doctor in the House; by 2010 most were *House* (only a fifth pre-1948). Sunderland, for example, refurbished all but one of its GP surgeries and health centres and built four new 'one-stop shops' offering healthcare, housing and homelessness advice. Labour's legacy was many more modern, bright, welcoming NHS clinics that confidently proclaimed the health service to be sustainable into the future.

Computers, too. British doctors were not, despite appearances, antagonistic to technology either in the operating theatre or in GP surgeries. A 2006 survey by the Commonwealth Fund, an American non-profit organization, showed the UK ahead on electronic prescribing and electronic access to patients' test results. But Choose and Book, the IT system designed to let GPs book patients into any hospital or with any consultant, faced debilitating problems and patients still had to phone hospitals to make appointments. The government succumbed to grandiosity. Its vision was compelling, of patients and clinicians carrying round digitalized records, diagnosis at a distance, smoothing the glitches between GPs and hospitals. A single 'spine' would receive records from across England; any doctor could access patient records anywhere, eliminating all those lost notes, let alone bad handwriting. But the National Programme for IT proved to be too big and suffered serious delays, though, unusually, civil servants wrote the contract to ensure dilatory suppliers bore the costs of late delivery. Its overall cost by 2012 was projected to be £12.7 billion, but by March 2008 only £3.6 billion had been spent. The implosion of the grand scheme was partly the companies' failure, partly the software. It fell victim to a new panic about data security. Libertarians joined in revolt with know-nothings, poisoning the political air around what had promised to be a major advance. Successive studies by auditors said the original vision remained feasible, but NHS trusts looked unlikely to have care records systems till 2015. The spine crumbled into local and regional arrangements.

Big spending pumped up expectations, whereas a more cautious approach might have avoided hubris. What the NHS needed most was a cadre of clever, financially literate managers, backed by astute non-executives, working within an envelope of central directions and targets but allowed room to respond to local circumstance, clinical capacity and demand. Many might be trained doctors and nurses, the rest professional managers with a public service bent. Such a fine body of men and women would have taken time to grow and they needed to be well paid. Instead of hunkering down for a long haul, Labour ministers contracted a bad case of policy diarrhoea, as Professor Chris Ham of the King's Fund called it.

First came targets. Failure to meet the numbers could spell career death, and during the most frenetic period of targetry in Blair's second term, managers were reputed not to last much longer than 1940 spitfire pilots. Targets led to 'gaming', the polite word for fiddling the figures. However, targets did cut waiting times and that had been the public's principal demand in 1997. The Centre for Market and Public Organisation compared the 'targets and terror' regime in the NHS in England with the NHS in Scotland, where targets were not adopted. Average waiting times fell in England by twelve days more than in Scotland and by around fifty-five days for those who had to wait the longest. That is a difference; but was it worth all the fuss and professional antagonism?

The government published a national plan in 2000. Despite its Stalinist overtones, this was a consensual and popular document. It ended the internal market created by the Tories, where GPs bought care from competing hospitals. Instead, it envisaged a co-operative hub-and-spoke model, in which GPs referred patients to smaller hospitals, which, in turn, recognizing the limits of their competence, referred them to regional centres of excellence. The plan begot a new contract for GPs, linking payments to clinical and service objectives. The plan meshed with the report commissioned separately by the Treasury from the former banker Sir Derek Wanless, which made the case for a National Insurance increase to pay for increased spending. The Treasury's budget that year was the most popular in a quarter century, offering evidence that people were willing to pay more for causes they cared about. Labour seemed well set to create a creditable and popular health service.

But in the second term dogmatism took hold. What happened next was an exercise in disruptive health administration. It was as if within health policy all the tensions within New Labour were played out, notably the conflict between planning and markets, between competition and cooperation.

Patients were to choose the hospital where they were to be treated (the reformers only got round to choice of GPs much later in the day). From 2006 patients had a minimum of four choices and from April 2008 they could, in theory, choose any hospital in England, private or public, provided it met minimum standards and charged no more than allowed under the tariff, the fee fixed for each patient and each category of disease. In practice most patients preferred their GP to navigate the system; they wanted trusted professionals to advise them when they were ill. Labour talked as if getting care and treatment were like going shopping.

By 2010, academics found that competition had fostered better management. But it also jeopardized the shared purpose and automatic co-operation on which the NHS depended. Hospitals became trusts, to give them more autonomy, which risked turning patients into parcels to be sent shuttling from GP to hospital and back. A 'patient pathway' was the goal: for patients and their families it was often more like an obstacle course. They confronted a unified health service as a disparate set of providers, now told to be more competitive with one another.

In May 2002 Alan Milburn told the NHS Confederation he was creating a new NHS in place of the old 'monolith', in which 'there is greater plurality in local services with the freedom to innovate and respond to patient needs'. But the NHS could never be a market as long as it promised equal treatment regardless of income; in commercial markets those with money can buy more. To avoid that logic in healthcare, Labour gurus such as Professor Julian Le Grand of the LSE began to devise voucher and top-up schemes, which would have spelled the end of the NHS as a universal service.

High Blairism demanded fragmentation for the sake of competition. Labour ministers envisaged a new private sector, but were unclear whether it was to perk up existing services or replace all or part of the NHS itself. They were intent on its expansion. Private companies took on a few failing GP services, but most contentious was buying care from independent-sector treatment centres (ISTCs), for-profit mini-hospitals for production-line surgery on hips, knees and cataracts often using simple keyhole procedures. Labour commissioned thirty-six of them to offer NHS trusts hand-to-hand combat. But not on a level battlefield. To entice private providers, the Health Department promised ISTCs 15 per cent more cash for each operation. Investors were still reluctant, so the companies were guaranteed payment for a fixed number of operations, no matter how many they did.

The ISTCs helped abolish waiting times. Fast treatment in gleaming new suites pleased patients and surveys of quality were mostly good. But by 2010 private hospitals provided only 10 per cent of elective surgery, not enough to change the complexion of the service. They were not notably productive, on average 78 per cent full against an NHS occupancy rate of 95 per cent. In 2009 their operations were still costing an average 11 per cent more than the NHS for surgery.

Borrowing from Thatcher-era proposals, Labour invented health's version of the academy schools: the foundation trusts. Autonomous and competitive, foundation hospitals – the idea was even extended to ambulances and mental health – were to be run on commercial lines under governing boards for which elections would be held. The theory was ropey and the practice mixed. In most cases the voting was confined to patient activists and staff and tailed off after initial enthusiasm – though Labour claimed 1.5 million members of the public had enrolled. The idea seemed half-baked, especially after the Treasury squashed the Blairite bid to give foundation trusts borrowing powers. Who was supposed to compete with the ambulance trusts — the local taxi service or the WRVS? A measure of enterprise was welcome, as one of the first foundation trusts, University College London

Hospitals, proved when it bought a private hospital to expand its cardiac treatment and cut numbers waiting. The new hospital allowed UCLH to do some 2800 revascularizations per year, twice its previous capacity, and the NAO certified the deal was cost-effective.

We visited a friend several times at the bright, newly built UCLH during his treatment for leukaemia in 2008–9. Like most NHS anecdotes his was a mixed story, the highs eventually overcoming the lows before his death. What he needed and his family wanted was kind, prompt, clean, safe and above all consistent and coherent treatment from friendly NHS staff. They often got it, but those 'patient level' qualities were not the object of the government's agitated policy-making. Labour barely tried to link hospital reforms with the felt experience of patients and their families. Ministers insisted that competition drove up quality, efficiency and responsiveness in the public sector and that the public wanted choice. Most evidence said the public wanted access and reliability. The economics textbooks said competition might drive down price; but it also threatened quality, which in health is everything.

What if Labour had not bothered with 'reform' and instead had just expanded provision, while still insisting on results, quality and patient contentment? Later health secretaries Alan Johnson and Andy Burnham calmed competition, the latter declaring the NHS would always be the preferred bidder against private firms. (He had to withdraw the promise when he remembered EU competition rules, but he lodged intent.) What if Labour had concentrated on GPs, instead of sitting the mighty hospitals even more firmly at the fulcrum of healthcare? Too late, towards the end, the Department of Health commissioned studies of how better to integrate patient care.

Not that Labour had not tried to beef up primary care. They had dismantled the Tories' fund-holding GPs but promptly reinvented 'practice-based commissioning', which looked remarkably similar. After Labour invented Primary Care Trusts (PCTs), they were reorganized twice and then cut in number by mergers. Regional health authorities were abolished and replaced by twenty-eight strategic health authorities, which in turn were reorganized into ten regions – which looked remarkably like what the NHS in England had started with. Back to square one. Nameplates and reporting lines changed constantly. The public health director for the South West had held his job since 1994, but between 1997 and 2005 had to reapply for the same post seven times because of reorganizations. Each change of letterhead and job title cost months in advertising and interviewing as managers wasted time worrying about their own jobs. Experienced people left, robbing the service of its deep memory. Ideologues and policy advisers in Westminster rarely consider such practicalities.

Labour forgot that the doctors and nurses carry the NHS ethos: lose their trust and you run the risk of their infecting patients with their discontents. Of course professionals could be self-interested, inefficient and incompetent. The inquiry into children's deaths at Bristol Royal Infirmary in the 1990s that reported in 2001 left Labour with an ample agenda for regulation. Blair would ask why some surgeons took a week to do three operations when others did thirty in the same time. Florence Nightingale had posed a similar question about comparative death rates in London hospitals on her return from the Crimea. Variation in performance was both a safety problem and a source of inefficiency. But it was not something to be cured from a prone position in Downing Street. Performance management at a distance is tricky.

For most patients GPs were the NHS; coverage improved vastly as their numbers grew by 4000. Practice nurses had more to do and their productivity rose. As for the doctors, the British Medical Association ran rings around ministers and civil servants when it negotiated a new contract meant to ensure that payment matched results. The Quality and Outcomes Framework (QOF) that was agreed in 2004 cost the Department of Health £1.76 billion more than it had budgeted. Much sniggering accompanied the comprehensive conning of swaggering, macho ministers. Civil servants predicted GPs would hit 75 per cent of the contract targets;

they immediately scored 90 per cent. Pay shot up by 58 per cent over three years. In real terms GPs' average income rose from about £58,000 in 1997 to over £110,000 in 2008–9.

The 2004 contract said more patients were to be screened and those with chronic diseases offered better support. GPs did start identifying diabetes and cardiovascular disease earlier and they treated patients faster. Cholesterol was checked, statins prescribed, depression monitored and the campaign against smoking renewed. Surgery consultations lasted longer, up from an average eight to twelve minutes. But at what price? 'As far as the public and taxpayer are concerned,' the NAO said, 'the benefits they should have been expecting to see have not materialized to the extent they should have done. From their perspective, it's not a good deal.' Also, by paying a paltry £6000 GPs could hand back any obligation to be on call at night and weekends. PCTs had to do expensive deals with other GPs or private firms, which often resorted to foreign locums – though a study by the NAO found six out of ten patients rating the new service positively.

The government vainly hoped better doctoring would cut admissions to hospital. In Hammersmith and elsewhere, GPs sat in A&E, helping filter the genuinely ill. The government looked for ways round the stagnant service offered by some GPs. It opened ninety walk-in NHS Centres in high streets and closer to where people worked. GPs had grumbled when in 1998 the government created NHS Direct, a phone and internet service run by nurses giving advice, attracting over half a million calls and three million hits a month to its website. The NAO praised the speed of its launch. A 2001 review found 'very few' callers got an engaged signal, though one in five had to wait more than half an hour for a nurse to call them back. It was hard to detect any impact on hospital admissions.

In its latter years in power Labour switched the focus to patients, their rights, safety and quality of care. A new NHS 'constitution' introduced in spring 2009 was underwhelming; the rights it conferred could not be legally enforceable unless the NHS were to become a paradise for ambulance-chasing lawyers, but it did strengthen the idea of minimum standards. The distinguished surgeon Ara Darzi, a Labour peer and minister, made a diagnosis. But the profession did not like his prescription of 152 health centres or polyclinics, diagnostic centres run by GP and nurse collectives, one for every PCT. They were to open at times to suit people who worked during the day – a challenge to most surgeries, which slammed their doors at 6 p.m. and at weekends.

For London, Darzi planned ten mini-hospitals where consultants would come to hold sessions, to get a grip on the often still poor and unscrutinized work by GPs working alone in ill-equipped surgeries. Surgeries were private businesses, so PCTs had no right to close down bad GPs; the only answer was to woo patients away to better services. Local GPs grumbled that the new polyclinics were not always well sited; they had to be built wherever land was affordable.

The government sought to enfranchise patients by training, for example, diabetes patients to manage their own treatment. These 'expert patients' were credited with better management of symptoms and with attending fewer GP consultations and using A&E less.

These measures marked the beginning of a better primary service, relieving hospitals of needlessly expensive non-specialist work, a goal unrealized since 1948. Had Labour started out in this practical direction in 1997, patients' experience would have improved faster. PCTs rank as one of the might-have-beens of the era. In 2009, the Care Quality Commission said 48 per cent were only fair or weak; the Commons health committee lambasted them for squandering 14 per cent of the NHS budget on paper-pushing 'commissioning' (the figure was contested). What enterprising managers would want to run a PCT when they could be running a mighty hospital? PCTs were supposed to be the powerhouse deciders, lynchpins of the internal market. They held the money to buy the best possible services for their local population and Blairite ministers vowed they would do 'world-class commissioning', a spurious claim since other countries did not do primary care commissioning. In fact, they were the weakest link.

The PCTs ran untidy but indispensable services such as district nursing, chiropody, speech and language therapy, community mental health and sexual health services. Contract them out, the reformers cried. But not-for-profit companies selling their services to PCTs made no financial sense to the nurses and midwives supposed to run them unless they kept their NHS pension rights, and if they did, they were no cheaper. Floating off community services made little sense either, when the problem was how to integrate care around patients.

A burst of regulatory engineering accompanied the pro-market fling. Labour created so many new arm's-length bodies that they then had to set up a separate 'council for regulatory excellence' to keep them all in line. The Commission for Health Improvement transmuted into the Healthcare Commission, then finally into the Care Quality Commission (CQC) as policy shifted. But only weeks after it passed a CQC inspection, tables published by Dr Foster Intelligence, a company co-owned by the NHS, exposed Basildon and Thurrock hospital for its above-average death rates.

Countering criticism that the new foundation trusts could spin out of control, the government created yet another regulator called Monitor to approve applications: 126 had been successful by February 2010. Hospitals scrimped and squeezed to pass the financial tests, an approach that came unstuck for patients in Stafford and Cannock Chase hospitals. The Mid Staffordshire foundation trust had ticked all Monitor's boxes but still contributed to the preventable deaths of 400 patients and offered thousands of others shockingly bad care. All England's hospitals were to qualify for the status within a couple of years. In reality, half never looked like they ever would.

One of Labour's regulators had foreign visitors queuing to admire it. The National Institute for Health and Clinical Excellence was set up in 1999 to mobilize scientific and clinical consensus around the effectiveness of drugs and treatments, and assess their cost before recommending their use by the NHS. 'It made the NHS more equitable,' the Centre for Economic Performance judged. NICE guidelines 'helped to prompt a more uniform uptake of new drugs and technology across the country'. Its enemies were Big Pharma, the drug companies, which were powerful political players because of the size of their UK investment; they used patient advocacy charities to lobby against NICE. Late-stage cancer drugs were most controversial. The tabloids stamped in outrage, provoking a public who found arguments based on risk, probability and opportunity cost hard to grasp. 'I cannot believe that my life is being measured in pounds,' said an anguished cancer patient in a case the media highlighted in 2005. But governments had to. Ministers usually backed the scientific legitimacy and reputation of NICE and held the line when they judged an expensive drug added minimal extra chance of life. Big Pharma itself began to avoid referring new drugs to NICE: if rejected in Britain, other countries followed NICE's lead and refused them too.

Despite such recognition of their craft, despite all the buildings and their own higher pay, some surveys found only 3 per cent of doctors 'favourable' in judging the state of the NHS: 70 per cent were 'critical'. But in international comparison, primary care physicians in the UK emerged as positive. As with teachers, the government had to balance respect for professional judgement and a legitimate push for performance. Did Labour go badly awry? Had Labour chivvied and reorganized them less, clinical staff might have smiled and encouraged their patients to feel better about the improved NHS. All too typical were the words used by Simon Gray in *Coda*, his account of his cancer year published in 2008, which described a session with a nurse: solemn, unforgiving, insensitive, frowning, scowling, indifferent and blank.

Labour's 'choice' programme had not swung patients' opinion one way or another; they asked for quality, short waits and clean, pleasant local hospitals with kind and caring staff. They were satisfied, with 91 per cent of those treated in hospital consistently rating the quality of care as good to excellent. The same proportion were satisfied with their GP surgery or health centre. But Ipsos MORI's Ben Page also noted the 'I've been lucky' syndrome where people regarded their good experience as exceptional. The public – whose experience as patients would have been intermittent – mixed their views of the NHS with their wider take on politics and events. Satisfaction with the NHS in 2008 was higher than it had been since 1984: 51 per cent said 'very' or 'quite' satisfied, 17 percentage points more than in 1997. Often views about the NHS became a proxy for people's political sentiments. Yet the salience of health fell. In 1997, six out of ten regarded the parlous state of the NHS as their principal concern, spiking at seven out of ten in early 2000, which was why Blair made his abrupt sofa announcement on funding. Health anxiety then dropped sharply, reaching its lowest levels under Labour by 2009, when only one in ten put the NHS anywhere near the top of worries – trumped easily by the economy and crime.

People still found plenty to concern them. As they forgot about waiting lists, they worried about superbugs; hospital-acquired infections were an old problem and their resurgence indicted hospital management and nursing standards. True to form, the government issued a target: the incidence of MRSA cut in half by 2008 and of C. *difficile* by a third by 2010–11. The NHS, with its often foreign and low-paid cleaning staff, rolled up its sleeves. MRSA was cut by 57 per cent by the end of March 2008 and C. *difficile* by 41 per cent. But pity those undergoing surgery in the one in eight trusts where MRSA infection increased during the same period.

MRSA shows how Labour never managed to change the tenor of the 'NHS conversation'. Alarm was followed by panicky response. The public could not be brought to triage their own demands: they wanted better results and they liked sparkling new prestige hospitals, but often rebelled when old and familiar institutions closed or services were reconfigured. Labour got a bloody nose early on when plans to shrink Kidderminster Hospital and remove its A&E led to the election of a local doctor, standing as the 'Save Our Hospital' candidate for Wyre Forest. He ousted the sitting Labour MP in the 2001 election and won again in 2005, before losing to the Tories five years later.

The NAO said victims of life-threatening injury faced

'unacceptable' variations because the NHS lacked 24/7 modern trauma units with specialists on call. The auditors stated that of the 3000 deaths in hospital from major trauma each year, an extra 450 to 600 lives could be saved across England. But, a clincher, such units could only work if smaller A&E suites elsewhere closed. Uproar. Labour MPs and even, disgracefully, cabinet ministers were so alarmed at scare campaigns against closures they joined protests in their own constituencies. As health secretary, Alan Johnson poured balm on the wounds, referring plans to an independent panel that eased closures through but stopped a few. The example below of closing the A&E at Chase Farm Hospital in Enfield showed how important clinical opinion could be in winning over the public.

If, on most indicators, the NHS had improved since 1997, why did Labour reap so little political reward? One reason is that people 'pocket' public service improvements, redraw their baseline and expect more – and Labour encouraged them by failing to link benefits, costs and tax. The public wanted to live longer and get sick less, but complained when the government tried to chivvy them to cut smoking, eating and drinking and exercise more. Yet one sign of Labour's stewardship was the growing popularity of the NHS among those who could afford to go private. Numbers paying for private operations fell during a decade of rising disposable income. As NHS waiting times fell, so use of the private sector shrank – even allowing for the rise in private cosmetic operations and tummy tucks.

But the public's views cannot be the arbiter when so much of what a health service does is out of sight and rarely in the public mind. Take mental health. The WHO European Regional Director for Mental Health, Matt Muijen, speaking in 2006, asserted that mental health services in England were better funded, structured and supported than anywhere in Europe: 'No country has it all as England has.' Waiting times for cognitive behaviour therapy fell, but were still too long for GPs, often left with no choice but to prescribe drugs to the clinically depressed.

Public demand required expensive preparation for epidemics,

even if they never quite materialized. Much criticized for not 'joining up' services, the government did well on H1N1 flu, as an independent report confirmed after the election. After the first case was reported in Mexico in April 2009 and the first UK case in Scotland later that month, the Westminster and devolved governments, the NHS and other public bodies moved swiftly to stockpile vaccine (132 million doses), alerting GPs and nurses to prepare for the worst.

The trends were benign, and Labour's stewardship pushed them along. Infant death rates halved and mortality from disease fell by over a third between 1996 and 2007. Put simply, our chances of living longer rose as the likelihood of dying from disease fell. The 2000 NHS cancer plan was an impressive mustering of targets and leadership. Cancer mortality improved at pretty much the same pace in France, Germany, Australia and the US – though England spent 5.6 per cent of the healthcare budget on cancer, compared with France's 7.7 and Germany's 9.6 per cent. Five-year survival rates for colorectal cancer diagnosed between 1995 and 1997 were better in England than in Denmark, but worse than those of the European leaders. The gap did not shrink. The UK continued to spend relatively more on cancer research, for example developing the new prostate cancer dug Abiraterone.

Yet for circulatory disease – especially heart conditions – the relative rate of improvement was striking and brought the UK to the same position as Germany, Australia and the US. The cause was statins, cuts in waiting times for heart surgery, and quicker and more effective treatment of heart attacks. In 2001, only 24 per cent of stroke patients received thrombolysis (clot busting) within sixty minutes of a call for help; by 2010 it was almost 70 per cent. That took investment, which included seventy-two extra catheter laboratories; GPs were paid to improve recording of blood pressure. The NHS got round to a national strategy for strokes by 2007, emphasizing anti-cholesterol drugs and prevention. Since 2006, stroke patients' chances of dying within ten years fell by 4 per cent.

In their own terms Labour failed on the count of equality.

Access to care continued to depend on postcode, despite NICE. How many years you lived, and your chances of contracting disease and surviving it, remained closely linked to class and income. A government with egalitarian ambitions barely closed the health gap, despite directing more NHS money to the poorest places. Health spending, like education, turned out to be no panacea for lifetime disadvantage. The NHS could not mitigate basic inequalities in income and life chances. Poor people have poorer health, and no health service can overcome that.

If Labour leaves any lesson, it is this: avoid big new institutional changes and push on with improvement on the ground. Ministers wasted time, political energy and money on non-stop reorganization. But on central targets most managers, analysts and even eventually many doctors were agreed: they worked, combined with shed-loads of money. Some were perverse, some pointless and there were too many – but the important ones did force staff to keep pursuing basic goals.

Looking back to that 1997 electioneering ploy about 'saving the NHS', the government delivered. Labour killed – perhaps anaesthetized would be a safer judgement – the zombie that had been lumbering around health discussions since the late 1970s: replacing a tax-funded service free at the point of use with insurance and private funding. Ending waiting lists and brightening wards, it cemented the NHS ever deeper into the collective sense of what being British means, even if that included never-ending complaint.

The verdict from Chase Farm Hospital

Enfield is not where Labour would have chosen to tell their NHS story. We returned there because we had closely monitored public services in the borough for the *Guardian* for the four years from 2001. More a basket case than a showcase, Enfield health had bombed when the Tories first drew up league tables. Chase Farm Hospital was notorious before and after 1997. Originally a Victorian orphanage – the clock tower remains –

then a treatment centre for Second World War wounded, it had never been an NHS star. When the *Guardian* first visited, Chase Farm's A&E was packed with patients on trolleys, most waiting far longer than the target four hours. Cases backed up because 'the system' failed to arrange home care for older patients. Waiting lists grew and it took longer to get patients from A&E into wards. In 2003 Chase Farm only just met the deadline for treating patients who had been waiting more than a year. Minutes before midnight on the eve of the new financial year, patients had been rushed into operating theatres. Such absurdity brought targets into disrepute, said some; others concluded that nothing electrified failing hospitals like targets.

When Averil Dongworth took over as chief executive in 2004, she was the twelfth in eleven years, each defeated by the challenge. Her chances of success were as near zero as Chase Farm's star rating – regulators awarded it no stars for longer than any other hospital in England. The public complained about cleanliness, and infection rates were high. When the star system was scrapped, Chase Farm was rated 'weak' on quality and financial management. But under Dongworth, who had run the primary care trust in next-door Barnet, the hospital hit every target. In October 2009 the Care Quality Commission rated Chase Farm good for both quality and finance, and put it in the top thirteen most improved. An inspector said facetiously, 'I declare, officially, that Chase Farm is no longer a basket case.'

Dongworth, born and brought up in Omagh, Northern Ireland, trained as a nurse in Barnet. She is a large, forceful, funny and cheerful woman, witty and caustic with an infectious enthusiasm. She had dropped out of school without A levels. 'I was a dizzy seventeen-year-old with no plans. I had wanted to be a vet, but girls at my school were not allowed to do science.' She drifted into a temporary job in the catering department of a local mental hospital where a ward sister spotted her potential and suggested she go into nursing. She applied to six hospitals in London and was accepted by Barnet with no qualifications and no interview. 'I had no vocation whatever,' she says with a laugh. 'But from the day I hit the wards, I just loved it. Nursing was for me.' She became a ward sister at twenty-one, and the night nursing officer at the Whittington Hospital in Islington at just twenty-nine. She was the first nurse to become a hospital general manager.

Labour was ever keen on upgrading qualifications, so now every nurse must be a graduate. Dongworth took an MA at Ashridge Management College. 'I was the only public sector manager there and it exposed me to management theory and private sector managers.'

Hanging on her door was a healthcare assistant's uniform she donned from time to time to walk the wards. Few recognized her because in medicine's caste system, the lowest rank is invisible. One day she berated a junior doctor for failing to keep his arms bare to the elbow and smothered in anti-bacterial gel. He rounded on her arrogantly at this presumption. She told him tartly who she was and that if he didn't obey the infection control rules, he would be out of a job by the afternoon. That sort of story whisked around the wards within hours.

What Chase Farm needed was leadership: strong, consistent and stable. She supplied it. For her first years everyone kept assuming she would be gone by the next Monday morning like all the others. Now headhunters rang trying to poach her. But she was right, it was not done yet. The hospital still carried a historic debt of £18 million. Chase Farm made an operating surplus in 2008 and expected to make £4.5 million in 2010, but the old borrowing (within the NHS) was a problem with ever-tightening budgets ahead.

She helped hammer out a plan to reconfigure three hospitals in North London. Barnet and Chase Farm had amalgamated and their services were to be rationalized with North Middlesex, Chase Farm losing its A&E, keeping only a daytime walk-in treatment centre for minor injuries. It would do pre-planned surgery from the waiting lists, specializing in cardiac and cancer cases. Its maternity unit would also move. Doctors in the hospital supported the plan and they tried hard to persuade the public in noisy local meetings. It would be safer for emergency cases to travel further to a hospital with a full 24/7 complement of specialists.

Healthier?

But a Save Chase Farm movement took off and two members were elected to Enfield Council on its ticket. They lost their seats in the 2010 borough elections, but the campaign won the backing of the new Tory health secretary, Andrew Lansley. Within days of taking over he vetoed the reconfiguration. He may regret such populist decision-making.

As for Dongworth, she remains a case study in the latent talent within the NHS and the vitality of its management. As chief executive of Chase Farm she was paid £170,000 a year. That was by no means top of the league – the head of Guy's and St Thomas' in central London was on £270,000. Too much? Labour ought to have anticipated the Tory–Liberal Democrat coalition in examining public-sector executive pay and trying to base it on a set of principles.

Non-political, Dongworth still had strong views. In 1997 she was chief executive of City and Hackney health authority: 'Frank Dobson came in as Labour's first health secretary and made mental health a first priority. We got money right away, so we closed down a terrible Victorian mental hospital that was more like a prison than healthcare and we opened up a bright new facility at the Homerton.' On targets, she was one hundred per cent in support, despite all the grumbling from the professions. 'Take the four-hour maximum wait in A&E. Well, just ask the patients how they used to feel, waiting forty-eight hours on trolleys in corridors. I say to my staff, is that what you would want for your relatives?' But what of the research that shows a depressing number of nurses in England say they would not want to be treated in their own hospital? 'That question was asked cold and the answer was misinterpreted. A lot of them meant they wouldn't want to be treated in a place where they were known, and their medical record seen by employers. Most nurses are proud of where they work.'

That led to a theme she often returned to: we have 'great public services we often undervalue'. She blamed the press, which she loathed with a passion, partly because of her experience with her local paper's obstinate and deliberately misleading campaign against sensible reorganization. 'The question is how to get the public engaged with the services they've got. It's the same with schools and the police – if only people would take a hard look at how good they are, instead of relying on the odd negative story exaggerated in the media.'

As for Labour's NHS reorganizations. 'Going in a circle? No, I'd say three or four times round in a circle.' If she stays on during the Con-Lib era, she will have more circuits to do.

CHAPTER 3

The economy under Labour

'I just want my money out,' Thea Hardy from Crystal Palace told reporters as she joined a shuffling, angry queue outside a Northern Rock branch, showing how formerly phlegmatic Britain could panic with the best of them. The day the good times ended was 14 September 2007. The subsequent recession caused UK national output to fall 5 per cent, a larger cumulative loss of output than in any other post-war recession. Labour went from impresario of capitalist prosperity to doughty Keynesian mobilizing the state to fill capitalism's deficiencies. Neither of course was the whole story.

Brown strode into the Treasury in 1997, a Moses stern enough to soothe bondholders' century-old fears about the Left, his tablets commanding prudence and public-spending constraint. But this upstanding prophet fawned on financial power. This Labour chancellor would petition Her Majesty to confer a knighthood on Alan Greenspan, a devotee of the cult of the capitalist superwoman Ayn Rand.

Capital will be safe with Labour, Brown had told the boardrooms in the City and Canary Wharf. And so it proved to be. Corporate taxation was kept low – it was second lowest among the G7 in 2009. Profits beckoned, as the state divested itself of air-traffic control and defence research, pushed contracting in health and IT, guaranteed returns for the companies owning water, nuclear and train companies and (though this changed later) soft-pedalled on competition inquiries in defence, communications and energy. Brown was Guizot, the nineteenth-century French prime minister who told his country 'enrichissez-vous'.

The bargain was meant to go two ways. Cosset the golden goose and she will keep laying. The City and business were to grow jobs and revenue, while Labour eased the plight of the poor. No need for vote-jeopardizing redistribution if the chancellor's coffers were full and government had more to spend without adjusting tax rates. No official document ever spelled it out but this was the 1997 version of Wilson and Callaghan's 'social contract', theirs with the unions, Blair and Brown's with business and finance.

So did Labour's bargain produce the goods and did the growth justify the attendant inequality and instability? The UK economy was worth £830 billion in 1997 and £1140 billion at the start of 2010. In real terms it grew by a fifth. If that sum were shared out equally, everyone would have had £3840 per capita more in January 2010 than in May 1997, measured in 2009 prices. Those years of growth and recession added only enough to buy a third of a new Ford Fiesta, a week in Lanzarote for six, a breast-enlargement operation, a year's university tuition or a year's social housing rent. Averaged over the Labour years, annual growth in GDP per capita was 1.6 per cent. The 1948–98 average had been 2.2 per cent. Labour bucked no trend.

The recent past now looks like an eighteen-year cycle, gathering momentum after Black Wednesday in 1992 and ending as the economy started growing again in 2010. The UK outpaced rivals during the bubble, but the recession pushed it back down the rankings. Even then, measured in purchasing-power parity, UK living standards per capita were still higher in 2010 than in Germany, France, Italy and Japan.

Labour's tenure was a game of two halves. Towards the end of the first, in late 2006, the OECD praised the UK as 'the Goldilocks economy'. Like the little bear's porridge, it was neither too hot nor too cold. A month later, would-be president Nicolas Sarkozy came to London to canvass votes from the French diaspora, many in the

City, and spoke enviously of the Anglo-Saxon model of capitalism. If the clocks had stopped on New Year's Eve 2006, Labour's stewardship might have looked positive. Take Manchester. Its centre was transformed, its trams, bridges, proud public spaces showing the high levels of public investment in the city and in Salford. Unemployment when Labour took power was 8.4 per cent. In January 2007 it was 3.8 per cent. More money was swishing around the city but not far from the bright lights of the city centre, the people of Openshaw and Hulme still depended heavily on benefits; not for them the new jobs in hip bars and hotels. Gross disposable household income rose from £9905 in 2000 to £12,291 on the eve of recession.

If the UK had a formula it was still Thatcher's: the costs of employing people remained lower in the UK than elsewhere in Europe – workers were more 'flexible'. During the recession, unemployment remained relatively low, at 8 per cent. But the social costs of a low-wage economy are also destabilizing, putting extreme pressure on households and communities, helping explain idiosyncratic British worries about crime and disorder. Socially disruptive mass migration pegged down low wages. The British model was only one of the ways to trade off inequality, social disruption, job creation and prosperity. The Germans had higher unemployment, but treated those out of work more generously because, right and left, they valued 'social solidarity'.

The UK formula started with consumption. Growth kept going because people spent more than they could afford. The ratio of UK savings to GDP was the lowest of any OECD country; the proportion of private disposable income saved fell from 12 per cent in the early 1990s to zero in 2008. Guizot had said make yourself rich by hard work and thrift. Brown all but said: do it by pushing up your credit card balance.

What Labour brought to the party was jobs. Well over half the 2.2 million new jobs created in the UK between 1998 and 2007 were public sector or in charities and firms dependent on public contracts. State and 'parastate' employment rose from 6.2 million in 1998 to 7.5 million in 2007. These jobs did not crowd out opportunities that otherwise would have arisen in private firms. Instead, you could argue, as does Professor Karel Williams of Manchester University, that Labour was 'filling in for the incompetence of the private sector to employ'. Between 1997 and 2007, London's regional GDP increased 6.4 per cent a year, against 3.5 per cent in the North East and 3.1 per cent in the North West. Manchester prospered, but the gap remained; without government it would have become a chasm. One reason why unemployment did not rise as sharply in the recession as in previous downturns was the public sector. In the three months to October 2009, for example, an extra 23,000 NHS jobs pushed up employment opportunities, in many cases for women. Another academic study, looking at Dundee – the jam and jute city once famously dependent on international trade – remarked that with four out of ten jobs in the public sector, the city had been 'de-globalized', making its regional economy both less open and more stable.

Labour's trick was to detach living standards from incomes. During stable, low-inflationary growth, people readily took on more debt while running down their savings. When nearly seven out of ten households owned their own homes, property inflation created a widespread sense of being better off, with added ease of borrowing. The wealth illusion depended on the banks lending on higher multiples of income to finance consumption. Bankers were the alchemists of Labour-era prosperity. Ministers turned a blind eye to financial excess so long as it filled Treasury coffers and in return kept consumers and house-owners happy. With at least some vestigial memory of the part bankers had played in their history – in 1931, the 1960s and 1970s – Labour might have been more wary.

Finance's share of GDP in the UK economy rose from 5.3 per cent in 2001 to 9.1 per cent on the eve of the recession. Finance generated foreign earnings and contributed 35 per cent of all corporation tax paid in 2001. However, its share of corporation tax fell to 27 per cent in 2008, a sign of how unsustainable such revenues were. Banks were never going to help Labour on the jobs front, finance accounting for only one job in twenty-eight. In the decade after 1997 employment in Great Britain in banking and financial services did rise, but slightly, from 978,000 to 1,054,000. Compare that with manufacturing, where the job count fell from 4,050,000 in 1997 to 2,820,000 in 2007. It turned out that the finance sector's largesse was temporary.

Labour had swallowed an ideology. That was the word used by Adair Turner, chairman of the Financial Services Authority, to describe the assertion that liberalization of short-term capital flows was both necessary and benign. Market intelligence was dumb. In 2007, the crash imminent, the credit default swap market was 'revealing' that the risk of a major bank defaulting had hit its lowest ever level, a message backed up by banks' share price. Labour never got it, nor the point made by American economist Joseph Stiglitz. He argued that the banks practised ersatz capitalism: when they had become 'too big to fail' they had stopped being genuine commercial entities.

Labour had divided supervision between the Bank of England and the new Financial Services Authority, with the Treasury hovering in the background. But this triple overview was irrelevant when the government decreed 'see no evil' in the City; the problems were political, not regulatory. The FSA was expressly told to put profitability before sustainability. All were complicit in letting the banks' boards run riot. After the crash, the FSA started raiding suspect bankers at dawn. Imagine the demonstration effect if, five years earlier, it had sent the heavy mob into RBS.

Even after the crash, it is not clear how much Labour understood. Brown, in his maddeningly airy way, avoiding personal responsibility, said the UK was paying a one-off cost for globalization. Typically, he never explained the reasons for the bust, but got away with it because the response to the crisis from the other political parties was uncomprehending and inept. At the 2010 election, Labour's strongest card was the way they handled the financial crisis followed by their Keynesian textbook response to recession – bringing forward capital spending and keeping to planned increases in public-sector jobs and spending, at the expense of an increase in the deficit. Darling and Brown were praised for their phlegm and pragmatism. But you could read their unstinting application of public money in rescuing the banks as the opposite of 'statism'. As William Keegan put it succinctly in the *Observer* (16 May 2010), 'Having given us the debt crisis, and passed the financial and private sector's debts over to the public sector's balance sheet, the financial sector now has the audacity to complain about the public-sector debt crisis it created.'

Labour's catchphrase came out of the neoclassical economist's playbook; it was flexibility. In labour markets, that meant people's willingness to accept low wages and insecure employment. In financial markets it meant reluctance to tax and regulate, in case the golden goose found her wings and flapped off to nest in Zurich. Flexibility meant not joining the Euro, for which Blair's enthusiasm was idiosyncratic and short-lived. In retrospect non-entry looks preordained, given public opinion and Rupert Murdoch's power. In 2003, at his most bullying, Brown had dared the Cabinet to read his 2000-page examiner's script on the tests he had set for entry. His defiant setting of the exam and equally defiant announcement of the negative result said everything about his French-speaking, Italian-holidaying next-door neighbour. After the recession, Brown could claim he was right. If, as Blair had wanted, the UK had joined in 1997, growth would have been slower, the bust might have come sooner and without sterling depreciation recovery from recession would have been harder. But the economy might have been better balanced and, who knows, Iraq less likely. That is academic: Brown had already taken his decision on the euro when Labour entered office. It was to make the Bank of England independent, not to hand authority to the European Central Bank.

Bank independence was the high-water mark of Labour's embrace of the neoliberal idea that the economy was best governed by expert rules, not cack-handed politicians. Because of the deference paid to economists and bankers, a theory became an axiom. The crash showed the extent to which nobody, especially economists, had a clue what went on under the bonnet. The Bank's vaunted success in keeping prices down turned out to be a local version of a worldwide trend. During the bubble, the Bank governor Mervyn King shared the serene conviction of his American counterpart Alan Greenspan that the wisdom of the markets would always prevail. In critical months during 2008 the Bank miscalculated the risk register between inflation and systemic failure. 'The origins of the crisis,' King asserted (*Guardian*, 20 January 2010), 'lay in our inability to cope with the consequences of the entry into the world trading system of countries such as China, India, and the former Soviet empire – in a word globalization. The benefits in terms of trade were visible; the costs of the implied capital flows were not.'

Though uttered by the banker, those words encapsulated Brown's view. In it the state was a cipher, a plaything of 'forces' and flows. Both men seemed unaware of the paradoxes. Both China and India were state-driven economies. Besides, if the crisis were to be resolved, only states could act and, in the UK case, did act. Labour made the Bank of England independent in the belief that only central banks can be trusted to ensure strict monetary discipline and keep inflation down. But the reasons for low inflation were global – notably, cheap production in China and raw material prices. A sudden oil price spike in 2010 pushed UK inflation up too, proving that Bank independence and money supply had little to do with it. The 'explanatory' letter King was bound to write was vacuous.

A sympathizer would agree that the incoming Labour government did feel an acute need to expiate a reputation for financial mismanagement, earned in the 1970s when the IMF had to be called in. Yet of the four occasions since 1945 when the state ran a budget surplus, Labour was the party in power on three of them. Profligacy with the public finances had been a Tory vice, as it was with the US Republicans. The 'structural deficit' made much of in the 2010 election had been bequeathed to Labour by the Tory chancellor Ken Clarke. This refers, simply, to the gap between what the state takes in taxes and what it spends. In the decade after 1997, Labour increased public spending by 1.2 per cent of GDP (which of course was growing). It raised taxes by 2.3 per cent of GDP, which is why Brown could boast about paying down the accumulated borrowings of the state – the national debt. But watch the timings: spending was starting to run ahead of receipts even before the recession and the bail-out that pushed the deficit to 9 per cent of GDP. It was not that Labour, having masochistically worn too tight a corset for the two first years, then tore off the garment with burlesque abandon. As the brakes came off spending, the government failed to make a political case for matching it with extra tax receipts. Labour leaders colluded with the public wish for American tax and European spending, and that, combined with the crash, produced the huge rise in state debt – to £890 billion in 2010.

Brown's tablet from Sinai had said national debt should stay below 40 per cent of GDP. Labour repaid debt from 1998 to March 2001, pushing it below 30 per cent in 2001–2. If national debt then rose, by 2007–8 it was still well under 40 per cent (at 36.5 per cent of GDP, the second lowest among the big economies). The Treasury had plucked that 40 per cent limit out of a hat; no formula or economic theory specified it. But once lodged, it became a reference for the dealing rooms and buyers of UK government debt – and they started to twitch when the Treasury projected national debt would nearly double by 2011–12. Darling's first budget in 2008 said debt would fall steadily over the next two decades. In fact the worsening in the public finances saw the projected debt rise beyond 75 per cent of GDP by 2014. But other countries lived happily enough with such a ratio. Here Brown's exaggerations did their damage. Markets, and not just currency and bond markets, pullulate with sentiment and subjectivity, whatever the textbooks used to say about them maximizing knowledge; they also remember and resent what former chancellors told them.

The charge against Labour cannot be that it overspent. It fixed essentials in the public realm, work made urgent by earlier Tory imprudence; the necessary expansion of health and education spending was willed by the public. The problem was how the extra spending was paid for. The indictment says Labour failed to adjust that spending to the reduced rate of growth obvious after the first years of the new century. A sheepish Treasury mandarin,

Sir Nick Macpherson, acknowledged it. 'With the benefit of hindsight, the surge in revenues in the late 1990s may have been more cyclical than it appeared at the time: and it was this assessment that informed the spending reviews early in this decade.'

The personal crashed into the prudent. Will Hutton (*Observer*, 13 December 2009) argued that Brown's wilful refusal to raise the money for spending increases after 2001 stemmed from his fear that unpopular tax increases might jeopardize his dream of succeeding Blair. When Blair stayed on after 2005, scuppering his grand plan, Brown still avoided necessary tax increases or spending restraint, waiting for his coronation. A measure of Brown's profligacy was successive revisions in forecasts for the gap between spending and outlays – bending the 'golden rule' he had inscribed on the tablets he carried into Number Eleven in 1997. In 2000, the Treasury projected stability or even a surplus. On the eve of the financial crash eight years later, the annual deficit reached 2.7 per cent of GDP, about what Labour inherited from the Tories in 1997.

Labour's response to the crash would have been more financially comfortable if during the previous decade bedside reading in Number Eleven had included *Matthew 7:24–27*. This recounted the parable of the man who built his house on sand. When the rain came, the streams rose and the winds blew and it fell with a great crash. Public borrowing between May 1997 and the first quarter of 2008 totalled £161 billion; the UK government borrowed more than that in the single twelve months between April 2009 and April 2010. Windfall tax gains from the booms in the City and house prices were not going to support the rafters in a hurricane. Labour's budgets – in 2000 or 2002 – could have been 'you pay for what you get' moments of truth. In retrospect the 2005 budget was Labour's last chance, pre-recession, to say: here is the bill for services rendered. That year we interviewed Andrew Dilnot – just moving from the Institute for Fiscal Studies to become principal of St Hugh's College, Oxford. He spied a watershed for the welfare state. People wanted more and more health and education. If the state were to satisfy them, it had to spend more, which meant either raising taxes or cutting non-welfare spending, such as defence. Cut defence, after 9/11? 'That means – if we're not going to see the role of the state decline – we have to see tax increases.'

Labour got by thanks to Tory taxes. The IFS estimated a third of the increase in tax revenues as a share of GDP since 1997 came from tax started by the Tories and continued under Labour – such as the fuel and tobacco duty escalators. A third came from Labour's own tax increases and a third from growing incomes or 'fiscal drag', where earnings increases push taxpayers into higher tax brackets.

When it did increase National Insurance in 2001, clearly earmarking it for health, the public applauded. The pollsters called it the most popular budget for twenty-five years and this could have been a lesson for Labour. NI was, after all, a kind of income tax. If voters are to support an increase, they have to connect it to services received. A Fabian commission on tax in 2000 asked people if they would pay an extra 1p on the basic rate of income tax to pay for general spending: 40 per cent said yes. Whether they would pay to earmark money for education: 68 per cent said yes. All that sounds somewhat abstract now that it is going to require a 6p in the pound increase in income tax to get debt down to what the National Institute for Social and Economic Research calls manageable levels – but it is a reminder of lost opportunity.

Still, over the ten years from 1997, the share of tax receipts coming from income did rise, including NI and council tax. The balance of tax shifted slightly away from pleasure – drinking, smoking and gambling – and from motoring. In keeping with the retailing spirit of the times, the tax-take from consumption fell as a share of total tax. To get the money in, Labour depended on housing and finance. Banks provided a slug of corporation tax, then there was housing stamp duty, inheritance and capital gains tax, and VAT from buying paintbrushes at B&Q. In 2002–3 these receipts were together equivalent to 3 per cent of GDP. By 2007–8 this had risen to 4.25 per cent, and that growth accounted for half the increase in total current receipts over these years. Inevitably they weakened in the recession.

When Labour came in, tax amounted to 35 per cent of GDP.

It is worth pausing on that figure. Anti-statists liked to conjure up a government behemoth consuming the nation's hard-earned produce, with Gordon Brown intent on fattening the beast. Yet under Labour the tax-GDP ratio peaked at just over 36 per cent in 2001 then fell, before picking up, returning to 36 per cent in 2007–8. It had risen well above that level during the high days of Thatcherism, from 1980 to 1989. The UK's historical challenge and Labour's political challenge was that the national appetite for services and transfer payments was higher.

Labour's most striking early move was to cut capital gains tax from 40 to 10 per cent, raising it after the crash to a still modest 18 per cent in 2009. Part of the implicit bargain with the City, this was a bonanza with far-reaching effects. It was Brown's friend, the Labour donor Sir Ronnie Cohen, who told him total receipts would rise on the back of tax cuts. Instead, heroic venture capitalists got their accountants to reclassify income as capital gains, avoiding sizeable slabs of tax.

Labour's most catastrophic tax change, in 2007, sprang from Brown's desire for a popular inauguration as prime minister. He abolished the 10p rate that he had brought in as a way of cutting tax for the lowest earners. Now even low-earners would have to pay 20p tax, the proceeds used to cut the basic rate to 20p for all but top earners. He wanted to bribe the majority of basic-rate payers, hoping tax credits would compensate low-earning families. The change came into force in April 2008, just as the Crewe and Nantwich by-election was in full swing – and the middle-middle Englanders Brown had expected to celebrate hated it. They were were outraged that the poorest would have to pay for their tax break. Labour lost Gwyneth Dunwoody's safe seat.

Even at the peak of the housing boom, inheritance tax was due on only one in fourteen estates but media campaigns amplified homeowners' and legatees' fears. Labour quailed. Even though Labour had already adjusted thresholds to keep the incidence of inheritance tax broadly the same for ten years, in a fit of panic in the autumn after Brown became prime minister, they proposed cutting it.

Labour ministers called tax a 'burden' when they should have joined the diary-keeping MP Chris Mullin in promoting it as 'the subscription for living in a civilized society'. They might have been tougher with the free-riders. HM Revenue & Customs (HMRC) estimated the gap between what taxpayers owed and what they paid at 8 per cent of GDP or £40 billion, compared with American estimates of 14 per cent and Denmark's 6 per cent. Tax-avoidance expert Richard Murphy said it was likely to be nearer 20 per cent, or £100 billion. The government, like the Tories before it, put menacing posters in bus shelters urging citizens to shop benefit cheats. It ran great data-matching exercises to trace over-claims and fraud by tenants and disabled people. But it dealt with serious tax cheats gingerly. It posted no warning posters in City champagne bars.

The gap was caused by legal avoidance, illegal evasion, work in the black or hidden economy, deliberate non-payment and errors. But HMRC must not impose a 'disproportionate burden', Labour declared, agreeing that the UK should not expose tax cheats, as happened in the Republic of Ireland. Only after the crash, barely months before they left office, did ministers allow HMRC to put more offenders' names into the public domain. As for making all tax returns public, as in Finland, the government's political imagination failed. It did blow wind into HMRC sails. New disclosure rules in 2004 allowed the tax authorities to take swifter action on loopholes; court rulings gave them access to 400,000 offshore bank accounts held by UK residents, 100,000 of which were not declaring income or interest. After the crash, in a stable-doors exercise, rescued banks had to list where they sheltered their money – one had 500 tax-haven subsidiaries. In April 2009 HMRC set up a High Net Worth Unit, looking at complex share and property dealings. The Germans had shown the power of shame when in 2008 they started buying stolen computer discs containing Swiss and Liechtenstein bank records. At last, as a result of the recession, the UK cut subsidies for the Isle of Man, forcing its toy-town government to put up taxes.

Spending on public services (excluding pensions and cash benefits) amounted to a fifth of national income when Labour took power. Amid claims of oversized government, the alleged army of pen-pushers, overpaid nurses and park-keepers made up just a fraction of the economy by financial value. They represented about 20 per cent of the nation's total workforce, which included, as well, all those squaddies, police officers and prison warders the Right usually wants to employ in even greater numbers. Labour pushed spending on services up to a pre-recession peak of about 25 per cent of GDP. In other words, it shifted about one-twentieth in the balance of GDP, leaving aside the response to recession and bank bail-out. It doesn't sound revolutionary, nor was it. To have asked the public to cover its cost would not have taken Leninist verve.

Instead, Labour seemed almost to admit the futility of public spending. In a letter to the CBI and TUC in 2000, Brown said 'government can sometimes do best by getting out of the way'. That chimed with the dominant neoliberal doctrine that UK competitiveness depended on less government. Business wisdom said the UK was over-regulated, and Labour had added to the burdens. The *World Competitiveness Yearbook* put the UK about 20th in its charts, the US top, the UK ahead of France. One of its criteria was 'management practices', where the UK ranked very low. How far was government the culprit? According to the Advanced Institute for Management Research, over-regulation helped explain the persistent gap between UK business productivity and elsewhere, other reasons being deficits in innovation, skills and the quality of managers. So the private sector was also the problem. The French regulated business, yet French workers were more productive at work. Even though real GDP per capita grew faster in the UK than in France or Germany, GDP for each hour worked showed the same gap with France as a generation earlier, in 1979. An old question in UK economic history was one Labour never really answered. Problems of growth and productivity stemmed from the way companies and their managers performed, but what could government do from the outside to improve them? When, after the crash, the dogmas of 'shareholder value' crumbled, a Labour view – any view – might have been a reference point in debate.

*

Labour did both deregulation and intervention, which seemed to reflect business's own lack of coherence. Typical was Philip Bowman, chief executive of Smiths Group, who in one breath bemoaned 'red tape' and excess tax and in the next demanded support for business and, by the way, more state-funded research and development (*Financial Times*, 25 March 2010). Labour tried to oblige, turning the Department of Trade and Industry (DTI) into the Department for Business, Enterprise and Regulatory Reform. Business Links was only one of a portfolio of schemes, many carried through by regional development agencies (RDAs), putting smaller companies in touch with research, promoting training and dishing out grants. The Centre for Economic Performance found 'no compelling evidence' that RDAs helped or hindered.

Labour wanted to boost firms by making workers cheaper, but it knew that productivity depended on making them (more) skilled. Labour had swept to power proclaiming work the best welfare, fervently telling swing voters it was no longer the creature of the unions or soft on welfare loafers. Its interest in work carried through into some eye-catching initiatives, benefiting women and part-timers with flexible working times. But it mixed the signals.

In opposition Labour had promised to end the UK's opt-out from the Social Chapter of the Maastricht Treaty, which in theory meant more protection for workers. Ignore it, Blair told business audiences, trust us to look after your interests. According to the employment specialist Robert Taylor, 'union leaders were to be treated with politeness; at best they would enjoy a minimum respect and some informal access to Downing Street, as well as relevant government departments. But this did not mean they would be able to negotiate any special bilateral deals to their advantage at the expense of capital.' The Cabinet had nonetheless to sing a reassuring tune to the unions, which had paid for the piper's election and became more not less important in funding the party. The 1999 Employment Relations Act assisted unions in negotiating recognition. They pressed for and got extra workplace rights for individuals, more paternity and maternity leave, and better compensation for unfair dismissal.

Accords worked out at a meeting between party leaders and unions at the University of Warwick in 2004 made big concessions, notably to unions representing public-sector workers. Yet at the same time ministers were intriguing in Brussels with East Europeans against rights for agency workers. They also fought to keep the opt-out from the EU working-time directive introduced in 1998 to prevent people working over forty-eight hours a week. Eventually the UK adopted it, leading to a short-lived media panic over doctors' hours.

Average weekly hours worked were falling, from 37.9 in 2000 to 36.8 in 2009 – but the figures came from official surveys that tended to undercount migrants and chip-shop owners who lived where they worked. Still, an hour's less work a week was something, even if a fifth of British staff still worked more than forty-five hours a week, high by European standards. Talk of flexi-working from home and IT's impact was largely just talk. The Work Foundation found over 75 per cent of the staff of larger organizations still worked on one site. Only one in fifty worked from home. When recession struck, a lot would have liked to work a lot more. ONS reported 2.8 million people, a tenth of the UK workforce, were 'under-employed' on top of the 2.5 million unemployed. During the recession, BT, Ford, JCB and others had cut working time – and pay.

'More employers need to be persuaded of the value to their businesses of employment-related education and skills training,' the NAO observed plaintively. The prize was enhanced growth: boosting the proportion of trained workers by 8 per cent could increase UK productivity by 0.6 per cent, as measured by value added for each hour worked. Government initiatives included subsidies to employers (Train to Gain), and further education expanded mightily. But grand promises made in 1997 about the quality of the workforce went largely unrealized. Its upskilling was, Professor Richard Layard noted, Labour's 'greatest failure'. The IFS concluded that the gap between the UK and other major European countries, let alone the US, was 'persistent' – with a given level of labour, we produced less. The gap had narrowed since the mid 1990s but increased again after.

Skills training was a telling example of how markets do not work. The state either had to levy taxes to pay for training, or force companies to band together for the greater good. But even confronted with clear evidence that employers could not or would not add value to their own staff by investing in training, ministers dithered, unsure whether they had any mandate to buck 'market forces'.

If the banks offered the most egregious example of the government allowing itself to be steamrollered for the sake of growth and revenue, housing came a close second. In presiding over a bubble in prices, Labour did not even pretend that the wider economy benefited; investment was misallocated and capital squandered. The necessity was political. Labour were never going to challenge the national passion for house-price inflation that soared everywhere, in England, Scotland, Wales and Northern Ireland. Brown's responsibility is all the heavier because the Treasury was fully aware of the problem. In the 2003 budget, he declared: 'Most stop-go problems Britain has suffered in the last fifty years have been led or influenced by the more highly cyclical and often more volatile nature of our housing market.' And so intoned an expert chorus. Housing was the Achilles' heel of the UK economy, according to Andrew Farlow of Oriel College, Oxford in 2002: 'We would be better served by a market not prone to bouts of speculative excesses, by advisers who put their clients' interests above their own, and by monetary policy that takes the possibility of housing bubbles seriously.'

In Spain and the Irish Republic, low Eurozone interest rates helped stoke property booms – but the UK still had such a boom outside the zone. Tight planning, land supply and, above all, inadequate taxation of income and capital gains caused house-price inflation. Calming the property market would require increases in stamp duty, capital gains tax and a massive building programme. Remortgaging – people withdrawing equity from their homes – fuelled a quarter of the increase in nominal GDP from 1997. The government sought stability by encouraging fixed-rate loans; variable loans made up two-thirds of the total.

But, as with tax, what was missing was a politics, or narrative, to make sense of what the government said or did.

Why had we learnt so little from earlier bubbles and busts? The ratio of house prices to earnings rose to 5.5 to one by the eve of the crash, an all-time high. The gap was met by credit, which bank executives and directors supplied. Their control of their companies' revenues meant they personally faced no risks so felt no need to give their corporate risk registers any substance, as we later found out. Vince Cable was prescient when, five years before the event, he argued for new prudential rules and control on loan-to-value ratios for banks and mortgage lenders.

Labour did away with mortgage interest relief, which the Tories had already cut back. In other circumstances this might have restrained borrowers, but interest rates were low. Demand pulled, but contrary to market theory, supply did not respond. The profits of housebuilders soared, yet they built relatively few new houses. The average cash price of homes rose 117 per cent between the fourth quarter of 1999 and the end of 2009. If you were seeking somewhere to live in Newham, not previously reckoned the most desirable London borough, you would have confronted an increase of 190 per cent; the Olympics may have had an effect. It was not just London. Plymouth in the South West and Moray in north-east Scotland, plush York and ex-industrial Sheffield all saw big rises too. House prices had fallen by 14 per cent in the early 1990s. Under Labour they rose 68 per cent in real terms. Recession was barely a blip, as prices dropped 16 per cent in 2008 but rose 6 per cent the next year. The crash strangled the market as the volume of sales dropped. But prices soon recovered, up 1.2 per cent in January 2010.

As well as housing, the other great gap in Labour policy-making was around companies. In opposition it talked of encouraging commitment and boosting productivity by making employees shareholders. Remember Will Hutton's stakeholder society, briefly taken up by Blair? Once in power, corporate self-interest won. If firms malfunctioned, if they paid their boards too much and misallocated capital, that was none of the government's business. Misbehaving companies would (eventually) go bust or the mergers and acquisitions market would swing into action and predators would take them over. This was the myth but, where companies did go bust, it was the state that had to try to hold family and community life together.

The crash showed the cost of ignoring company board-rooms. The performance of the directors of many banks and finance houses had been 'at least defective and at worst incompetent', according to the Morgan Stanley mandarin Sir David Walker. But some physicians never heal themselves. Successive inquiries into company governance had no effect. The government commissioned a study in 2003 from Sir Derek Higgs, chairman of Alliance & Leicester, and a report for the Treasury by Paul Myners, a former chairman of Marks & Spencer, on the governance of pension funds. (Their subsequent fates differed. Myners became a Labour minister with, at last, a nice line in threats about the scale of City greed. The merger tide swallowed Higgs's company and it went bust along with the rest of RBS.) Government reforms were self-defeating. The remuneration committees it had insisted on became a means of further inflating top pay. A new shape for boards did not lead to better behaviour. Labour tried to strengthen the arm of dissident shareholders, giving them extra rights to push and probe. However, the Northern Rock board reached the end of the worst year in its history, nationalization pending, by paying its chief executive a salary of £760,000 pro rata till he departed, plus a bonus of £660,000. So much for shareholder power.

Evidence piled up that mergers and acquisitions did not secure prosperity, either for workers affected, or in aggregate. Germany and Japan did not allow takeovers in the British style yet they kept exporting and manufacturing. Reticent over mergers, Labour did have a vision of the future of British industry. Science was to support and expand the base of research and the state would help build bridges between laboratories and commerce. The renamed Business, Innovation and Science department included the universities; this was supposed to lead to better coordination. Brown praised 'clusters' of high-tech firms around Cambridge. Business collaboration with universities improved after a report from Richard Lambert in 2003 – the former *Financial Times* editor himself a mass of contradictory impulses. Here were elements for a white paper Labour never got round to writing, about the 'developmental state' where government nudges, leads and inspires private enterprise and investment.

Instead, state intervention co-existed uncomfortably with a hands-off, free-market approach. Adam Smith had warned: turn your back and business fixes prices and colludes on sales. Labour's enthusiasm for regulation of market competition waxed and waned. In telecoms, the regulator was encouraged to be an instigator of competition. Competition policy was sharpened in legislation in 1998 and 2003. But on the way Labour abolished the power to intervene in a takeover if the wider public interest was threatened. The classic case was the £11.7 billion transfer of Cadbury, a national brand, to Kraft, an American corporation with no interest in UK employment or the brand's Quaker heritage. Business secretary Mandelson 'hit out' at Kraft, judging the deal to be in the interests of neither company but then did nothing. The recession led to Labour's deathbed conversion to a policy on takeovers, but it was late in coming: only a third of the components in a JCB digger are now made in the UK, when it had been 96 per cent in 1979.

By the last lap even Brown, the prophet of globalization and markets, was talking up the role of the state in supporting manufacturing. In the winter of 2010, he gave Vauxhall loans and guarantees allowing its 4700 UK workers to escape large-scale redundancy. Compare this with Labour's response when the board of BMW decided to abandon Longbridge in Birmingham in 2000. After one of the UK's remaining vehicle makers, MG Rover, collapsed just before the 2005 election, the DTI made great show of brokering its transfer into Chinese ownership. Which meant, to no one's surprise, the end of vehicle manufacturing in MG Rover plants. With the tacit encouragement of ministers, careers advisers in schools told young people that factories were finished – to the chagrin of the UK's manufacturers. Snake-oil merchants flogging the 'weightless economy' wafted into Downing Street seminars. As if willed by Labour, manufacturing declined faster than during the Thatcher years, when Labour had passionately deplored deindustrialization. Manufacturing amounted to 20 per cent of the economy in 1997 but 12 per cent in 2007, its decline fostered by sterling appreciation during Labour's first term. Fittingly in Labour's economy, construction, estate agency and property rose from 12.6 to 16.2 per cent. By 2010 only one in eight of Coventry's working-age population of 194,000 was in manufacturing, compared with over one in two in the 1970s.

Growth was to be the antidote to debt and deficit, Mandelson said at Labour's spring conference in February 2010, and the future was bioscience, medicine, advanced manufacturing, precision engineering, creative industries and – a new undertaking – 'this is not going to happen without active government working hand in hand with enterprise'. Finance was notable by its absence from the new Labour vision. Mandelson now called for flexible EU state aid rules to allow support for cutting-edge companies, French style. When he was European trade commissioner, he had singled the French out for criticism for supporting such companies as Alstom and Areva, multinationals responsible for large chunks of transport and nuclear generation, in the UK as elsewhere.

Come the 2009 budget, £405 million was available to support wind and marine energy to 'establish the UK as a market leader in renewables technology and advanced green manufacturing'. The trade department put hundreds of millions into venture capital funds to support young companies that found it hard to raise money in the markets – though auditors worried at a lack of evidence about whether UK plc (start-up division) benefited. Treasury officials said they had a coherent plan that embraced schools and universities, and research and development, awarding a new tax credit in 2001. R&D tax credits were worth £700 million a year, backed by evidence from the OECD that credits did encourage private investment and the UK's regime was among the world's most attractive.

*

Manufacturing had always been a regional affair. The number of sizeable public companies with headquarters outside London fell sharply, with the North having only 26 listed FTSE 350 companies in 2009 against 38 in 2000; 211 of the 350 were based in London. Steve Denison of PricewaterhouseCoopers had no hesitation in drawing the conclusion – business, or capitalism, was passing the North by. 'They draw non-executives increasingly from a pool around London. Listed businesses like to have blue-chip, blue-blooded non-executives.'

Since the 1930s Labour had believed in regional policy – government trying to steer economic activity to one place rather than another. Some interventions – the Humber Bridge – were more obviously connected with vote gathering than others. Labour had to reconcile their enthusiasm for globalization with Redcar's well-being. The Indian owners of Corus, the steelmaker that had picked the bones of what was once British Steel, decided in 2009 to close the blast furnace and most of its Teesside production site, with the loss of 1700 jobs. Redcar's unemployment rate, already 9.6 per cent, could only increase. On BBC's *Question Time* (18 February 2010) the dry-as-dust free-market economist Ruth Lea was speechless in front of an audience of about to be ex-steelworkers. Why did market collapse in the City demand relief from the state when a dubious decision by a foreign company brought forth no government action?

Labour's answer had been a weakened form of regional support, delivered through arm's-length agencies. Instead of bribing companies to stay put or move in, they would provide sites and under-the-counter subsidies. A combination of regional aid and urban investment funds served to keep leaky and damaged ships afloat. Take Coventry, where since the turn of the century Jaguar had stopped assembling cars, Peugeot had made 2300 redundant when it shifted production to Slovakia, and Ericsson earmarked its research centre by the M6 for closure with the loss of 700 jobs. Between 1997 and 2006 the output of the city's production industries had fallen by £700 million, offset by £687 million in business services and £627 million in the public sector. Perhaps Labour's covert industrial policy was expanding the public sector, and not just in Coventry. Half the growth in and around Blackburn and Darwen came from public administration, education and health.

By the end, Labour was talking of a 'rebalancing' of the UK economy. But for all the 'world-beating' boasts, Labour had for years ignored warnings of how far Britain was falling behind the Germans in making wind turbines and solar panels. In nanotechnology in 2008, UK investment per capita had been a third of the American level and a quarter of the German.

The Labour era, at least from 2000, saw growth in spending that will not be matched for a long while. Underlining just how much Labour was a 'freshen up' government, the annual average percentage increase in total investment between 1999–2000 and 2007–8 was just over 16 per cent, compared with minus 5 per cent between 1979–80 and 1996–7. That spending was the point of a story about tax that Labour never got round to telling the public. They were left oblivious, and the gap between spending and tax revenue grew in consequence.

For the UK economy, it was largely business as usual under Labour. Growth rates were the same as or even below their level in the years when chancellors and prime ministers were not haranguing us with the dreadful inevitability of globalization. GDP per head grew by £3840 between 1997 and the start of 2010, measured in 2009 prices. That was 20 per cent more. If the clock had stopped on 31 March 2008 it would be nearer 30 per cent. Was the benefit from Brown's vaunted opening to the world enough? Average unemployment from 1992 to 1997 had been 9 per cent. Between 1997 and 2007 it was 5.5 per cent. Such performance was matched in other countries. Yet again, the UK had found no elixir.

Verdicts from the boardrooms

At the end of the decade bankers became the King Rat villains, cause of the catastrophe for so many unemployed and repossessed families. They had amassed huge economic power but seemed to rejoice in their unaccountability. In corporate board-rooms, panjandrums paid themselves what they liked, regardless of economic performance. Directors' rewards skyrocketed from forty-seven to eighty-one times the average of workers in companies, uncorrelated with corporate success or even, astoundingly, share prices.

Bankers were shameless but shy. Try winkling one out and they retreated like hermit crabs. But here is one willing to talk – on terms of strict anonymity. 'George' is a very senior figure in investment banking. Even anonymously he would not divulge his earnings: perhaps they were just too shocking to speak out loud. 'Money has gone silly in the last few years,' he did admit. New recruits to his bank fresh out of university started on £30,000. Why pay so much when so many want the few prized places in this bank, 1200 applying for twenty-five jobs? The 'market for talent' myth seems to start at the bottom, where classic market theory would surely decree that steep competition for jobs should deflate, not inflate, starting pay. No, high starting pay denotes status for the institution, the opposite of how it works at the other end of the earnings scale.

In his late forties, Oxbridge-educated after private school, George reflected on what had happened. 'I can't honestly say any of us saw it coming, understood it or acted on it.' So it was only with hindsight he could look back and say, '[F]or fifteen years there was massive liquidity in the system. It just mushroomed with private equity and hedge funds, an explosion of money as a commodity. With asset prices rising, for as long as growth lasted anyone doing moderately well could borrow and make returns of 100 per cent. There was a very poor understanding of risk. But even if individual bankers had wanted to jump off the train, it would have been very hard for them to try.' He recalled one Cassandra who kept warning and calling the top of the market, but as the market went on inflating upwards, he was ignored: he was fired a month before the crash.

He had mentioned 'silly money' and 'ridiculous bonuses' as causes of the crash, and on the day we spoke the front page of the *Financial Times* reported the chief executive of Reckitt Benckiser pulling in £92 million. George thought nothing could be done: it was just the way of the world. 'These people are quite mobile, they can just go. There is a market place for top talent who can just say "I'm worth it."

'You can't turn the clock back to when CEOs were paid maybe ten times average pay. The old values of the twentieth century are gone.' So what can be done? 'You could tax non-doms a lot more. They wouldn't leave: London is the most attractive city, speaks English, it's safe and pleasingly cosmopolitan. You could stop rewarding people for failure. But no, you can't restrict pay. There is no right sum, £1 million, £6 million? Maybe better education will increase the pool of talent and that will down the price.' But already he had more 'talent' knocking at his door than he could use and the price still rose.

What about his own pay and his family? He had two young children not yet in their teens, at private schools, and they lived in one of London's most desirably leafy districts. Did he ever worry about his children growing up immensely wealthy, far beyond the lives of most of their fellow citizens? 'We live very modestly,' he says. But he did worry about their future, expecting the next decade to be 'very tough indeed'. He wrung his hands over values. 'I think often about where would be the best place, the best society for them to grow up. Sometimes I think France, which despite everything seems to get the balance of life right.' But not, he thought, Britain. It would not be over-taxation that sent him away, but the search for a better life in European countries with stronger, more cohesive social values. The irony is that those precious commodities have often been achieved elsewhere by decades of higher taxes, more regulation, less inequality, a smaller gap between top and bottom and better social investment.

On the other hand, the high performer of the decade was the John Lewis Partnership, owned by its staff. It prospered and grew, never over-borrowed, escaping the perils of the crash. Its executive chairman, Charlie Mayfield, joined in 2000 and was promoted to chairman in 2009 at the young age of thirty-nine. An angular man with chiselled good looks and a quiet, earnest demeanour, he has the bearing of his background, a Scots Guards captain by the age of twenty-two, serving in Northern Ireland. Later he put himself through an MBA at Cranfield University, had a spell at SmithKlineBeecham marketing Lucozade and Horlicks before joining McKinsey, the consultants. Now he had become an apostle of mutualism, a promoter of better ways of doing capitalism, eager to seize on the lessons of the crash to point to short-term shareholder profit as the cause of the crisis. New businesses needed new forms of ownership, he suggested, and 'the public limited company may not be it'. Known for modesty, rarely giving interviews, he kept a low profile, in keeping with the collaborative style of the partnership's ethos.

He lived with his wife and three children in Newbury, Berkshire, waking at 5.50 a.m., in his office by 8 a.m. and not home again until eight in the evening. He only talked to us as part of an initiative to promote mutualism at a time when after the crash he was alarmed that returning to 'business as usual' seemed the narrow goal of policy-makers.

The past decade had been exceptional. John Lewis grew by 70 per cent, nineteen shops increasing to twenty-seven, with more in the pipeline. The other side of the business, Waitrose, doubled its share of the food market, growing from 120 to 230 stores, with plans for a host of local convenience shops. Customers parted with £6.3 billion across the partnership's counters.

Labour's era 'was a valuable long period of stability and retail enjoyed a very benign environment'. The crash 'was frightening. Sales dropped instantly by 10 then 20 per cent. Customer behaviour was extreme as people's confidence was severely shaken. It was a reminder of how fragile customer demand can be.' But the panic reflex wore off within a short time as most people realized they would keep their jobs and economic disaster had been averted. People were more inclined to turn to traditionally trusted shops. That 'never knowingly undersold' promise, worth its weight in gold, was underpinned by the trustworthiness of employee ownership. The partnership had been cautious on borrowing in the wild years, so it was now well placed for the thin years. That grounding was maintained by the council of seventy elected employee representatives who met twice a year to agree strategy. How unlike fly-by-night, get-rich-quick temporary shareholders flitting from company to company in search of the next quarter's fastest profit, regardless of a company's long-term well-being.

Did Labour's fiscal stimulus help, the enormous sums pumped into the economy to keep it afloat and to keep people in jobs? 'The hard thing is, we can never know. It can't be proved. But it certainly delayed and softened the effect of the price we shall have to pay for the last ten years. Unemployment is lower than expected. The 2.5 per cent cut in VAT put another £12 billion straight into people's pockets so the average household had £10 or £12 more a week to spend, and we could see that made a difference.' How has his own life changed in the last decade? 'I've grown up a lot, learned a lot. Above all, I've come to appreciate the great challenge and potential of having a better way to run business.'

Mayfield's own pay was no pittance, fixed by trust deed at no more than seventy-five times the average earning of the partners. That was £750,000 a year, plus the same percentage annual bonus as all employees, depending on the profits of the year. In 2009 it was 15 per cent for one and all of the 72,000 partners. Chief executives of his rank routinely got a 100–150 per cent bonus, but not John Lewis. 'Bonuses produce very bad incentives for short-termism. They are also incredibly divisive within organizations.' He commented, 'Employees here are not treated equally, but they are treated fairly.'

Was this a freak that could never be a model for other companies? John Spedan Lewis was a philanthropist who set up the partnership when he inherited the business from his father in 1929, the year of the Great Depression. Hard to imagine plc shareholders succumbing to a similar fit of spectacular generosity. No, he said, all kinds of companies could be converted to mutuals. 'But the idea does require flexibility and imagination on the part of lenders to lend for employee buy-outs. Business Links, the government advisors to business, should be primed to help make it happen, but they don't even have it in their vocabulary.

They never consider plurality of ownership.' The legal world had little experience of how to set up a partnership, and business degree courses did not teach it. 'If the owner wants the highest possible return, or buyers want a private equity type deal, then you get huge debts and great vulnerability, as we've seen. But owners can get a good return with an employee buy-out. Governments should be creating a framework to encourage it. The tax regime inadvertently discourages it. It is a more stable form of business that government should welcome, taking far less risk over the cycle.'

The first of John Lewis's seven founding principles is worth contemplating: 'The partnership's ultimate purpose is the happiness of all its members, through their worthwhile and satisfying employment in a successful business. Because the partnership is owned in trust for its members, they share the responsibilities of ownership as well as its rewards, profit, knowledge and power.'

Acme Whistles' verdict

Manufacturing shrank faster under Labour than under Margaret Thatcher. All around the West Midlands, firms closed as production moved east. Yet in a Birmingham side street stands the Acme Whistles factory, thriving against the odds in its trading niche. Is it in business because of, or despite, the government? It seems appropriate the building has a preservation order. The workshop felt almost untouched since its founding in 1870, with its narrow walkways and external wooden staircases. The founder's wooden workbench stood inviolate.

Acme offers eighty-three types of whistle: train, bird and dog, crow whistles and a pig grunt, navy and scout whistles, women's self-protection whistles, swanee and tin whistles, orchestral whistles, comic pantomime whistles for when the dame's skirt blows up, megaphones, hunting horns and, above all, whistles for referees in every sport. The Thunderer and the even louder Tornado are standard Football Association issue. Men and women sat at benches and polishers, dipping whistles in the plating rooms, doing old-fashioned factory work where the relatively small run of any one model ruled out savings from more mechanization.

The firm employed sixty-five people in spring 2010, turning over £9 million a year. It had been a popular place to work, with virtually no staff turnover, many retiring from here after twenty or thirty years; waiting lists of people who wanted jobs, any vacancies going to friends and relatives of employees. Depending on skill, pay averaged £20,000 a year, more than you would get in services in the West Midlands. This was a well-balanced work-force with a mix of white, black and Asian staff, reflecting the neighbourhood.

Old Joseph Hudson had struck lucky in persuading the Metropolitan Police to abandon their Victorian warning rattles and adopt his whistle. He took a party of officers – you can just imagine them in their top hats, brass-button uniforms and mutton-chop whiskers – to Clapham Common and blew loud enough to be heard a mile away. Since then 45 million Metropolitan whistles have been sold to 120 police forces around the world. In *Titanic* Kate Winslet was spotted in the icy sea blowing an authentic Acme Mates. Cashing in, the firm found the original die used for the White Star line and rapidly made the whistle again, selling 350,000 replicas. So, with clever marketing and a sharp eye for new opportunities, it flourished.

Born and bred in Handsworth, Acme owner and manager Simon Topman had moved to live only a few miles away in Sutton Coldfield. He attended Handsworth Grammar School, did not do particularly well and afterwards took jobs with Birmingham Dairies, Mappin and Webb the jewellers, a brass ornament maker, and a pipe fitting and steel plates company, before coming to work at Acme in the late 1980s. When the Hudson family died out and the factory was put up for sale, he bought it with venture capital participation. Now his wife and his two daughters in their twenties work here too, a family business once again.

He watched the factories close around him. 'Tool-making, paintbrushes, jewellery, it was awash with manufacturing round here. Now there's no rolled brass in Birmingham. Think of that:

I used to get it round the corner, now I have to go to Italy. I could have got tools next door and polishing equipment when this was the "City of 1001 trades" but not any longer. The shake-out has been brutal.'

Making things in China cost less. Whistles were 50 per cent cheaper; he had been there to look. 'But I wouldn't get the quality. I'd spend almost as much hiring people to put the whistles right when they arrived. And – the Chinese would copy us. They'd be making for us in the daytime and then making exact copies for themselves at night. I've seen plenty of Birmingham manufacturers really regret it. Chinese prices are rising now and some firms are repatriating work with the devalued pound, but it can be difficult once you've scaled down.'

Was Topman political? 'I never vote, never have.' But when we pressed for views, back came a rich, ambiguous mix, informed by his extensive non-business life. Topman's complaint about Labour is not over sterling, taxation or even the 'burden of regulation'. Intriguingly, it is cultural. 'They talked down manufacturing. They said it was all over and globalization was inevitable. It was really unfashionable, political death for any minister to talk up anything as old-fashioned as making things. They never said they believed in us. Waves of these negative messages coming from the top meant no one wanted to invest either. Fathers I know in manufacturing told their sons it was all over, lots took early retirement and sold out rather than buy new machinery and invest in the future.'

But he registered a policy shift, too. Around 2005 he felt Labour lost interest in business. 'The atmosphere changed, hard to say why. Something atavistic, back to Labour's old days. A lot of the equalities legislation was difficult, because business feared they didn't know when they might trip up and fall foul of it, seeing hard tribunal cases where employees won horrendous sums over small matters. It made everyone nervous.' He thought the regional agency Advantage West Midlands started taking a new tack. 'It stopped being primarily for industry and business and it was given social targets, ticking boxes that confused their purpose – targets for ethnic minority business start-ups, or easing unemployment.'

Topman was president of the Birmingham Chambers of Commerce and joined the DTI's small business council. Fellow executives moaned about over-regulation but he usually saw the point of the rules. He helped draw up new dispute-resolution regulations to stop cases going to tribunals, only to find they were not compatible with guidelines from the Advisory, Conciliation and Arbitration Service. 'There we were, three businessmen, experienced and practical, thought we knew it all and we got it wrong. It was an eye-opener. It showed us just how hard it really is to run the country. Business people, my members, often get above themselves and think they can run everything.'

Outcry greeted the Labour proposal to give employees the right to request flexible working hours. 'My members all thought this meant they would be forced to give flexible working, while a lot of the unions didn't realize until later that it was only the right to "request" flexibility.' But it was a really good solution – and it worked. He had already done it in his own factory. 'I told my staff to go away and work out what hours they all wanted to work and come back with an agreement. I said how much work I needed, and it had to be in the right order as work is passed from one bench to another. I said if they came back with three options I'd tear them up and decide myself: they had to agree everything amongst themselves. So they chose to work 8am to 4.30pm every day and Friday afternoons off, with only half an hour for lunch – and everyone was happy. I build in extra flexibility if people need other time off for family or religious reasons. I need to keep my people happy – it takes six months to train up someone new. I'd be mad to let anyone go because of working hours. I said that to other businesses.'

As for the government, his judgement was more positive than negative – except for Labour's failure to promote manufacturing. He looked ahead with some foreboding, worrying that the disappearance of the RDA would leave the West Midlands with a weaker voice. He worried cuts could destroy much of the regeneration of Aston that he has worked so hard on over the last ten years. Despite everything, Birmingham still made things. Manufacturing's demise had been overstated: companies downsized by outsourcing services – cleaning or back office – so the shrinkage in people apparently engaged in manufacturing looked worse than it was. 'Late in the day, Labour came round to it. After the crash and discovering the City wasn't everything, they started to have an industrial policy again. It's not too late, not yet.' He cited a joint venture with acoustics researchers at Birmingham University to make a highly sensitive whistle that sits in the back of a firefighter's suit. The failsafe whistle had to go off if oxygen flow started to fall but be under eighty decibels to avoid hearing damage. 'The world's your oyster as a manufacturer in Britain, but you need to specialize.'

PART TWO

Life in Labour's Britain

CHAPTER 4

Mood music

'Whatever people say I am, that's what I'm not': the title of the Arctic Monkeys' 2006 album caught a public mood that stymied persistent government attempts to define Britishness. Blair arrived with a toe-curling riff on 'Cool Britannia'. Brown chipped in with a version owing more to Edward Elgar than *X Factor*. In one mercifully forgotten speech he called for a British national motto to be emblazoned on every school and public building – something Kiplingesque, perhaps. Maybe he should have persevered, because *If* topped the polls for favourite poem.

John Major had rhapsodized about Orwell's old maids, warm beer and county cricket, to be greeted with derision, and not just because he had confused mythical England with Britain. Yet the need for a narrative of nationhood grew as Britain became more contested territory. Migration and devolution strengthened the case for finding signs and symbols of who we were. Old, unthinking British empiricism would no longer do and Labour knew it. They spent generously on arts, culture and knowledge, insisting recipients made efforts to rope in children, minorities and the many who never frequented galleries, museums and concerts. Labour were seduced by potential representations of oneness, notably the Millennium Dome and the Olympics. But their cultural efforts lacked a connecting thread. Labour could not spin it, because they lacked a sense of national trajectory, of where the UK was moving from and to. They were not even sure about their own story. Even Labour's cut-down version of social democracy depended on social solidarity and a mutual willingness to pay tax and help others: appeals to 'fellow Britons' had to have more in common than physical occupancy of islands, the disunity of which the historians were now emphasizing (Norman Davies's *The Isles* was published in 1999). But descriptions, let alone visions of 'Labour Britain', were hard to find.

At first, Labour's arrival stimulated chatter about a New Britain. Within months of the 1997 election, Demos, the flighty blue skies think-tank, reported on new ways to market UK plc. Trade on culture, it said, exploit the Royal Shakespeare Company and the universities. That sounded old-fashioned – despite the forward-looking glories of British science – so the bright young things of Demos threw in Hoxton clubs and White Cube cutting-edge art. American *Vanity Fair* had published a special edition on Cool Britannia with Liam Gallagher and Patsy Kensit on a cover emblazoned with 'London Swings! Again!' There they all were – the hot Brits, Alexander McQueen, Damien Hirst and *Loaded* magazine. Was that it, national unity in contemplation of Hirst's pickled cow?

Politics mixes badly with culture. Harold Wilson had tried to surf the Swinging Sixties and Blair reprised with a reception for the in-crowd. If briefly flattered by an invitation to Downing Street, Noel Gallagher soon changed his tune: 'If I could be arsed enough to vote now it would be for the Liberal Democrats.' What prescience. Yet the Gallaghers' hometown, Manchester, was a regeneration success story and remained a music Mecca after Oasis ran dry. Labour's pop music moment ended in a damp patch when the lead singer of Chumbawamba – whose pedigree included poll tax protests – threw a jug of water over John Prescott during the 1998 Brit awards. Hot Brits went their way, Hirst to be the City slicker of the art world, McQueen to global triumph and suicide. Fashion and modern art turned out to be markers of British distinction during the Labour years and government policy played some part; Labour tried on occasion to tell a story about the 'creative industries', but hesitantly.

Mood music

Civic anxiety about new arrivals and non-voters motivated ministers. They called in politics professor Bernard Crick to devise a citizenship curriculum for English schools. From 2004 new citizens were ceremonially inducted, after they had graduated from language classes and passed a test on life in the UK. 'How many parliamentary constituencies are there?' was a question many British-born citizens would have fluffed. The newcomers welcomed the civic handshakes and posing for photos in front of a portrait of the Queen.

Brown, worried about Labour in Scotland post-devolution and Scottish identity in Britain, announced a citizens' summit to come up with a defining 'statement of British values'. Labour loved these grand and expensive exercises in testing the popular mind, commendable in concept but largely a waste of time in practice. Consultation dragged on around the country till February 2010, when it was quietly dropped.

Brownian nation-making notions were embarrassingly vacuous, jingoistic and banal. Like a superannuated public-school headmaster he suggested 'fair play and duty' for the national motto. He even proposed a daily oath of allegiance from children. It was a good question – in a globalized world, in countries pulled apart by commerce and capital movements – where were the ties that bind? But Labour, wedded to globalization, could not contemplate the ways in which trade and migration had dissolved bonds of allegiance and solidarity; it could not accept, at least before the recession, that government might need to temper commercial exuberance. Take football. Boys in both the Blair and Brown Downing Street camps bonded over their teams. But clubs were the playthings of footloose owners. The vulnerability of football identities became evident as clubs were asset-stripped and, like Portsmouth, left bankrupt. Carpetbaggers took over Manchester United and Labour said not a word until electoral expediency in 2010 prompted vague musings about clubs as cooperatives of fans.

In football as in popular culture we came together to celebrate celebrity. Among his many painful clips Brown must wince at appearing before the cameras while visiting India in 2007. On the nation's behalf he solemnly apologized for a clash in the *Big Brother* house between two famous-for-fifteen-minutes attention-seekers. Yet something was going on here. In the spat between Shilpa Shetty and Jade Goody everyday behaviour suddenly intersected with policy and diplomacy. With her insult, Goody had transgressed in a way that showed sensibility was shifting. Rudeness and boorishness might be acceptable but racial disrespect was not, in a way Goody was too clueless to comprehend. Here was terrain more familiar to Labour. Their new equalities laws embedded stronger individual identities based on disability, sexual orientation, race and religion. But these were fissiparous, sources of social and national division. The government struggled to reconcile 'cohesion', individual rights and the new insistence on respect for the group or cultural identity. To say Labour's thinking was fuzzy and their policies confused is true – but so was everyone else's.

The public willed confusion between politics and entertainment. So of course Blair enquired about the 'Free Deirdre' campaign (only to find it was a *Coronation Street* storyline). Despite his incurable woodenness on camera, Brown completed the colonization of politics by celebrity with a lachrymose appearance on Piers Morgan's show in 2010. Perhaps he cottoned on that being British now meant weeping together. Upper lips softened and public tears proved sincerity. Blair intuited how sentimental the country had become when on the morning after Princess Diana's death he both captured and stimulated public grief. 'She was' – gulp – 'the People's Princess' legitimized the flowers, teddy bears and poems strewn over that fateful week. Within months national park authorities were pleading with walkers to stop pimpling pristine mountain tops with an acne of memorial cairns. Diana's death and funeral merged folklore and fiction; for many Michael Sheen became Blair as Stephen Frears' 2006 film *The Queen* replayed the events – not the last example of screenplay creating reality. Perhaps Blair's greatest achievement was saving the House of Windsor from itself. The death of the Queen Mother in 2002 reprised Diana's death in a minor key, as an estimated 200,000 filed past the matriarch's catafalque.

Mood music

The government willed collective remembrance, with memorials both kitsch (animals in war in Park Lane) and banal (tourist deaths in Bali). Woe betide ministers and television presenters who did not don the requisite mourning or wear a poppy. Armistice Day grew in salience, even as those with living memories of wartime fell away. Harry Patch, the last surviving serviceman from the 1914–18 war, distinguished mainly by his longevity, was given the rites of a great hero.

Even such a bling-master as Blair understood materialism could divide rather than unite. Labour's problem was elemental: was economic growth the be-all and end-all? Money's handmaiden was celebrity. Teachers worried that children replied 'famous' when asked what they wanted to be. But in another of the decade's national moments of coming together – the TV talent show – at least aspiring singers and hoofers had to work at it. Whatever model sportsmen did off the pitch, the likes of David Beckham, Wayne Rooney and John Terry laboured hard at their craft.

Still, graft got less attention than being Waggishly rich or famous or beautiful. Beauty mattered more with the rise in makeovers and growing use of cosmetic surgery by women and men. In 2009 the British Association of Aesthetic Plastic Surgeons recorded 22,041 procedures carried out by its members, up 34.6 per cent since 2004. However acquired, money was to be ostentatiously enjoyed in bling and brass, branded handbags or Saturday-night stretch limos.

For bling you needed to shop, and retail was a very British engine of growth. The physical renewal of Britain's cities during these years hinged on Gap, La Senza, Costa and the Body Shop. Critics worried that the urban fabric was being privatized, with ostensibly public space now policed by security firms. Unfortunately timed for the start of the recession, caverns of consumption opened with the Westfield shopping mall in London's Shepherd's Bush, Bristol's Cabot Circus and Liverpool's Paradise Street development, anchored by a John Lewis store. Labour had long before thrown their lot in with a different chain, Tesco. Ministers courted and hero-worshipped its chief executive, Sir Terry Leahy – knighted during a decade when that honour, scuffed and scratched, was damaged further by its award to the self-righteous destroyer of capital value at the Royal Bank of Scotland, Sir Fred Goodwin.

If being British meant shopping till you dropped in clonal high streets, it also embraced drinking till dawn in Wetherspoons; 500 of them opened on Labour's watch. When England's football fans went to Euro 2000, drink fuelled the riots in Charleroi and Brussels. Starting with the Football (Offences and Disorder) Act 1999, Labour tightened controls on who could travel; 3180 orders forcing fans to surrender their passports for the duration of a tournament were in place in November 2009. Over the years, Brits started to lose their reputation for foreign drunkenness. In 2008–9 over 100,000 English and Welsh club fans went to 49 matches elsewhere in Europe with only 30 arrests. Despite copious amounts of vinho verde and Sagres, arrests of England fans at the European finals in Portugal in 2004 fell to 70, and in Germany and Austria in 2008 England's fans appeared saintly next to rioting Germans and Poles. Here was culture change indeed.

Bingeing had been blamed on restrictive licensing laws. If pubs did not chuck punters out all at once, chief constables predicted that fewer drunks would fight in city-centre taxi queues. Labour obliged with the 2003 Licensing Act, allowing bars and pubs to stay open for twenty-four hours. The binge went on. In 2009 the Commons' culture committee observed that 'relaxation has not diminished law and order problems, merely moved them two hours later'. Numbers of pubs continued to fall, 2000 closing in 2008 alone, reported the trade association. But pubs had been closing since Victorian times and 57,000 still remained, sufficiently lodged in the popular imagination to sustain *Eastenders*. However, they no longer smoked in the Queen Vic. The smoking ban in public buildings transformed how the country smelled. The law enacted in England in 2007 was one of Labour's most radical legacies. Pubs complained, but the public celebrated.

But what if smoky pubs inspired poets? Government intersects with culture randomly, except when it knowingly pays artists public money. Labour did a lot of that, some extravagant observers even comparing its benefaction to that of the Florentine Medicis. Total assistance to the arts can only be approximated since the £500 million formal arts budget in England in 2010 was complemented by local and regional grants. Add university spending (the research element of which rose) to that pot, and a proportion of the (increased) BBC licence fee, and you got substantially more support for artistic life, from orchestras to new radio plays, poetry, music and drama of all kinds. Defined public spending on the arts rose 70 per cent in real terms over Labour's era, and it showed.

Labour's great boast was free entry to museums and galleries. True, they prevaricated and only after the second election victory removed all charges for the national collections. Numbers of children admitted to the now-free museums and galleries rose steeply and satisfyingly. That, in the government's eyes, was a measure of cultural success. Labour saw no conflict between excellence and wide, class-blind participation. Grants were dispensed on the proviso that museums, orchestras and dance troupes would reach out and bring in new audiences and under-represented social and ethnic groups, which by and large they did.

Dusty old glories were revived, some too long the preserve of curators and Casaubons. Oxford's Ashmolean underwent a spectacular transformation. The reopened medieval and renaissance galleries of the Victoria and Albert were greeted rapturously. Kelvingrove in Glasgow, Middlesbrough's Institute of Modern Art, Manchester's Whitworth and City art galleries, the Imperial War Museum North in Trafford and the People's History Museum in Salford all showed fresh faces. Individual museums had their own trajectories, following the ups and downs of temporary exhibitions, and the balance of government grants, sponsorship and donations varied. The lottery paid for much of this building, Labour breaking the covenant that said it would only pay for extras, not substitute for public spending. But look at the new buildings, some planned pre-Labour. The Walsall art gallery, the Lowry Museum, the Salt Mills in Bradford, the Sage Centre and the Baltic in Gateshead, Tate Modern and the International Slavery Museum on Albert Dock in Liverpool – most were triumphs. Run-down cities ached for the 'Bilbao effect' – what Frank Gehry's spectacular Guggenheim Museum had done for that depressed industrial city in Spain. Labour bought heavily into cultural construction as an instrument of regeneration.

Which helps explain the Millennium Dome. Blair shared a taste for grandiose display with the project's Tory instigator, Michael Heseltine, who had once brought an unlikely garden festival to run-down Liverpool. Here was national symbolism and urban regeneration in the same package. In his giant tethered-down frisbee in Greenwich, Richard Rogers – for a while Labour's in-house urbanist, at least till he starting saying uncomfortable things about inequality – delivered a remarkable building. Opening on time was an achievement. In its first months the dome attracted more paying visitors than any other British pay-to-view exhibit, although still barely a third of the twelve million forecast.

But this entered the annals as a Labour disaster. Many made their minds up on the notorious opening night. Along the Thames the 'river of fire' passed so fast onlookers claimed it never flashed at all, while at Greenwich a security glitch trapped celebrities at turnstiles for hours, among them the Queen. She was not amused. Before long the dome's tacky contents were removed and the structure stood vacant amid tumbleweed. Later, resurrected as O2, it recorded spectacular attendances – 420,000 for the appearances of Prince in 2007 – and the venue was partly redeemed, if not the net public investment of £1 billion.

Undeterred, the Cabinet bid for the 2012 Olympics. It was the same mix: a laudable wish to regenerate wasteland, a longing for some symbol of Britishness, overreaching ambition and uneven project management. The bid was a creature of the bubble years, an extravagance in the lean years. Ministers had no clear idea how much public money was being committed, and many of the promised 'wider benefits' were afterthoughts.

Mounting the games was to cost the taxpayer £4 billion, with £700 million to come from the private sector. Then it was £9 billion offset by £165 million from the private sector, which fell again when failed contractors had to be bailed out in the recession. A paltry £100 million was to be raised from sponsorship of the events themselves. The government had promised no money would be stolen from the National Lottery: by 2009 the costings said 23 per cent would come from the Lottery, much of it taken from local sports and arts.

As for the promised cultural Olympiad, there was no money. Fencers and practitioners of peripheral sports also complained but these were fat years for athletes: the available funds were to buy gold. Labour gave generously to UK Sport to fund runners in the run-up to Beijing in 2008: money works in sport and Britain brought home 47 medals, coming fourth in the international medals league table. The 2012 target was the same, fourth, and second in the Paralympics.

At least you could count medals. Achievement in the arts was less tangible but the critics were generally impressed. At the end of the decade Mark Lawson in the *Guardian* proclaimed a 'golden age' for the theatre, and expanded subsidy must have played a part. He meant performance rather than new plays, though Labour, in a perverse way, stimulated a new strain of contemporary-historical plays; people went to the theatre to boo Jack Straw on stage (*Stuff Happens*) or have financial meltdown explained (*Enron*). The critic Michael Billington heard a depressed, pessimistic tone in the decade's drama, often to do with Iraq: 'One of the multiple paradoxes of Blairism was that it enhanced the financial security of theatre, thereby enabling it to examine the failings of our society and the plight of western culture at large; which is precisely what writers like (Alan) Bennett, (Mike) Leigh, (Richard) Bean and (Tom) Stoppard did in a series of vauntingly ambitious plays' (*State of the Nation*, 2007). At the National Theatre, the Arts Council grant covered about a third of spending at the start of the decade. The National's turnover expanded by £15 million between 2002 and 2009 and state support kept pace, rising by £5.5 million in cash. Private funding of the arts rose from £454 million in 2003–4 to a 2007–8 record of £687 million – but was then badly hit by the recession. Here was a telling example of symbiosis. 'Public and private money go absolutely hand in hand,' Colin Tweedy, chief executive of the lobbying group Arts & Business, acknowledged.

Labour had had a soft spot for film ever since the Wilson government started supporting the British Film Institute – its former director, Wilf Stevenson, was a Brown aide. This time around, Labour established the UK Film Council, through which the industry benefited to the tune of £665 million plus tax reliefs. During the election, Richard Attenborough led a posse including directors Danny Boyle (*28 Days Later*) and Paul Greengrass (*Green Zone*) in praising the government's 'significant and valuable impact' on British film. Labour's relationship with popular music was rockier. Feargal Sharkey, chief executive of Music UK and formerly of the Undertones, may have been right in saying 'the music thing is something we are really bloody good at' (*Guardian*, 29 March 2010). But no one was quite sure why. Labour tried to help by moving to control illegal file sharing – one of those policies always likely to generate more antagonism than support. In 2005 it also extended licensing to cover an estimated 8000 extra premises, among them small venues playing live music. Ministers promised exemptions, but a survey of small venues for the DCMS in 2007 found a drop in their number leading to protests from guitarists and vocalists.

Governments can influence the 'where' of cultural life. In 2000 the extravagantly refurbished Royal Opera House was unveiled, with Covent Garden's Floral Hall transformed into a new semi-public space, thanks to £178 million of Lottery and Arts Council money. But what goes on stages or concert platforms or into galleries or sculpture collections rarely had a discernible, even indirect relationship with politics and policy. The flourishing of a mystical, intensely Catholic composer such as James Macmillan during these years was mere coincidence. Yet public or BBC commissions sustain creators. Anish Kapoor and Antony Gormley are among the artists who benefited.

Labour renamed the ragbag Department of National Heritage created by the Tories the Department of Culture, Media and

Sport – still a ragbag. The Britishness question was whose heritage, the people's or the power holders'? Labour did not want to ask, insisting instead that whoever's heritage it was, the people should have more access. In 2008 the Public Accounts Committee worried about a 20 per cent decline in schoolchildren visiting English Heritage sites. Also in the quango's custody was Stonehenge. Labour's years saw grand and controversial plans for roads around the monument, first underground, then overground. By 2007, the decision was that no new road would be built. Druids were happy enough; nationally they recorded increases in membership.

Dressing up for the solstice was a valid act of faith in a relativist age. Under Labour, faith became almost fashionable. Early on, Blair had been asked whether religious belief guided his deliberations, but before he could answer, Campbell flashed: 'We don't do God.' Yet the prime minister made no secret of his Christian adherence; his wife and children were Roman Catholics and the only surprise on his conversion soon after leaving office was that the Pope did not require much by way of penance for his having fought wars and approved abortion.

Campbell was right in a narrow sense. Though the government retained powers of patronage in the Church of England, no obviously Blairite bishops were appointed. To most observers Rowan Williams, the archbishop appointed to the see of Canterbury in 2002, was the meritocratic candidate, highish in practice but liberal in social philosophy, having had a spat with the previous archbishop over his views on homosexuality.

As for belief at large, there had been no reason in 1997 to suppose religion was likely to play any larger part in British politics. Only 12 per cent of the population were deemed regular worshippers in any faith, Druids included. If the Church of England had once been the Tory Party at prayer, now its pews were more evenly divided between the parties. It retained its twenty-six bishops in the House of Lords, who swung debates on such issues as the right to die.

Suddenly, 9/11 made religion political. Even without the attack, shifts in the geology of belief in Pakistan and the Middle

East might have shaken the sons of Muslim families settled in the UK. The shoe-bomber, Richard Reid, arrested after attempting to blow up an American Airlines plane to Miami in December 2001, exemplified a new pattern, where young British-born people were radicalized through contact with Wahabi extremism and sent to Pakistan for training to return as human bombs – this was before the Iraq invasion. Labour, as puzzled as the rest at the translocation of fundamentalism to Luton, set itself the subtle task of policing areas of Muslim concentration while persuading adherents into moderation. Disaggregated, internally pluralist and non-hierarchical as it was, Islam nonetheless pullulated with transmitted resentments. Labour had, in a sense, to create such a thing as British Islam, by giving recognition to often self-appointed spokespeople. They wanted to get Islam inside the tent. But it also seemed the government was actively encouraging transcendental belief, albeit for its this-worldly effects. In November 2009, John Denham, the communities secretary, launched yet another set of 'interfaith initiatives designed to increase social cohesion'. 'Faith is a strong and powerful source of honesty, solidarity, generosity – the very values which are essential to politics, to our economy and our society.' But sectarian faith also dissolved common identity. It was an odd spectacle: a government made up of non-believers advocating prayer in aid of group identity.

Labour were led into dangerous territory. In seeking to protect identity, they offended the British value of free speech. The Anti-Terrorism, Crime and Security Bill of 2001 purported to protect Muslims by means of a new offence of 'incitement to religious hatred'. Wasn't this the offence the ayatollahs had said Salman Rushdie had committed and for which he deserved to die? Opponents mustered. But in the 2005 manifesto Labour promised to criminalize incitement to religious hatred, which became law in the Racial and Religious Hatred Act 2006. The revised aim was to stop the BNP using the indentifiers Muslim and Islamic as proxies for race in their hate-leaflets. The new law was inert. Were Labour too hasty in legislating? Perhaps, but similar conversations were as animated in other countries. In France, Belgium and the Netherlands secular and national identity was held to be compromised by Muslim dress, especially face covering; about some things the British remained tolerant, or perhaps merely indifferent. Labour, as a quid pro quo to the free-speech lobby and as a sop to faiths that resented Christianity's unique protection, used the 2008 Criminal Justice and Immigration Act to abolish the offence of blasphemy in England and Wales. The courts had already discarded it; after the BBC broadcast *Jerry Springer: The Opera* in January 2005, the fundamentalist group Christian Voice failed to persuade the judges to convict.

And on such religious totems as abortion and stem cell research, rationalism ruled OK among Labour ministers. The worldwide scare over the Y2K millennium bug has become a classic of media hype and public gullibility – there was panicky talk of machines stopping and planes falling out of the sky. Ministers kept their cool and in October 1999, a couple of months before the witching hour, the NAO reported that the non-profit company Action 2000 set up by Whitehall to check IT systems had flashed only a couple of amber risks. 'A major achievement, the risk of major failures arising as result of the millennium threat is now low,' the auditors opined, and so it proved.

Bug worries lessened even as exposure to malicious software grew. The internet 'happened to' the government; only a few MPs exhibited strategic grasp of the explosion. In 1999 over ten million people in the UK had access to the internet either at work or through home PCs. Ten years later 70 per cent of the population had access, most on broadband. But hold the hype: since the Victorians, successive generations have believed their world spun faster. The internet did not topple Saddam; bankers would have overreached whether or not transactions were conducted online.

Labour knocked together a digital strategy of sorts, but you sensed ministers running to catch up both with markets and with people's self-exploration online and in social media. Blair never learned to email while in office and Brown's handwritten scrawl became notorious. The government pledged universal access to broadband services at two Mbps by 2012 paid for by a 50p monthly levy on fixed phone lines, a plan abandoned when the government ran out of time before the election. Access? The Thornton Estate in Hull was the subject of an optimistic proposal floated in 2009 for priority broadband cabling – a run-down estate where, despite community projects aplenty, residents remained poor, low-skilled and riven by differences in ethnicity. As ever, Labour found it easier to consider the symptoms of poverty – no broadband – rather than the root cause – no money.

Labour suffered – as their successors will – from a blogosphere churning out bilious rumour, conspiracy theory and silliness. Britain online was not kinder and gentler. Culture pulled in opposing directions – reason, science and experiment tugging one way while faith, conviction and opinion pulled the other. Ben Goldacre, the *Guardian*'s debunker, did not lack for examples of abuse of statistics and gobbledegook charlatanry. Yet science had never had it so good, on the back of a two-thirds increase in government spending. Scientists' productivity rose as measured by citation per paper and universities made progress in transferring research into commercial applications. The brain drain reversed: the UK became a favoured destination not just for postgraduates but also for established American researchers. Not enough, some scientists said; spread too thin, said others, across rapidly advancing frontiers in bio- and nano-technology and – hugely expensive – particle physics.

Labour said the state would support research on the understanding that – as set out in the 2000 white paper *Excellence and Opportunity* – a proportion of it could be commercially exploited. Beyond the argument over what that share should be, Labour's touch was assured; even before the recession changed ministers' minds, the government had a vision of marrying state funding with an export-orientated capitalism that actually made things. The matchmaker was (Lord) David Sainsbury, whose philanthropic generosity based on grocery millions extended to supporting the Labour Party; he was an effective science minister who was allowed to stay in the job long enough to get things done. Labour updated Harold Wilson's 'white heat of the technological revolution' in the *Science and Innovation Investment Framework* published in 2004. It sought to marry state investment, intellectual excellence and commercial and practical gain. The social sciences did enormously well in these years, too. The authors of social programmes as ambitious as Labour's recognized that they needed to know about the dynamics of a changing society. The Millennium Cohort study caught up with the Conservative drought years, with its lifelong investigation of every child born in two weeks during 2000, following on the 1946, 1958 and 1970 studies. The great *Understanding Society* inquiry, launched in 2008, covering 40,000 households, to be re-interviewed each year over at least five, was a true monument to the government's inquiring spirit.

A new acronym was STEM – science, technology, engineering and maths as a group of studies deserving extra support. Even as university places were cut in spring 2010, the government insisted universities favour STEM subjects, and vice-chancellors, mindful of the larger grants attached, were more or less willing. Incentives were built into postgraduate programmes. Students came forward in higher numbers in biological and mixed sciences, but less so in physics, chemistry and engineering. Sainsbury looked ahead, observing that the UK had a reasonable stock of STEM graduates but the twenty-year decline in numbers taking A level physics spoke of 'potential problems'. This was manpower planning of a kind of which Wilson would approve.

But was it enough? Even Thatcher had recognized the standing of UK science and the worth of public support. In the decade from 1997, the OECD reckoned gross spending on research and development in the UK increased only marginally as a proportion of GDP. However, that sum meant large cash increases in the science budget and in 'civil' spending on technology and science, with a fall in defence R&D. Sainsbury's successor as science minister, the businessman Paul Drayson, praised UK scientists for squeezing more from every pound spent on research. But university scientists jibbed at Labour's utilitarianism, which demanded practical 'impact' from research. Labour invested at least £800 million in supporting technology transfer up to 2007, and a further £429 million was scheduled for the years to 2011 – paying for innovation funds, seed corn for start-ups and a Cambridge–MIT programme.

If Labour's generosity went unthanked by arts and science, the reason was ministers' insistence on a pro quo for the many quids they put in. What scientists, academics, clinicians and theatre directors like is freedom – to spend as the muse or the fire of knowledge leads them. Scientific autonomy, a precious principle, took a heavy hit when emails among climate scientists at the University of East Anglia were hacked, and the price of their knowledge was shown to be a clubby arrogance about letting opponents see unhelpful evidence.

Self-regard in clubs was not confined to science. Here was something that ought to have concerned Lord Triesman – the Labour Party apparatchik and minister turned chair of the Football Association – but he stayed quiet before departing in disgrace in 2010. Labour's role, as big money washed into sport, was that of an ineffectual assistant referee, fated to wave the yellow flag and be ignored by everyone on the field. During the 2009–10 Premiership season, chickens came home to roost, some of them among the cooing pigeons in the rusting roofstand at Portsmouth's Fratton Park. According to David Lacey, the *Guardian*'s veteran football correspondent (9 January 2010): 'The Premier League, founded on avarice, is now on the edge of a precipice. At one end Manchester United and Liverpool are burdened with debts imported from America while at the other Portsmouth are struggling with financial problems involving person or persons unknown, such is the Byzantine nature of their latest ownership.'

Still, foreign cash had perked up attendance: during the 2008–9 season 37 million attended football matches in England and Wales, up from 29 million in 2003–4, figures last seen when *Hey Jude* topped the charts. Few would turn the clock back even though parochial fans habitually exaggerated the quality of the Premiership over the Bundesliga or Serie A. Yet in Germany, clubs were obliged by law and custom to maintain local and mutual structures, and to keep gate prices down; in Italy, the plutocrats were at least home-grown and, in the case of the president of AC Milan, Silvio Berlusconi, Italians could even vote against him. What English club football exchanged for money, new stadiums and foreign players was fairness, stoicism and localism. A similar story unfolded in the gents' games of cricket and rugby union.

Labour intervened occasionally, protecting events of national significance by insisting they had to be shown free-to-air. But it stood transfixed as huge sums were committed by such peculiar hybrids as the FA (a private club with public responsibilities), despite knowing that if catastrophe happened, the state would be forced to pick up the pieces. Labour bailed out the £757 million Wembley project, and the stadium did get built, though it has yet to win the place in 'national' affections that the Cardiff Millennium Stadium, opened in 1999 also with Lottery support, quickly did. The government flapped as the governance of the English FA became a Brian Rix farce.

But through a combination of government, clubs and cultural change, football became a more pacific sport to watch, just as standards of behaviour on the field broadly improved. By the 2008–9 season, the total number of people arrested in connection with all international and domestic football matches involving teams from England and Wales was 3752, and only 354 of those arrests were for offences of violence. Here was progress.

Cue Bill Shankly – 'some people think football's a matter of life and death. I can assure them it is much more serious than that.' Sport supplied community allegiance in a fissured world. Football taught globalization – if that meant the England national team being managed by a Swede or an Italian – but it never seemed to leak into greater enthusiasm for the UK's place in Europe. In a different league from football, Labour's emblematic sport turned out to be Formula One motor racing, which spilt oil on Blair's spotless reputation when Labour took money in exchange for manipulating their own policy on banning tobacco advertising from sports sponsorship. A champion, Lewis Hamilton, demonstrated the prevailing selfishness by announcing he was going to live abroad in order to avoid paying UK taxes, about which the government said not a word in rebuke. So this was a British sporting hero: sheltering your earnings by moving abroad.

Labour's navigation of the boundary between culture and commerce pitched and rolled. Twenty-four-hour drink licenses were bad enough, but what would Philip Snowden have made of Labour's love affair with what the former Labour chancellor had called 'the second greatest curse of the country'? Like the Dome and the Olympics, roulette and blackjack were supposed to regenerate the poorest districts, as ministers talked fantastically about casinos to rival the Bellagio in . . . Salford, Luton and Swansea. Imagine *Ocean's Eleven* playing out on the Manchester Ship Canal. Thousands of jobs would be created in the Sun City of Europe, drawing gamblers and their money to this offshore, unregulated gambling den where the poor inhabitants would, as in a Navajo reservation in Arizona, get to wait on tables and serve the drinks. Labour ministers climbed into bed with Las Vegas gambling magnates, raising eyebrows in the US where the government was just then prosecuting British businessmen for running internet gambling sites that had been made illegal in America.

A consortium of charities, churches and anti-addiction lobbies pleaded with Labour to do likewise, instead of expanding gambling. But ministers saw only a win-win, combining easy tax revenues and urban regeneration. For the first time the government allowed gambling advertisements on television. Never mind the evidence that high-value slot machines in these casinos were highly addictive. In 2004 there were an estimated 370,000 gambling addicts, and an OECD report showed that the poor gambled away a higher proportion of their incomes than the better-off. Labour believed in equal opportunity to lose money.

The site for a super-casino narrowed down to Manchester or the increasingly beleaguered Blackpool. The two councils fought like scavenging dogs but Brown took away the bone when he arrived as prime minister. However, a further sixteen casinos were still to go ahead, each larger than any in existence in Britain.

By the time Labour left office, the first two of them were under construction in sun-kissed Great Yarmouth and glamorous Nottingham, palm-bedecked queen of the East Midlands. Leisure Parcs, the company that had bought tracts of Blackpool in anticipation of the super-casino, sold the tower and Winter Gardens to the council. It still hoped, like Margate, Hastings, Morecambe and other forlorn English seaside towns that had seen better days, that strategy and regeneration pots could somehow mitigate alteration in leisure habits and the British weather.

From 2001 gambling tax came from bookmakers' gross profits rather than bets laid by punters. The UK gambling industry – the one located outside the City of London – boomed, but winnings were not pouring into the Treasury. Betting was moving into new exchanges, interactive television, mobile phones, online and offshore. In 2009 William Hill and Ladbrokes moved abroad, threatening to cut the tax take. Labour could have followed the American example. Congress dealt with the new phenomenon by banning online gambling altogether, stopping US credit-card companies paying out to gambling sites. Instead, in 2010 the government said it wanted to give more power to its new quango, the Gambling Commission, to regulate online operators who would be required, for example, to contribute to the levy paid by UK bookmakers to support horse racing. It seemed the government just wanted to clear space for free enterprise, no matter how socially harmful.

Oscillation between freedom and restraint marked Labour's tenure. Their attitude towards sexual orientation fell firmly on the former side. Gay knights were feted in Downing Street under both Blair and Brown; gay rights were made law. Out politicians, brave at first like Chris Smith and Ben Bradshaw, were later reassuringly banal, among them the Foreign Office minister Chris Bryant. Bryant represented the Rhondda, but how culturally distant he seemed from a former parliamentary neighbour, the MP for Caerphilly, Ron Davies. Twelve years on, the furtiveness of his 1998 career-destroying moment of madness on Clapham Common seemed utterly anachronistic.

Section 28 was a discriminatory clause in a 1988 Act passed

during a spasm of Tory moral panic that forbade councillors and schools to 'promote' homosexuality. Largely unused, it was a textbook case of the irrelevance of statute law in affecting deep movements in public attitudes – homosexuality was becoming normal, inside families, in popular culture, even fractiously in the pulpit. Still, the law remained an affront.

Abolition of the Scottish counterpart to Section 28 was delayed by interventions from both a Catholic cardinal and an evangelical Protestant in the shape of the bus and coach magnate Brian Souter. Labour's first minister Donald Dewar stuck to his guns and repeal was enacted in Edinburgh in 2000. It took three more years before the Westminster parliament followed suit. Local government minister Nick Raynsford declared: 'For over a decade, Section 28 has cast a cloud of confusion and ambiguity over local authorities' ability to support and provide services to the whole of their community. Repeal means that this cloud has lifted.' Why did it take so long?

One reason might have been Labour's legislative busyness. In 2001 it had equalized the age of consent for gay sex at sixteen years. In the same year same-sex partners were given equal rights under the Criminal Injuries Compensation Scheme, after a bomb in a gay bar in Soho revealed that some of the victims were not eligible. The Civil Partnership Act of 2004 gave gay and lesbian couples the same tax and legal rights as married heterosexual couples. They were able to register their partnership in an official ceremony and acquire the same right to inherit one another's pension and pay no death duties on their shared home. Old buffers and bishops in the Lords tried to wreck the vessel but the ship steamed on amid a spate of celebrity partnerships. The news value of 'gay marriage' wore off within days.

If Labour freed sexual expression, they also confined it. The police reported that pornographic imagery was getting more and more extreme. The 2008 Criminal Justice Act 2008 made possession of extreme images an offence. 'Sex workers' denied exploitation, but lapdancing – sexual teasing that did not always stop short of prostitution – had exploded on Labour's watch. Lapdancing clubs were encouraged by the 2003 Licensing Act, which took them out of the category of establishments requiring a special sex encounter licence. Local authorities therefore lost the power to stop them setting up in high streets and even residential areas, however much local people protested. Women often had to pay to work in such places, recouping the cost from what happened in the private rooms. After much campaigning, new legislation in Labour's final year did give councils back licensing powers, but only after lapdancing had become socially acceptable.

Labour were sexually confused. Lapdancing elicited no condemnation from ministers but they proscribed the buyers of kerbside sex after another campaign. The Police and Crime Act 2009 shifted criminal liability away from prostitutes, regarded as victims of exploitation, placing responsibility on clients, who had to ensure sex was voluntary and prostitutes were not controlled by a pimp or trafficked, which amounted to rape. The reform was passed despite strong opposition from those who protested that a client could not be expected to know – but that was the point. The courts had long required buyers to exercise care and caution in making sure they were not purchasing stolen goods, which are a lot less intimate and invasive than sex.

Intermittent attempts to amend the abortion laws drew thousands of messages to MPs organized from the pulpit, but psephologists never found a single seat lost or won by such free-vote questions. In 1990 the Tory-dominated Commons had cut the legal date for termination from twenty-eight to twenty-four weeks, and during Labour's tenure attempts were made at further reduction. Although votes were always free of party whips, the Labour-dominated Commons imposed no new restrictions. But campaigners failed to bring equal abortion rights to Northern Ireland, where abortion remained banned and women had to travel elsewhere in the UK for private treatment.

It was unclear, by the end of the Labour government, whether such regional differences were to be celebrated or if they affronted basic ideas of fairness and rights. Northern Ireland showed just how puzzling Britishness remained. In the 2010 election its voters could not even cast a Labour vote. But how fair is it to accuse

Labour of lacking a 'national' narrative, or of having imposed no cultural stamp on the epoch, no -ology or -ism? Their era felt like a creative time, in fashion, music and on the stage, and Labour investment played a big part in making space for innovation.

Labour did believe fervently in the power of the arts, just as they did in education. They desperately wanted people to have more, and set themselves targets for visits and visitors. In 2009, about 51 per cent of people in England had visited a museum or gallery in the previous twelve months, and about 45 per cent took part in some sort of arts event. The probability is they were the same kind of people who did culture as in 1997, except twelve years later opportunities were much expanded and crucially, for the big museums, entry was made free. But it was also typical of the times that the in-phrase became 'cultural and creative industries': the arts to become money-spinners, culture and commerce combining in mystical union. Indeed, by 2009 the culture industries made up 8 per cent of GDP – a considerable contribution and significantly around the same amount as the City and financial services, including all high street banking and insurance.

Another catchphrase was knowledge economy – trying to capture the commercial importance of ideas and experiences that were also significant in themselves. Labour had the glimmerings of a vision of Britain, open, innovative, arty, keen on the pursuit of knowledge and endowed by public money – and very cheap at the price. Labour bequeathed something much richer than they inherited, but had not painted a national transfiguration.

The clubber's verdict

Policy, politics and pogoing – until the recession and beyond, clubbers kept on dancing without a thought about Labour, Westminster, wars or welfare. For many, well-being was not an earnest think-tank debate on the causes of happiness – it was a night out, preferably out of your skull.

Mood music

Scenes come and go; within a few years Hoxton Square was so over, though Manchester kept its vibe. It was incarnated as a media label in the late eighties and early nineties as Madchester, thanks to the Hacienda, The Smiths, the Stone Roses and Happy Mondays. But Factory Records, motor for much of the music scene, went bust. The Hacienda closed down the year Labour came to power, plagued by gangsters and protection rackets. By then music and property development were holding hands. The boom years were kind to Urban Splash, a hip regeneration company that built bright flats in derelict warehouses and deserted stretches of Manchester. Its founder, Tom Bloxham, won architectural awards as he spread out to revive run-down districts in Salford, Bradford, Liverpool and Sheffield, and restored Morecambe's Midland Hotel, which reopened in 2008 in all its art deco splendour.

The IRA bomb that wrecked Manchester's city centre in 1996 came to mark a turning point, since when hotels, restaurants, bars and clubs blossomed, new trams trundled and, rescued from dusty dilapidation, the city's Victorian civic monuments stood proud. Manchester University was hotly popular as students pretended the excellence of the courses attracted them, when everyone knew it was the raves.

The Warehouse Project was among the Hacienda's progeny. It was set up by Sacha Lord-Marchionne, thirty-eight, a boyish, elfin type who would pass for ten years younger, as maybe he needs to in a Peter Pan business. He was a schoolboy of seventeen when he first ran his own regular night – 'Scandalous' — at the Hacienda, which gives him iconic credibility with ticket-buyers who were then still in reception class. He started out in an early factory bought for an Urban Splash renovation. There was Paradise in the old Factory Records office, then Sankeys in a disused soap mill and the Boddingtons brewery beside Strangeways. The authorities soon put a stop to 3000 people raving until 5 a.m. to techno music pounding the corrugated-iron roof underneath the jail. 'Prisoners used to throw down their requests out of the windows, it wouldn't do.' Incidently, Boddingtons' fate was emblematic of the destruction of local identity: taken over by Inbev, 'the world's largest brewer', Boddingtons' association with the city snapped and the bitter branded the 'cream of Manchester' was transferred to an anonymous factory estate in South Wales.

Lord-Marchionne and partners conceived of a three-month festival, its edge to come from not knowing when, where and even if. 'We'd lost our way and that's never going to happen again. This will always stop when people least expect it, when it can't get any better.' The festival ran weekends September to January when Manchester's vast student population of over 87,000 had money from their loan cheques in the run-up to Christmas. 'We found that's when we made money, and we spent the rest of the year trying not to lose it, when students are running out of cash and working for exams or away on summer holidays. Not being there all the time makes people value it more. Not knowing if, or where or anywhere, stops it going stale.'

Touring the city looking for empty venues, Lord-Marchionne found a car park under Manchester's main station. Piccadilly Arches was an old air-raid shelter with twelve-foot-thick walls, able to absorb thumping drum and bass that would rattle the gates of hell. They had to wait for the last cars to drive out of the exit barrier on Friday nights, when they had just two hours to carry in the bars, booze, flat screens, speaker stacks and Portaloos and turn an unprepossessing underground car park into a state-of-the-art party venue for 2000 long-sold-out ticket-holders.

He had the measure of the city council and the (Labour majority) councillors had the measure of him. 'If you said to most councils I want to run raves under your train station, not many would say "Right, OK", would they?' he says appreciatively. They may not have got the music or the DJs but they knew music was a Manchester brand, and more might have heard of the Hacienda than of the Hallé. Because Lord-Marchionne ran safe events with police hired in as heavies he was invited to become vice-chair of the council's Pub and Club Committee. The motto on the town hall clock reads, 'Teach us to number our days'; Lord-Marchionne and his hedonists might interpret that as *carpe diem*, probably not the intention of the city fathers.

Mood music

He was born in leafy Hale and attended Manchester Grammar School. Already in the sixth form he was running nightclub nights. Ugly Duckling, his company based in an elegant glass office in a glitzy new canal-side Urban Splash development, has enjoyed Labour times. 'Never better. In recessions people always want pleasure. Ticket sales are up for us, though bar revenue is down. Students haven't got so many jobs as they had, but they've still got loans, haven't they?'

He sang the praises of the Greater Manchester police. 'The city was a scary place back when the Hacienda was shut down in 1997. You could see the gangs in there, all standing under the balcony. The problem was really bad with guns and everyone paid protection. Now no one does. If anyone tries it, the Tactical Aid Unit is in there in a flash. They'll slap on an Asbo and that person won't try it again. The police have it all locked down these days and that's a big change in the last decade.'

His family were Tory and he professed not much interest in politics. 'The John Major government was pretty crap so I voted Labour 1997, really excited for a bit, not for long.' Local Manchester politics is all that matters. 'Whatever happens, so long as Manchester stays Labour everything's fine with me because they and the chief executive are so understanding. I can really work with them.'

Did anything in national politics touch him during this time – the Iraq war, for example? 'Um, well, to tell you truth, all I thought was panic. What if they have conscription like World War One and Two? How can I get myself out of it and would they have a special exemption for entertainers?' Hedonists were ever thus, the leavening in the bread, the joy in the streets, me-first individualists. The Labour years had plenty of them, and gave plenty to them too.

CHAPTER 5

Migrants, homes and places

'They just aren't civilized,' Beryl Comer reported. 'They aren't used to using an indoor bathroom, as they think it's dirty, same place as cooking, so they'll do their business right out there in front of you, don't mind who's looking. The men all stand out in the street all day and all night, big gangs of them, twenty or thirty, and it's intimidating. And they make such a noise out there all night. We had a meeting when this started, everyone kicking up. When I go down to the post office for my pension, I see them handing over £2000 or £3000 to send to Romania. Where do they get that?'

Benefit and passport fraud were answers and possibly child trafficking. A couple of months before, police and Manchester Council had mounted an operation in November 2009 and taken a number of Roma children from the terraces in Gorton into care. In the previous two years upwards of a thousand people from Romania had moved in, causing mayhem in this network of neat red-brick terraces with their back doors giving onto gated alleyways. Superintendent Paul Savill, who led the operation, said to the press: 'I want to stress this operation was not intended to stigmatize the Roma who have settled in our community. They have an absolute right to live here.'

That was the voice of officialdom as modulated during the Labour years – absolute avoidance of anything that could be interpreted as prejudice. But why Gorton of all places? One of

Savill's police colleagues told us, 'It seemed to happen overnight, a few came then hundreds more, most from a single village. Since 2007 they've had permission to come and they can claim benefits for children.' This part of Manchester offered some of the cheapest rental housing in the EU, rows of terraces where landlords crammed properties to the roof. 'Three families in a two-up two-down,' he said.

Labour's migration problem was that large numbers arrived without a back story. Their impact, as in Gorton, was greatest in poorer areas. Ministers and think-tanks remarked airily on the benefits; the costs were often specific, local and unrecognized. If Labour had openly acknowledged the extent of the arrivals, and the problems – however transitional – they might have convinced more people. But the absence of a Labour housing policy meant they could not respond in the most obvious and direct way, by building more places where residents, their children and new arrivals could all live. For a government concerned with fairness, migration was a test: how were its benefits and costs to be distributed? Labour failed it, by overdoing the advantages, which had a definite class profile to them, and underplaying the costs – which might have been mitigated by active assistance to areas affected, especially more housing.

In 1997, 350,000 migrants arrived to live in the UK for at least a year and in 2005 that rose to an estimated 565,000, though many migrants migrated again. In 2007, the official figures said 340,000 people emigrated from the UK and 577,000 people arrived to live for at least a year, giving net immigration of 237,000.

But in 2007–8 the figure rose again. Some 1.27 million applications were made to visit the UK, including 459,000 family visits and 344,000 from students. How many of these visitors would remain? Over-stayers could only be guessed at. The Labour Force Survey estimated that non-EU nationals in jobs in the UK doubled between 1997 and 2009, at least. In early 2009, that meant 1.2 million non-EU workers out of a total UK workforce of 27.8 million. Statisticians projected the UK population would rise to 70 million by 2029, powered by young migrant families. Already, one in four babies was born to a foreign-born mother.

On Beryl Comer's street in Gorton the authorities had tried to integrate the arrivals. Translators explained British laws to the Roma families: no speeding cars, motor insurance compulsory, children to attend school, use bins, no rubbish in the streets, no noise. The local schools were inundated and late in the day the council threatened to prosecute the landlords for overcrowding. 'If a sudden influx happened again, we'd know what to do,' Damien O'Reilly, the local police inspector, said. 'Truth was, we were a bit slow off the mark, didn't quite know what to do. Now we'd stop the landlords packing the houses, apply the regulations, make sure right from the start that people arriving here all know the rules and how to behave.' Greater Manchester had the third largest regional share in immigrant settlement after London and the West Midlands. In a pre-election briefing, the Centre for Economic Performance declared – in that supercilious tone often adopted by academics and commentators on migration – that the evidence of the value of inward migration was positive or at worst ambiguous, and anyone who suggested different was veering towards racism.

But that was not how it felt in Gorton. Its residents, moreover, were Labour's people. At the 2010 election no BNP candidate or other extremist stood here and the swing against Labour was only a mild 1.5 per cent in favour of the Liberal Democrats, hardly worth a second thought to the sitting MP Gerald Kaufman. Migration changed people's lives on a daily basis, but it was not something they had been asked about, it just happened.

Migration touched the common sense of orderliness and fairness. In Gorton, back alleys that had been scrupulously clean, with a little garden and wooden flower boxes for each back door, were now filled with rubbish. Beryl unlocked the gate for us to show that morning's tipping. A couple of soiled duvets are bundled up, and there's a dripping old carpet, and dirty water ran down the cobbles from a blocked drain. 'Perceptions are not reality,' Bobby Duffy of Ipsos MORI kept reminding those who read his polls, which so often showed the public hugely overestimating the scale of migration. In 2006, four out of ten rated immigration their highest concern. Many were angry and frustrated at their inability to speak about what they witnessed daily. Blunkett later asserted that the Cabinet had spent hours discussing the subject; he did not say so at the time and the political class steered clear. A typical poll – for Communities and Local Government in 2009 – found 77 per cent favouring a cut in immigration. Yet large numbers also said integration was going well and 84 per cent attested that their own neighbourhood was a place where people from different backgrounds got on well together.

Irene, in her eighties, is one of Beryl's Gorton neighbours, her front room almost impenetrable, piled high with stuff. She pointed through the window: 'Across the road now they are all foreign people, Polish and all sorts, only five British left in this street, but we do sign language, and they're very nice. My alarm goes off sometimes by mistake, and they come out and ask if I'm all right. I wave and they smile but we can't speak.'

Poles and Roma were legal migrants within the EU, but where they settled and whether they spoke English had a decided impact on how others felt. Stop and listen on the ancient Market Square in Boston and the ethnic transformation of this corner of Lincolnshire is audible. Brown's stuttering conversation about Britishness made even less sense when Home Office ministers had periodically to admit they did not know how many people lived in Britain legally. Labour's stance was hard to fathom. They were pro-migration, partly because of their deference to business – which wanted cheaper labour – and partly because they had converted to the modern doctrine of diversity. A more Asian, a blacker, a more mixed Britain was, Labour believed, a better Britain. Such beliefs were reputable, but party spokespeople rarely articulated or defended them in the cut and thrust of debate. The people might have been responsive but, like tax, migration was treated as something that went on under the counter.

Barbara Roche, the Home Office minister, declared outright that 'immigration is a good thing'. If so, why not welcome asylum seekers? Ministers strove to separate asylum and 'economic migration', but the two merged in the public mind. The government had inherited a backlog of asylum cases from the Tories in 1997 and – oddly unprepared – missed the chance to call an immediate amnesty to clear the list. Computer failures, staff cuts and increased numbers seeking refuge or a better life in Britain pushed applications up. Those awaiting adjudication grew to 125,000 by 1999. Applications rose from 32,500 in 1997, to reach a peak of 84,130 in 2002, before falling back to 24,000 in 2009.

Applicants were predominantly from war zones, whether or not they personally were at political risk. Television pictures of able-bodied young men scrambling over fences at Sangatte to clamber aboard trains compounded the endemic confusion between individual and collective circumstances. If war afflicted Kosovo, did all Kosovars have a right to come to the UK and plead for asylum? When did the need for asylum end? Should refuge last only as long as the besetting emergency, so letting Iraqis and Afghanis return to countries made safe by British arms?

Perhaps ministers themselves simply did not understand this dimension of globalization. They tried to make the UK as unattractive as possible without rejecting what they still, high-mindedly, defined as the UK's international obligation to offer asylum. Yet their failure to stem numbers created an impression of state incompetence and uncontrolled borders. The government could not remove large numbers of those judged by tribunals to have no right to stay: their status as illegal immigrants with no right to stay or to work was officially tolerated because there was no other option. They could not be put on planes back to countries such as China that refused to accept them. Instead, they were dispersed to cities with empty housing. 'The whole thing was mad – give them a voucher and put them on a bus,' recalled an insider and loyalist, Nick Pearce, who was Blunkett's special adviser at the time. No wonder sudden influxes in Glasgow and other poor areas caused resentment.

Legislation in 2002 withdrew welfare support from asylum

seekers who did not apply immediately on arrival – a move later overturned by judges. 'Less eligibility' made the government look harsh. Blair, in super-hero mode, had stepped in, announcing on *Newsnight* in February 2003 that asylum applications would halve within a year. By 2005 applicants were being processed rapidly, in part because of tighter restrictions on visas and in part because fewer were arriving from the Balkans and Sri Lanka, where conflict was tailing off. Still, 'few removals of failed applicants are being achieved', the NAO found, and the gap increased between unfounded applications and removals.

The public pushed asylum seekers out of mind as the government criminalized their status; Yarlswood in Bedfordshire was a latter-day concentration camp for children as well as their parents. Turning away bishops bearing Christmas gifts in December 2009 did not speak well of British values. Ending up in a camp did not deter migrants much either, as asylum seeking rose again in 2009.

Labour's failing was lack of explanation: if trends were inevitable, why not admit it? If they were mutable, why not act? Ministers asserted the general economic benefits of people coming to work in Britain, but would not parse them according to who won and who lost. Plumbers, cleaners, gardeners and nannies served the well-off as businesses and employment agencies exploited cheap labour. Farmers and gangmasters flourished.

Boston, dominated by the tall tower of St Botolph's church – the Stump – is history-rich but poor. Its centre is pockmarked with vacant properties, charity shops and near-the-edge eateries. It exemplifies globalization as fate, an unplanned 'force' overwhelming the place. Perhaps migration could have been an opportunity to be exploited for communal benefit, but Boston politics were decrepit; the town council had been seized by the Boston Bypass Independents, a party agitating for a relief road.

In the rich loam fields around the town, agri-business ruled. The big growers and packers used to bus in workers from the Midlands, and bus them out again. But the expansion of the EU eastwards together with Labour's commitment to ultra-flexible employment prompted the gangmasters to set about recruiting in Poland. Locally they bought up terraces of houses, cramming migrant labour into them, charging high rents and making a lot of money on the accommodation.

'How do you begin to control that situation?' the council leader asked plaintively. Government projections of the effects of poorer, people-rich countries joining the EU were risible. 'I went to a presentation by a government adviser on migration in 2004,' a council officer reported. 'He said we project total net migration into the UK of 10,000. We've had 15,000 into Boston alone.' Portuguese settlers were followed by an East European influx into Fenland. Between 2004 and 2009 the number of young East Europeans living in the UK grew fivefold.

During the Labour years Boston income per head had risen, as everywhere else, but still remained £90 less per week (gross weekly earnings) than the UK average. High employment rates did not produce higher income. Because employment law was flexible – a coy way of saying in the UK it was easier to hire and fire staff – French, German, Spanish and other job-seekers came and often stayed. Brits of course also worked in Paris, Madrid and Frankfurt am Main but on the Paseo del Prado your waiter was not going to be a UK migrant. British plumbers did not fix the blocked drains of Wroclaw. The UK was far from unique; mass migration affected the Netherlands and Sweden and 13 per cent of Germany's population was foreign-born.

Getting into Britain to work legally had become easier. By 2009, 14 per cent of the population of working age had been born abroad, compared with 8 per cent in 1995, 6.8 million people, up from 2.9 million. Labour extended the Tories' policy of encouraging those with desirable skills – nurses, for example – to take jobs and settle. Council leaders in Slough and Peterborough challenged government claims that Eastern Europe migrants were transient and would go home in the recession. In Boston, young easterners came to stay, their children attending schools – four out of ten children in some of the town's reception classes were from migrant families. 'They saved our maternity unit,' observed Richard Austin, the Boston council leader.

Migrants, homes and places

Councils complained that the extra numbers failed to bring extra government grants to cover those services. Some areas were unaffected by migration – Merseyside and the North East, for example. Other areas were transformed – 60 per cent of the working-age population of the London Borough of Brent had been born abroad. The 2001 Census was a distant memory and its estimate that 4.9 million or 8.3 per cent of the total population of the UK were born overseas may never have been accurate anyway. When Boston protested at underestimates, the ONS said it recognized a total population for the area of 62,000, but the council put it nearer 75,000, taking its evidence from increased registration of migrants at GPs' surgeries and schools. Home Office minister Tony McNulty's 'best guess' was between 310,000 and 570,000 illegals. Some MPs became one-stop shops for migration casework, ministers getting (so a Commons committee reported) thirty to forty detailed letters about migration cases from MPs every day.

The public told pollsters they believed 22 per cent of the population were born abroad. Disparity between official numbers and belief was itself a social fact. Polling caught the variation between the local and the big picture: only 18 per cent of Britons saw immigration as a problem in their own area but 76 per cent saw it as a national problem. Working illegally in Britain also got easier. Universities needed foreign students for their cash and the authorities winked at the expansion of courses in marginal institutions the main purpose of which was revenue, visa fees included. Higher education policy clashed directly with migration control. The government tightened visa rules – students would in future be expected to speak English to GCSE standard. The Home Office issued 236,000 student visas in 2008–9, accounting for 30 per cent of people entering; it rejected 110,000 applications. How many stayed on?

Cynical or panicked, Brown talked 'British jobs for British workers' with no policy to back it. In 2009 oil-refinery workers at Lindsey in Lincolnshire walked out in protest at European contractors who arrived with their own workers, and paid them less, undercutting locals. The government stood back, impotent.

An expert committee was created to ensure foreign workers filled a genuine void. Professor David Metcalf of the London School of Economics, its head, said employers should be obliged to train locals at the same time, but this never happened. A £50 premium imposed on visas for foreign workers was supposed to go into a £70 million impact fund to be dispersed to police, schools, councils and hospitals feeling pressure.

Boston's council leader declared: 'No other part of England has suffered such a big change in such a short time.' Migrants tended to live in the town itself, where they were squeezed into too few properties. In Manchester, Beryl Comer regretted the consequences in Gorton. 'A lot of people are going from round here, if they can. We'd go too, but we've lived here forty years, brought up our children and our great-granddaughter in this house and we'd be sad to leave those memories.' Her husband chipped in, 'And frankly we couldn't sell anyway. We bought for £1100 and at one time it might have been worth a lot more when it had become such a nice little area. Not any more. The only people who would buy, very cheap, would be the landlords who would fill the house with more Romanians.'

Housing was one of Labour's weakest links. The equation was stark: house prices boomed, population grew, but little new housing was built. In this market, supply and demand were not operating. The government resisted the logic of state intervention, partly because rented housing sounded Old Labour, partly because it was scared by the large sums needed for subsidized house-building.

House prices had fallen by a third in real terms from 1989 to 1995, then rose rapidly after Labour took office. Despite the recession, the average price increase during its thirteen years was 7.5 per cent a year, compared with average annual inflation of 2.5 per cent. The ratio of average house prices to earnings rose, excluding new buyers. A Joseph Rowntree Foundation study in 2003 found thirty-three local authority areas – far from London – where a small home cost more than five times the average annual income of local working households with earners in their twenties or thirties. Yet, in this peculiar market, the real cost of mortgage payments fell as a proportion of income; it was not domestic mortgage lending which killed Bradford and Bingley and Northern Rock, but their exotic investments.

The Treasury commissioned an economist, Kate Barker, to state the bleedin' obvious. Reporting in 2004, she blamed too readily available credit, and the crash later proved her point. Supply did not respond because property companies bought land then sat on it, letting its rising value decorate their balance sheets and share prices. To keep house-price inflation at 1.8 per cent a year, Barker calculated that 70,000 extra dwellings should be built every year above and beyond already planned construction. In the second half of the decade, her projections looked more and more fantastic. From about 155,000 in 1997–8, annual housing starts for England fell, then rose to a pre-recession peak of 180,000, then collapsed to 90,430 in 2008–9, down 42 per cent on 2007–8 and 51 per cent below their 2005–6 peak.

That was the basic arithmetic, even before the government thought about greening the housing stock, improving the homes people already lived in or ensuring buyers could afford what the market demanded. House-price inflation was like a drug. In the year to April 2010, as if the crash and recession had never happened, house prices rose 10.5 per cent; we were swapping a more or less static stock of homes at ever higher prices, not so dissimilar, commentators pointed out, to a Ponzi scheme. Three-quarters of bank loans were going into property, not into building new homes, nor into productive investment. When 0.3 per cent of the population owned 70 per cent of British land, the rewards were bound to be skewed.

The government might have addressed the problem if it had anything like an urban vision – a strategic sense of how towns and cities might be. Housing was critical to basic quality of life, households' decisions about where to live, when and if to marry and have children. Time spent travelling to work rose, suggesting more people could only find accommodation further from their jobs. Prices made life hardest in London, where 1.34 million workers in 2009 spent more than an hour travelling between work and home, 385,000 more than in 1996.

Labour had an urban 'vision' of sorts – necessarily, given the areas that returned Labour MPs to Parliament. The North benefited from it. A report from academics commissioned by the office of the deputy prime minister in 2006, *State of the English Cities*, observed that 'sustained investment by the public sector had contributed to the renaissance of many Northern towns and cities'. Receding tides of manufacturing and mining had left towns in the north of England, west central Scotland and south Wales with plenty of houses. Often in a poor state of repair, they swamped the markets, sinking the prices Labour (and many of the public) now saw as the prime indicator of social progress. So the government offered to subsidize demolition. After five years and £2.2 billion, this housing market renewal had knocked down 10,200 dwellings, refurbished 40,000 and built 1100. The original idea had been to demolish 90,000 properties. It was a paradoxical measure, but expert evaluation said the gap in house prices between the neighbourhoods chosen for the scheme and surrounding areas had 'started to close'.

Labour hoped general economic growth would cure specific urban ills. Once, social democratic ministers would have relished regional plans and dreamed of new towns to cope with change – Labour's way in the 1960s – but the Blairites merely shrugged and said the market would provide. It did not, as the Barker report showed. Failure to build despite sky-high prices was an extraordinary market failure.

As for some overarching vision of urban Britain, Labour confronted political nemesis. London and the south-east of England produced GDP and tax revenue; that was where the jobs were, so that was where the housing should go. John Prescott presided over a policy of higgledy-piggledy expansion on the cheaper, flood-prone flatlands of east London and the cheap acreage around such East Midlands towns as Corby. The government itself would not build much, but would make it easier for developers. The Thames Gateway would realize a vision of renewal on straggling river sites in 'a world-class region with unrivalled locations for working and living and environmental sustainability'. But the project was under-capitalized; departments did not join up and the NAO complained that the government lacked a plan. The ratio of private to public, at £7 billion to £673 million, looked good, but the result was poor-quality housing and little improvement in transport and townscape.

The profligacy with which land was eaten up in car-dependent locations horrified academics and urban activists. They favoured rescuing run-down neighbourhoods and tightly restricting development on green fields. Labour wanted both, but within the confines of their restricted view of what the state should do. On one side, the government told the shires to assign land for housing. It proposed ten new 'eco towns', with about 15,000 people each, on brownish land such as ex-airfields outside urban areas – to be paid for by private developers. Here was a typical example of Labour's optimism that private beneficence would pour capital in for public purposes. The government's own advisers queried the finances, projecting that only three eco towns were ever likely to turn a profit for developers. Others would need tens of millions in public subsidy if they were to happen at all. A proposed community near St Austell in Cornwall faced a development deficit of between £60 million and £190 million. Then nimby locals started to mobilize against these Labour blots on their landscape. Reduced in scale, the towns went forward. In November 2009, a second wave of proposals added cash to develop plans for sites near Taunton, Yeovil, Lincoln and Gainsborough, Coventry, Leeds, York, Kirklees and Bradford-Shipley.

At the same time, urban areas were to be more intensely lived in; flats above shops were one short-lived initiative. Targets were set for 'brownfield' development on the back of a new database of previously used urban land.

Remembering its roots, the government grandly promised decent housing for all social tenants, and they would get it all the quicker if they signed up to transfer to the non-profit housing associations that Labour, like the Tories before, preferred to councils. Much housing was in a bad way, run down in the low-spending Tory years. By 2010 Labour had invested £37 billion in this Decent

Homes programme, installing central heating, new kitchens and bathrooms. In 2001 there were 1.6 million poor-quality homes in England's social housing stock, 39 per cent of the total. By the end of 2009, only 8 per cent remained unfit, a great achievement – and one that Labour oddly failed to talk about.

The programme still left 305,000 households living in houses and flats that were not 'warm, weatherproof and reasonably modern', with kitchens more than twenty years old and bathrooms older than thirty. The harsh line against councils running their own housing ended abruptly in 2009 when, as an anti-recession expedient, the government said they could once again build homes for rent and staked a modest expansion.

In a stylish report for the government the former chief executive of Birmingham, Sir Michael Lyons (later chairman of the BBC), urged 'place shaping' on local areas – councils were to envision how they should look in future years. But the look and feel of places depended on decisions made in corporate boardrooms or by migrant arrivals. Labour never quite reconciled their new enthusiasm for community self-government with the social and economic facts.

We confronted this gap in the South Yorkshire town of Rotherham, where one local man's sense of place was under assault by big commercial interests aided and abetted by the state. Andy Birk was the owner of Andrews the butchers in the Riverside precinct, under the shadow of All Saints' (the best perpendicular church in the country, according to Pevsner). For him, the identity of this particular place was being sucked out by the Tesco supermarket two miles away in the gigantic Meadowhall shopping mall. If that was not bad enough, a Tesco Metro had opened barely twenty yards away. 'Most of the shops along here have gone. The new retail units the council built haven't been let. It built this retail park half a mile away but the supermarkets don't employ half as many people for every pound spent as the small shops do.' A dwindling number of towns in the region, in Lincolnshire, Derbyshire and Yorkshire, had successfully kept away the supermarkets and as a result still had lively, thriving market-town centres. There were fewer and fewer of these, he declared, as he valiantly fought back with quality and variety. His prize-winning pies sat in a crusty row, pork, venison, game with cranberry. But it was the cheap cuts that also kept the shop going, 'the cuts you'll never find in Tesco'.

Before 1997, Tory environment secretary John Gummer had blown the whistle on supermarkets' locating on out-of-town sites reachable only by car, often destructive of the high streets left behind. Labour kept the policy largely in place, but got caught in an embarrassing confusion of planning and competition law after a tribunal struck down a bid by the Competition Commission to limit the number of 'Tesco towns', communities dominated by a single big retailer. Places such as Yiewsley on London's western fringe and Sheringham on the Norfolk coast had resisted, but multiple planning applications, and subtle pressure on puny district councillors, made the giant grocer hard to resist. The upside was often a Tesco Metro open late and at the weekends, offering choice and fresh produce. At £130 billion a year the UK grocery market was also a huge employer of precisely those targeted by the government's New Deals in low-waged, flexible jobs. Local identity, sense of belonging, a tradition pitted against esconomic advance, this was a conflict in Britishness that Labour never wanted to get into.

Community was the buzzword of the times, at least for the less well-off; the better-off apparently did not need it. Labour reached into their past and reinvented the community development programme of the late 1960s. Ministers devised a bold plan to hand £50 million over ten years to each of the thirty-nine worst housing estates. Residents would decide how to spend it, buying in expertise to refurbish blocks of flats, even develop and sell local property. Somehow housing was to parlay into broader social development and the New Deal for Communities (NDC) targeted jobs, school improvements, truanting, wardens and youth clubs. Cutting smoking, improving health, lessening visits to GPs – transformative magic was to be done.

This New Deal did improve the deprived areas, physically. And it galvanized some estate residents. Neighbours noted fewer abandoned burnt-out cars, run-down and boarded-up properties, less vandalism and graffiti. But community had a tendency to become oligarchy, with a handful of activists in charge. At best, about one in ten estate residents took part, higher than usual for such initiatives.

For Aston Pride NDC, high unemployment was the root of the area's problem. Simon Topman, the whistle factory owner, got involved as chair and claimed success: 'We tackled worklessness, not with training schemes but with real jobs. We asked employers what they wanted, how many they could take, and we found people that fitted.'

But if some NDC areas improved, they stayed poor. The New Deal left intact basic problems of skills, schooling, inherited deprivation and low income and – a new problem – migration. The Bradford NDC got more money for housing, schools, police and social services, but it secured 'little change in relative levels of economic deprivation', according to a study for Communities and Local Government published in 2010: the poor neighbourhoods of 1999 were still poor a decade later.

'Compelling evidence' was hard to find, evaluators said, but the lives of individuals had not improved in the NDC areas, even if the areas had. The conclusion exposed such Labour prophets of localism and 'community' as David Miliband and Hazel Blears. They advocated more community voting; but here was evidence it accomplished little when 'community' lacked money or control over the economic forces shaping its destiny. Labour talked a lot about social capital and 'place shaping'. But about the real capital that shapes places, and about the flows of people who shape place much more directly than town halls or community organizers, Labour had little to say.

The community verdict

Donna Charmaine Henry sat in the Hand in Hand pub, opposite the primary school on New Park Road, recalling when she first got involved, ten years ago. She was now chair of the Clapham Park

New Deal for Communities. It had been well funded, to the tune of £56 million, though what the board could spend was controlled by three anxious layers of government above them. The final year of the Clapham Park NDC marked Labour's ending too.

Henry never expected her life to take this turn. She is an elegant woman, born in St Kitts and brought up in Oldham, where her mother was a machinist. 'Since I've lived in London, my Oldham brothers and sisters call me Mrs Poshnobs,' she laughs, but she does indeed have an air of poise and refinement. She has lived on the Clapham Park Estate since 1975 and works as an optometrist's administrator. 'I never had anything to do with any community volunteering whatever. I came home from work, looked after my family, shut the front door of my flat and shut out everything outside,' she recalls. 'And there was a lot to shut out.' New Park Road was notorious for drug dealers and prostitutes plying their trade along the parade of shops, with frequent fights right outside the school in broad daylight.

How did she get involved? The first chair, a local builder and decorator, stopped her in the street out of the blue to ask her to join. 'I was so surprised I just said yes. I knew nothing about it, no idea what I was getting into.' A group of residents was rapidly assembled, later standing for election, most unknown to each other and knowing even less what they were in for. It was often a rough ride and many fell by the wayside, with only two originals still on the board. 'You have to have broad shoulders or you go home in tears. Rows, fights, arguments. The patience you need with people. I had no notion it would become twenty hours a week.' Unpaid, unrewarded, for years they all gave up most evenings, many weekends, their small flats filled with papers and files. Hardest was shouldering the blame from everyone on the estate who had seen the headlines about the fat cheque and wanted everything fixed right now. 'But it's been worth it, absolutely, for the things we've done.'

The board learnt community organizing the hard way, politics writ small and local. Anyone who thinks that 'community' is cuddly and consensual has never tried it. Political parties exist for good reason, to rationalize the inevitable disputes when more than two people try to agree anything. There was often vigorous opposition. But expecting democracy to flourish in a high-turnover, new-immigrant, partly non-English-speaking, low-voting, non-community was a high hope; it was often more Afghanistan than Ambridge.

Henry says, 'When I hear about people joining in and taking over everything themselves, it makes me really angry. It needs big backing by government.' The project had enough money for the resident-dominated board to buy in professional staff to run the programmes they wanted. 'We could have done nothing without that.'

She ruefully recalls the early days. Identifying need was easy. Clapham Park's 7300 inhabitants in dilapidated 1930s and 1940s blocks were plagued by crime at double the national rate. Local schools were well below standard, people were sicker than average, with a high proportion of single mothers and old people. Targets were set: all housing to reach the decent homes standard, property values to equal those in the rest of Clapham; crime cut to the national average, with fear of crime halved and sickness cut by a third. GCSE grades and adult qualifications must reach national average. Unemployment to fall and 85 per cent to be 'satisfied with the area'. Above all, three-quarters of residents must say they 'feel involved' in their local community – a larger civic commitment than you would ever be likely to find in Mayfair or Notting Hill. Professional organizers reckon on getting 2–4 per cent involved in most communities. So they were almost set up to fail.

The wonder is how much Henry and the others did achieve. They made superhuman efforts at learning committee procedures, prepared master plans and spreadsheets, and patiently led community consultations with demanding residents. Getting the vote out for elections to the board was hard. Spending money was slow, every penny passported from Whitehall through the Government Office for London and finally Lambeth Council. Monitoring and paperwork were a nightmare.

Julia Macfadden, one of the old hands, runs a greengrocer's in New Park Road and used to chair the crime group. A cheerful blonde woman in her late fifties, she helped oversee the dramatic change in the ecology of her street: she regularly used big scissors to cut the receiver off the public phone box that drug dealers and pimps were using. Her group helped set up neighbourhood policing on the estate. They hired estate community wardens, some of them residents; that was a transforming moment, along with the arrival of CCTV. The prostitutes and drug dealers have gone and forty crack houses were shut down in the first eighteen months. Julia dropped out when her husband became ill, but she says getting involved changed her life: 'I learned such a lot. It's given me strength to do things I never knew I could. You just try going through a project appraisal meeting. Horrendous. A lot got done, but no, not everything.'

The residents' big decision was to rebuild the worst parts of the estate. That meant transferring the blocks to a housing association that would be able to borrow and sell some of the land. Getting support – eventually 60 per cent in favour on a turnout of 78 per cent – was slow and the opponents kept up a permanent opposition: many had bought their homes and rightly feared the blight of a long rebuild. Then came the crash and the property developers' freeze. By the time Labour left office, only one fine new block had been built, not yet complete, two others were in construction, with a few blocks renovated. The bulk of the estate remains as it was, with no rebuilding timetable.

The decade had seen a flurry of employment, health, education and volunteering programmes. Organizers reckon 200 of the 3700 residents run everything. When the project comes to an end in 2011, a legacy charity with a small income would keep the Jobs Shop and the Timebank, swapping chores and favours, the internet community radio station, a bike repair project, youth schemes and coffee mornings for the elderly. A summer festival pulls in 1200 each year for outdoor food, music, sport and children's activities. We dropped in on a women's group meeting, struggling to devise events with less money. Mothers wanted outings, trapped on the estate, but they could no longer afford to hire a coach at £500 a day and travelling by bus with a score of prams was impossible.

What about those original targets? Local schools have improved greatly. The brightest change is two children's centres, the Maytree Nursery and the Weir Link Children's Centre, started by the sheer determination of neighbouring activists. According to a 2008 survey, residents' satisfaction was up, at 74 per cent. Many fewer felt unsafe walking at night – only 20 per cent. Nearly two-thirds thought the project has improved the area. A few more had gained qualifications, smoking was down, 3 per cent more were in work and 10 per cent fewer were living on very low incomes.

The Labour instigators of these schemes were sociologically naive, appearing to forget the rate of churn among residents. Over half the people here ten years ago have gone, which makes measurement of change impossible. People who get jobs tend to get up and go. People moving in tend to have extreme problems, making overall results look worse. Labour was seduced by the idea of captive 'communities' that could be fixed, but in reality they are fluid, mobile and unmeasurable.

Anyone visiting over the years would see how the energy of Henry and the other local heroes puts other places to shame. They have made the estate friendlier, with many more people greeting each other in the street than ever before. But as ever, the great majority did not join in – and many felt badly let down by the continuing failure to rebuild: renewal of their bad housing was what they wanted most, and most didn't get.

What happened at Clapham Park was a microcosm of New Labour, with its hyperbolic promises brought down to earth by hard, basic economic and social realities. One target was to equalize the value of property on the estate with the surrounding area. But the surrounding area became wealthier as property prices inflated, and the social distance between Clapham Park and well-off Clapham is wider than ever.

CHAPTER 6

Old and young

Labour created the first minister for children. Good idea. The government wanted the Department for Children, Schools and Families to wrap the 'whole child'. But on the ground this never happened. The criminal child stayed under the eye of the justice ministry; the sporty child was supported by culture, media and sport. The inspectors from Ofsted split the schoolchild from the abused child. Labour aspired to tie professional disciplines together and break down bureaucratic boundaries. Abuse cases in London and the West Midlands showed how distant remained their vision of joining up.

A new Children's Plan said the right things about integrating services and professionals, but the children's secretary, Ed Balls, was not a team player. He thundered out the same ambitious claims to be best in the world you heard in pronouncements on health, as if social policy was a kind of competitive sport. 'The plan aims to make England the best place in the world for children and young people to grow up,' he declared, but his plan lacked a timetable or priorities. Should progress on children's mental health services come before insisting teachers had a postgraduate qualification? The UK scored low in international tables (children in Wales and Scotland were broadly in the same position as those in England), and in 2007 Unicef placed the UK bottom of a league table for child well-being among twenty-one industrialized countries, and again in 2009 it was hardly better, at twenty-fourth out of twenty-nine countries.

Whatever they lacked in money or care, children did not go short of government initiatives. Most were aimed selectively at poor or 'problem' children. *Every Child Matters* set out Labour's plan in 2003 and became the Children Act 2004, except it was 'every difficult child matters'. The intention was admirable: to seize the jumble of criss-crossing schemes and agencies dealing with aspects of children's lives. This shake-up was the response to Victoria Climbié's death. The eight-year-old had been beaten and starved by a great-aunt and school, health, police, NSPCC and social services missed chances to save her. In the shadow of her death, the new act set up new council departments covering both schools and children's social services. In addition (Labour had a bad habit of over-egging every pudding), separate children's trusts were to pull together doctors, police, social workers and voluntary organizations.

The plan was multi-agency and multi-disciplinary working – teachers talking to social workers, school nurses sharing observations with after-school club organizers, GPs picking up the phone to head teachers. One tool was the database Contactpoint, which would register children, keeping track wherever they moved. Victoria Climbié had been shifted from one area to another, so schools and social services lost touch and her latest district knew nothing of her past. Now children would be flagged, and information exchanged. Here was a well-intentioned initiative that in an age of greater trust in government should have appeared merely sensible, harnessing IT to social protection. Instead, a paranoid age saw it as a nannying interference. The children's charities supported the plan, which began in January 2009, to reach all of England and Wales over the next two years. (Getting It Right For Every Child was a similar scheme in Scotland.) Contactpoint immediately identified children who had gone missing from school rolls. It would cost £224 million to set up and £41 million a year to run, but should save double that each year in time that was previously wasted chasing up records. The 2010 Conservative–Lib Dem government promised to abolish it.

Old and young

The focus on children risked marginalizing older people and adults with learning difficulties after the break-up of generic social services departments. But our colleague David Brindle, the *Guardian*'s public services editor, found 'a growing confidence previously all too often drowned out' in adult social care. Schools, encouraged to go their own way under Labour, resisted joining in. Children's trusts spent too much time filling in forms, especially those that would bring them bits and pieces of grants from the multiple pots the government created. Another casualty in the same Labour-controlled North London borough of Haringey where Victoria Climbié died showed how imperfect the new administrative model remained. Inquiries and trials after the 2007 murder of Baby P (Peter Connelly) caused an outbreak of rage against social workers, as if they were the killers. Even allowing for the cynical manipulation of sentiment by the *Sun* and such papers, popular anger was remarkable in its ferocity.

These cases were often cauldrons of ethnicity, poverty, religious practice, local authority shortcomings and conflicts of principle. Khyra Ishaq, a Birmingham girl starved to death in 2008, had been removed from school to be 'educated at home' – very much in keeping with the contemporary emphasis on parents' choice. Her mother's partner Junaid Abuhamza had himself been abused and witnessed his father beating his young sister to death for not flushing the toilet. The government seemed unable to find the language to rebut the suggestion, voiced aloud by relatives of child victims whose own moral responsibility was debatable, that the state should be more intrusive. That would have meant acknowledging the limits of intervention, and the permanent likelihood of neglect and abuse. The government put money and effort into social workers' training and pay amid eruptions of internet-abetted hysteria. Bureaucratic reorganization had accomplished little, in the public's eyes.

Labour's record on children had moments of brilliance but ministers were never coherent and failed to get their plans over to the public. Pre-school provision was a warren. Sure Start was free. All parents had a right to some nursery education for their children, from the age of three. Childcare was assisted, but care of an acceptable standard often meant parents topping up what the benefits system offered. Families not eligible for much help could find themselves facing bills for daycare for a two-year-old of £8500 a year. Compare this with Sweden, where no family was expected to pay more than between one and three per cent of its income, depending on the number of children – never more than £102 a month.

The New Deal for the unemployed and single mothers could never work unless parents had better access to childcare. Its absence was why most lone parents did not take jobs. Sixty years after the welfare state was created Labour added the missing cradle – care for the under-fives. Their motives were mixed: they wanted to get more mothers off benefits, but also stimulate children from poor homes, many of whom arrived at primary school well behind the average. The government's objectives were blurred but its reforms did offer parents cash and convenience, and a better start in life for their children.

In 1997 one childcare place – including after-school clubs – existed for every eight children under the age of eight. That doubled by 2010. The Childcare Act obliged councils to make places available but, to fend off the charge of statism, insisted most would be in private nurseries or charities. 'Places' sounds organized. On the ground – we looked in detail at Enfield in 2004 – parents confronted a welter of choice and non-choice: a Sure Start in Edmonton, council nurseries in the poorer parts of the borough, private nurseries in the better-off, well-regulated childcare in other women's homes and, beneath that, as always, dense informal arrangements between friends, grandmothers, aunts and cousins. The government could have created, even with the funds available, a network of public nurseries to the highest standards. Instead, under the banner of choice, parents were given childcare tax credits, a voucher for 80 per cent of the estimated cost of care, in theory to be topped up by parents. Private nurseries boomed. But many low-paid women still could not afford the care on offer, even when nurseries used low-paid staff, often young girls who themselves had failed at school. Where extended families lived in the same area – itself a problem where housing was scarce and migration and sell-off were breaking up older patterns of cohesion – grandparents might do the job unpaid, in the selfless ways in which families, especially their women members, always seek to cope.

When a child reached the age of three, things became clearer. Labour introduced a new right. All parents of three- and four-year-olds could take advantage of free nursery schooling, two and a half hours a day regardless of household income, and which the council had to make available. Hours were expanded to three by September 2010 and a last-gasp Labour promise was to extend free nursery to 250,000 of the more deprived two-year-olds.

The intellectual case for good nursery care rested on work by Professor Leon Feinstein of the London Institute of Education, showing how after the age of twenty-two months, a better-off but less bright child started gaining on the clever but poor child. Their developmental paths crossed at the age of six, as they headed for different destinies. Early years education could help those who were not talked to or read to at home and had barely grasped language so had little chance of being ready to learn to read when they arrived at primary school.

Commentators mocked when the government introduced a curriculum for early years in 2008 and Ofsted inspectors were sent in to check on standards. The intention was to guide nursery staff, still often untrained and low-skilled. Research showed nursery schooling only made a difference to a child's development if it was good quality. How much education was above that threshold, where it would repulse the influence of background and household income, was hard to judge. With typical exaggeration, the government declared that more children were getting the 'best possible' start in life; it should more plausibly have claimed that things were slowly getting better.

Ministers had visited Scandinavian nurseries where half the staff were graduates and all one-year-olds were guaranteed a good neighbourhood nursery. Promises were made to improve the skills of the nursery workforce in England, 98 per cent female, a third on the minimum wage. By 2015 there was to be at least one graduate in every nursery – still a distant dream in 2010. Councils maintained an England-wide elite of 460 beacon nurseries, but their survival was imperilled as councils themselves preferred private nursery places to meet government targets.

Few of Labour's innovations won such approval as Sure Start children's centres. 'They are the jewel in our crown,' said Graham Burgess, chief executive of the local authority in Blackburn with Darwen, where Sure Start was credited with raising the proportion of five-year-olds classed as good developers as the decade went on. At first the focus was under-fives from poor backgrounds, to bring them up to the level of their better-off contemporaries on starting primary school. For right-wing think-tanks it was social engineering, a bold attempt to decouple child, background and attainment. Born in Labour's early phase when 'evidence for policy' was all the rage, Sure Start followed a compelling social experiment conducted over thirty years in the US. Toddlers given intensive nursery education and family support did better in life than similar children outside the programme. They did not become rocket scientists, but they did grow up to be less likely to commit crime, need mental treatment, go to jail or lose their jobs; they were more likely to graduate, own their homes and have stable family lives.

The American results relied on intensive care in the nursery. To replicate this in all the UK's deprived areas would cost huge sums. Soon the original idea gave way to a looser ambition of expanding both nursery education and childcare in children's centres. Families of all social classes liked them, leading to complaints that the most deprived were missing out. By 2010 Labour had set up 3500 centres, juggling the middle-class interest with efforts to bring in depressed and mentally ill mothers, addicts and those 'hardest to reach'. The result was loss of focus. By the age of five many of their children were already too neglected, too lacking in early stimulation ever to catch up. The Audit Commission criticized the centres' record on improving children's health.

There was, of course, a target. By 2020 – that precious date when child poverty was to be abolished – 90 per cent of five-year-olds had to reach a good level of development. In 2007, 46 per cent of five-year-olds reached the standard and by 2009 it was 52 per cent. Their use of language was consistently the weakest point.

Infant mortality fell, but the UK's record remained poor compared with other countries. Progress stalled in reaching Labour's own target of cutting by 10 per cent the gap between children in better-off and poor areas. A child growing up in a deprived area was 19 per cent more likely to have bad teeth than the average child. Personal, social and health education became compulsory from 2009 – though in a last-minute swerve, children's secretary Balls caved in to the religious lobby and allowed faith schools to decide for themselves how they would offer sex education.

The government pushed mental health services for children and adolescents, with the promise that by April 2010, young people under eighteen would be treated in an environment suitable to their age, and those under sixteen would not be placed on an adult ward. Long waits for access remained. Some progress was made with children in care. A larger proportion of care leavers now had jobs or were still in education at the age of nineteen. But contrasts with their peers were stark. In 2007, 62 per cent of all children who sat their GCSEs obtained five grades A to C, compared with 13 per cent of children in care. Police were twice as likely to caution children in care aged ten or over; graduates from care were heavily over-represented among teenage parents, drug users and prisoners.

Being in care was considered 'dangerous' and ministers rarely challenged the stereotypes or a prevalent myth about children's safety. Never had it been safer to be a child than in Labour's Britain and the government could claim some credit. Few parents believed it. The number killed each year had dropped by 40 per cent since the mid 1970s – falling from 136 to 84 killings. Britain had been fourth worst in the developed world for child killings: now it was third lowest. The media and public believed something different. Crimes were real enough: tiny children in a Plymouth nursery were sexually assaulted by adults in an internet-coordinated attack. Yet despite the hysteria, sex crimes and offences against children did not increase.

Sympathy with afflicted parents and children did not justify the ugly outbreaks of prejudice and unreason. Ministers seldom tried to put individual cases in context or give parents a rounded picture of risk. After the murder of eight-year-old Sarah Payne in 2000 tabloids campaigned for a 'Sarah's law', disclosing the identity of paedophiles on the sex-offenders register living locally. Instead, from 2010 a new law allowed parents to check with the police if they were worried about who had contact with their children: pilots showed some children were being protected from predators.

Launched in 2002, the Criminal Records Bureau had to check on adults working with children; employers could now investigate a job-seeker's past. The murder of two little girls in Soham, Cambridgeshire by a school caretaker pushed public demand for yet more scrutiny of anyone in contact with children. But by the time tighter rules were drawn up, establishing an Independent Safeguarding Authority, with a new 'vetting and barring' scheme to cover any volunteer, the panic had passed. The public (as voiced by the media and internet) were now outraged by 'nanny state' interference. The scheme softened when distinguished authors such as Philip Pullman said they would not visit schools to read from their books if they had to undergo such ignominy. The government bobbed like a cork on the tides of panic, never able to explain the size of the phenomenon or educate a jumpy public and parents about risk.

Compiling evidence, the government backed a study of 19,000 children born in the year 2000 to allow comparison with other decades (except the 1980s, when the Tories took against social investigation and studies were dropped). Researchers looked at these Millennium babies at the age of nine months, at three and when they started school in 2006. Many did not go to Sure Start or get the full benefit of the new nurseries. The study showed a generation 'swimming against a tide of socially polarizing forces', with 39 per cent of a random national sample of children found to be living in poverty at some point in their first five years. Half the children had moved home. Cognitive and development scores followed the Feinstein pattern, with the bright but poor ones starting to be overtaken by the less clever but better-off children.

Mostly, parents wanted fewer children. By 2001 the birth rate had plunged to an all-time low, 1.63 babies per 1000 women of childbearing age. But by 2008 children were in fashion and the birth rate leapt to 1.96. Perhaps Britain was becoming an easier place to have children and hold down a job. The government greeted them with tax credits and higher child benefit, easing the cost of parenthood. Better pay and working conditions for mothers, more help with childcare, after-school and holiday clubs and the new children's centres made the difference. Not overtly pro-natalist, Labour were encouraging people to have children, welcoming each new baby with an endowment from the Child Trust Fund. Tiziana Nazio, an Oxford University sociologist, compared the rising UK birth rate with Italy, where it was falling. Part-time work in the UK was a factor. And public-sector working conditions: women there were more likely to have babies than those in the private sector. 'Women are more likely to think about having children if they have job security and flexible working patterns,' Nazio said.

Maternity support doubled in Labour's time – to nine months' leave, the first six weeks paid at 90 per cent of salary, then thirty-nine weeks at a weekly flat rate of £123. Only mothers with well-paid partners tended to take their full nine months. Labour gave fathers the right to two weeks' leave. Both parents could take up to thirteen weeks' unpaid leave to cover emergencies at home. A parental right to ask for flexible hours suited employers as much as employees.

Divorce fell, lower in 2008 than since 1975. Was it anything to do with Labour? The marriage rate was also dropping and divorce figures did not pick up the breakdown of partnerships. Labour largely steered clear of family moralizing. Louise Casey, the charity executive brought in by Blair to tackle 'respect', claimed poor parenting was a primary cause of crime and anti-social behaviour but this was 'a subject people in public life and in politics are afraid to take on'. She meant, of course, poor parenting among the poor.

The UK held its position in the European tables as least generous to new mothers. Even Albania and Belarus paid mothers relatively better and for longer after the birth of their children. Swedish mothers were on full pay for sixteen months. In 2010 the EU was trying to raise the minimum maternity leave in member countries but, true to form, Labour resisted. Amid loud protest from the CBI, Labour even delayed indefinitely their own promise to extend paid maternity leave to one year, which was supposed to start in April 2010.

If absent fathers paid for their children, as the law required, fewer mothers and children struggling alone would be poor. But many fathers remained on strike, refusing to cooperate and delaying or omitting payments. When couples separated, mothers' incomes plummeted and rarely recovered, while fathers' standards of living soon recovered as the taxpayer picked up their missing contributions. The Child Support Agency, a Tory invention, started disastrously when ministers ignored advice not to reopen old cases, causing a rebellion.

At first Labour had found it no easier than the Tories to get parents (almost always fathers) to pay and turn the CSA into a functioning collections agency. 'No discernible improvement' in Labour's first years, the NAO reported in 2001. The government tried to simplify the assessment formula, which had bedevilled the system in the Tory years. It spent huge sums trying to clear the backlog of cases and get the IT running. Fathers deliberately clogged the system by sending in new records of their income every month, requiring lengthy new assessments of what they owed. Between 1993 and 2006 it did manage to collect £5 billion, but it cost the CSA 70p to collect £1. Why, the auditors asked, was its use of enforcement so reluctant?

Labour took ages to improve the ramshackle administrative apparatus, but by 2010 the outlook was brighter. Fond of quangos, it added a new Child Maintenance and Enforcement Commission, which from October 2008 promoted voluntary arrangements between parents, with the old CSA stepping in for those who could not agree. Parents with children to care for could keep up to £20 a week of any maintenance payments they received, before losing any right to benefits. In 1997 the CSA collected only 58 per cent of payments in full, but 61 per cent by 2009. That year the new commission gained the power to confiscate non-paying fathers' passports and driving licences, without going to court. Would taking their wheels away produce the missing payments at last?

The proportion of children and older citizens in the UK population did not change much over the thirteen years. But demography was the scare story to come. The number of people over the pension age would rise from 11.8 million in 2008 to 15.6 million by 2033; the number over 80 would double by 2031 to 5 million. Actuaries started adding hours to expected lifespan for every day of our lives. Longevity might have been a cause for celebration. The prospect of a gently ageing society might have been the occasion for a national think-in about opportunities. Instead, in an unequal society, ageing was a threat, and 'demographic timebomb' became a frightening figure of political speech. The Tories had tried to exploit it in the 1980s, to cut state pension entitlements. In the 1990s the ordnance went away and the Major government told companies they could take a pension holiday and cease topping up their pension funds. Labour caught the blast when the new century dawned and pension fund managers realized stock could go down as well as up and those boring bonds and gilts suddenly looked a safer long-term investment.

In the 1980s the Tories abolished the contributory, state-backed second pension, created by the previous Labour government. Private pensions were then the rage, for those who could afford them; others assumed their company schemes would provide; for the rest, the state minimum. Labour presided over an awakening. Occupational schemes had miscalculated the length of time they would have to pay out to pensioners surviving for longer and longer. Private pensions had been mis-sold, both literally to those induced to opt out of the state schemes and figuratively to those who had believed the patter about them paying off.

In a parallel universe, pension reform might have been Labour's forte. All pensions systems ultimately had to be social democratic; even the most ironclad free marketeer had to accept the need for state provision and tight regulation. But if reforms were to last, a measure of bipartisanship was needed. Things started badly when Labour were accused of damaging private pension funds in 1997 by adjusting a tax break on corporation tax. With hindsight it probably was mildly damaging, but the funds' rhetoric was overblown. So, too, were persistent allegations that pension entitlements being racked up by public-sector staff were over-generous. But the state was accumulating hundreds of billions in liabilities and the government obfuscated when it might have fought prejudice with facts about the relative remuneration enjoyed in public and private sectors and the small average size of public-sector pensions. Reforms were needed but Labour went AWOL.

The biggest question confronting an ageing society was similar to that posed by Sir Nicholas Stern over climate change: how much would people cut consumption in the here and now for the sake of tomorrow? It was not one likely to be tackled by a government that believed its political fate depended on keeping the fires burning. The choice was either to save more now or extend working lives. From 2006 Labour, enacting an EU directive, stopped employers compulsorily retiring staff at 65. In fact, employment rates among men aged over 65 were gradually increasing to about a fifth, with a tenth of older women working.

The government commissioned a mighty report from its favourite *consiglieri*, Lord (Adair) Turner and Professor John Hills of the LSE, both clear-eyed and honest analysts. Their recommendation was to end the Tories' ill-advised cut in the basic state pension. Pegged to prices rather than earnings, it had fallen to 16 per cent of average earnings by 2008 – when Labour last left office in 1979 it had been 25 per cent; from 2012 the link was to be restored, provided (Brown said in an ominous caveat) the economy could take it at the time. Costs would be covered by raising the state retirement age to sixty-six for everyone in the 2020s. Women who had taken time out as carers and were the poorest in old age would be entitled once they had clocked up thirty working years.

Most radical was a new occupational pension: everyone would be automatically enrolled, the cost of administration would be low and employers would have to pay in 3 per cent. It was not compulsory to join the scheme – but it was reckoned inertia would ensure few people would opt out. The age of retirement would probably need to keep rising faster, with a review every four years to make sure pensions were keeping up with life expectancy. Later on, Labour tried to inject more equity into pensions by stopping the tax deductibility of pension contributions for those on higher earnings from 2011.

Labour's principal pension reforms were meant to address inequality. They introduced a future pension entitlement aimed at carers, disabled people and the low paid who had failed to accrue regular National Insurance pension rights. As many as twenty million people could gain extra post-retirement income in future if this reform were to stick.

The Blair–Brown rivalry played out over pensions policy. If Tweedledum could win praise over child poverty, Tweedledee determined to earn his by promising to end poverty among pensioners. Brown set no date. One of the biggest anomalies of Labour's 1940s welfare reforms had been the insufficiency of the basic pension. Recipients' income fell below the decency threshold, and first National Assistance and then Income Support had supplemented it for those with no other income in old age. Brown brought in a new kind of top-up in 1999. First called minimum income guarantee, then from 2003 Pension Credit, this was a means-tested payment adding to the basic pension. It pushed the income of the poorest older people above £130 a week minimum for a single person in 2010, compared with 1997's lowest guaranteed pension entitlement of £69 a week.

Older people, however, proved backward in coming forward, and in 2010 two million pensioners were still managing below the new threshold for Pension Credit. They were not claiming. Pension Credit did lift 900,000 old people out of poverty in the early years, and then it stalled. Pensioners were confused by separate forms for housing and council tax benefits; both were complex. Most of those eligible claimed something, so it was not necessarily pride that inhibited: 1.7 million pensioners, or 35 per cent of those eligible, failed to get all the money they were owed, worth up to £1.9 billion. The government created the Pension Service in 2001, and the new administrative machinery had a positive effect. For each pound spent advertising Pension Credit, £55 was paid out in additional benefits, the NAO reported.

In an ideal world, Labour might have recognized the elderly's need for care. But having created their one and only royal commission to examine the subject, the government ran for shore. When older people did not survive long after retirement from work, their income and care costs were manageable. Now they lived on and the numbers of those needing assistance grew absolutely, even as the general health of the elderly population improved. Relatives mostly provided care at home. Outside, private nursing homes, and charities and councils, offered an unpredictable menu, depending on where you and your relatives lived. Council home helps were free or cost a nominal sum, while homes charged and local authorities would reimburse fees on a means-tested basis.

So far so bad. Relatives' complaints never acquired political traction. Carers were too various and widespread to form a movement. Some two million people identified themselves as carers in the 2001 Census, a fifth of them providing care for fifty or more hours a week; Labour, of course, brought in a 'national strategy' for them, affording recognition if not much else.

Relatives with home-owning parents had a vested interest against any attempt to pay for care by liquidating property. Greater love hath no family members than for the valuable property occupied by their relatives.

In an NHS hospital, care was free. On entering a residential home, however, means had to be found and the nearest asset was usually the old person's home. Documentaries and articles stoked the outrage of middle-aged children fearing 'their' property was going to vanish in residential and nursing fees. In 1997 Labour set up the royal commission, chaired by Lord (Stewart) Sutherland, in an attempt at consensus. But it came up with an unpalatable answer. Care should be free for everyone, regardless of income, outside as well as inside hospital. A minority report expressed the government's view that this would consume billions in giving care to those who could afford to pay, money better spent on society's poorest. Here was a crux. Extending universal provision implied a big increase in tax. The alternative was charging, which in this case meant selling property. Labour funked it, trying to keep to the line that said medical care should be free, while hotel charges should be paid for. But was, say, Alzheimer's a medical condition when there was little or nothing doctors could do, and the monetary and emotional costs of care were huge?

Towards the end, Labour proposed a National Care Service. It was less than the sum of its parts, being only a right to have needs assessed, and to have the same proportion of care and support costs paid for wherever you lived – in other words, leaving a lot up to local chance. Talks were held between the parties to feel a way towards a consensus, but political self-interest won the day. Labour bequeathed care to their successors – a nagging problem on which neither ministers nor the public had a clear line, beyond a reluctance to face costs.

As well as cutting the number of pensioners in poverty, Labour ran a multitude of schemes to help older people live more active, involved, healthier lives. Better Government for Older People ran a scheme in Bolton around a new community centre targeted at Asian older people, offering advice sessions conducted in Gujerati and Urdu on their entitlement to benefits. In Oxfordshire the Campaign for Real Ale examined how pubs might become centres for older people's activities (other than knocking back pints, presumably). The government appointed the thinking man's pensioner Joan Bakewell as older people's champion, following the creation of similar advocacy roles in Northern Ireland and Wales. She spoke up when social care surfaced as a tiebreaker between the political parties in 2010.

By spending more on public services, Labour sought to earn a reputation as a friend of the elderly. But the government's reputation never quite recovered from Gordon Brown's 2000 budget, which increased the basic state pension by 75p. Raising the pension by pence, exactly in line with price inflation, was reasonable but politically irrational. Expectations had been raised. The economy was growing and an increase at this level exposed Labour's acceptance of what the Tories had done in breaking the link between the pension and earnings, leaving the pension to fall as a proportion of average household income. Barbara Castle, the Old Labour pin-up, came to the rostrum for her final appearance at a party conference to lambaste the government. Eventually Labour relented, but deferred the policy shift. They promised to reconnect the basic pension to earnings as part of the settlement that would see the retirement age move to sixty-five for women.

Before then the government had messily tried to make amends. Brown's budgets were studded with one-off sweeteners – on fuel, for example. Winter fuel payments worth £200 went to all over-sixties however well off, while an extra £100 went to the over-eighties, with free TV licences for the over-seventy-fives, as well a £10 Christmas bonus. These were gimmicks, all the more profligate for implying that all older households deserved support. Some did, but a growing proportion of pensioners were very comfortably off, the income divide among the elderly starting to mirror that in the working population.

International tables tended to make crude comparisons between basic state pensions – and the UK's were low. Once Pension Credit was added in, the comparisons looked better. It was a double-edged boast that there were now fewer poor pensioners than poor children. It was a better boast that for the first time in history the old were less likely to be poor than the rest of the population.

Carousel Sure Start's verdict

Carousel, a Sure Start children's centre in Braintree, Essex, was housed in an airy but solid, 1930s-built, former primary school. Outside, children had space and a static yellow playbus where they could roll and clamber around on soft cushions. Opened in 2006, Carousel covered a population of 1000 families with children under five, their gateway to all manner of services, available not just to under-fives but children and young people up to the age of 19.

This centre was run by the charity 4Children, on a contract to manage twenty-four Sure Starts across Essex. Of the 3500 that had opened by spring 2010, around 400 were contracted to charities such as Barnardo's and Action for Children, the rest run by local authorities and the NHS. They varied wildly in resources and how well they reached families in need. Some were hardly more than offices sign-posting parents towards services. Carousel was the ideal, how its Labour creators meant Sure Start to be.

Tracy Lindsell was the dynamo powering Carousel. All the best Sure Starts had people such as her, expanding horizons. The trick, she said, was to get out into the community and draw families in. This was a very deprived area. Unemployment, drink, drugs, single parenthood and domestic violence were all high in the surrounding estates, and so, unsurprisingly, was post-natal depression.

Mothers were reluctant to have anything to do with officials who had condemned, shamed or failed them too often. So it took all Tracy's sensitivity and ingenuity to cajole, persuade and entice them. But when news spread, others ventured in, to find a welcoming place to meet and where their children loved to come. The Strawberry Fields cafe, run by adults with learning difficulties, was open all day and so was the Stay and Play drop-in where children could play as long as they liked, without any commitment from nervous parents. Traveller families came, once she sent a minibus to collect them. Polish families who had stayed well away came in for a special play session on Saturday mornings with a Polish translator and Tracy was gradually persuading them to come in other days. English and IT classes were available. Little by little mothers who dropped in for a coffee were drawn to join parenting and health groups, to see the health visitor, to start training to get a job, and apply for childcare credits so they could take a nursery place.

Carly was well on her way to a life she had never imagined, thanks to Carousel. A teenager on drugs and self-harming – slashing herself – she got pregnant. Carousel holds antenatal clinics and GPs send women to the centre from early on in pregnancy. Carly had access to drugs treatment, a health visitor and advice, and gradually she set her life in order. 'In the end, getting pregnant was the best thing that happened to her,' Tracy said. 'She pulled herself together for the sake of her child, and we often see that.' Carly became a volunteer at Carousel and eventually she went to college, leaving her baby in the nursery there. 'The most important thing with teen mums was that they don't have a second baby soon. A lot do and that's what really sinks them. But Carly didn't and now she's studying and she wants to come back and work here when she's qualified. Her little girl is doing well.'

A paediatrician worked at Carousel full time. It made sense to be near families. Carousel hosted an audiology clinic and had a speech and language therapist, who helped nursery staff help children to talk. Holding antenatal clinics here meant mothers could be encouraged into the breast-feeding groups before they had a baby, learning from other new mothers. To fill nursery places Tracy had to help mothers confounded by the benefits system. 'I can always find a way,' she said. 'If a mum wants to use the nursery, I explain she needs to work or study sixteen hours a week and then I help fill out the forms and get her the childcare credits. There was no one else to explain how it all works and other nurseries don't do this enough.' Of the five million families who might qualify for childcare tax credits to help pay for registered care, only 57 per cent claimed.

Carousel had a unit for children excluded from school, an after-school and holiday club for children of all ages, and an evening youth club open every day of the week, plus services for children with disabilities, a clinic for bed-wetters and a pioneering mental health service. One way or another, every family in Braintree would be likely to come here. But the Data Protection Act was an obstacle. Although the hospital could tell a health visitor when a new baby was born, she could not share that information with the children's centre. All she could do was tell the mother about the centre and hope she chose to turn up. In addition, the centre employed a dozen outreach workers visiting families at home – once Tracy knew where they were.

This was how Sure Start should be everywhere. Anne Longfield, director of 4Children, was satisfied. 'We used to go to Sweden to look with envy at their children's centres. It's really only just struck me, we have a lot of centres now that are as good as that. I never quite believed it would happen. That's worth celebrating.'

If every family had a Carousel on their doorstep then the UK would indeed feel more like Sweden, able to catch problems earlier. It is hard to do justice to what a Carousel felt like, the ebullience of a Tracy, the determination to transform the lives of families in trouble, small children rescued. Studies show that poor families who were encouraged to read to their babies could improve their developmental score by months. 'It's my aim to flood my under-fives with words and books,' Tracy declared, augmenting research with her own observations. 'I aim to get mums really talking all the time to their under-ones. I know we can make all the difference, I know it.' How much difference may depend on how well Labour impressed on voters and future policy-makers the necessity of Sure Start and the need to make them all as good as Carousel.

PART THREE

Justice

CHAPTER 7

Crime

The likelihood of being a victim of crime was lower than at any time 'since records began', Jacqui Smith announced in January 2009. The first woman to hold the macho office of Home Secretary was stating a counter-intuitive social truth. Under the Labour government the chances of men being a victim of violence just about halved. Britain became a safer place for children and women too. Despite terror, knives, guns, Soham, paedophiles and abusive partners. And despite migration, a defining social phenomenon of the first decade of the twenty-first century, barely understood by the policy-makers but deeply troubling in the many neighbourhoods where it was experienced as social disorder.

Crime as measured in the British Crime Survey fell substantially: property crime by half from 1997 to 2008, violent crime by over a third. Though crime in the UK remained higher than elsewhere in Europe, after the crime wave of the 1980s and early 1990s, offending was by 2009 just below the level of the early 1980s. The success of the BBC television crime series *Life on Mars* – remember Labour's political stupidity in telling the public in the May 2010 election that David Cameron was like the wildly popular Gene Hunt figure? – was deeply ironic. The show was successful because people seemed to want to return to the imagined green pastures of the 1970s and because they believed that Hunt's tough policing worked.

Police recorded 4.5 million offences in England and Wales in 1997, down from a peak of 5.5 million in 1992. In 2008–9 they recorded 4.7 million offences. So crime rose? No, during Labour's first term the categories changed for the sake of more reliable recording. For example, 'pushing and shoving' became 'violence against the person' (about a fifth of all recorded offences involved violence, the rest mainly property crimes). The UK Statistics Authority ruled that you simply could not compare the figures for recorded crime before and after 2002. In 2005, the Audit Commission and Wales Audit Office reported improvements in crime recording by the police, data quality rising steadily year by year.

Crime's contours changed. It took new forms, such as suicide bombing and internet fraud. PricewaterhouseCoopers said in April 2010 that 'cybercrime' cost £10 billion a year and had grown despite the recession. The police also recorded an increase in offences involving violence against the person until the start of the recession – no surprise, since the Blair–Brown years oozed with booze. Recorded robberies rose, but burglary declined. More harassment on religious or racial grounds, said the police, but less violence from those causes.

But despite the statistics and despite what the chief constables wrote in their annual reports, people swore to pollsters that crime was rising. Ipsos MORI's register of our anxieties – the proportion identifying crime as what worried us most – was 25 per cent in May 1997, falling to a 20 per cent low, then beginning a jagged rise to 40 per cent during 2009. Already in 2000 a third of people were saying crime had risen since 1997, years of steep falls. By 2009 only a fifth of voters thought crime was not rising.

Deconstructing the public's wilful refusal to believe is not easy, and Labour barely tried. Of course the newspapers and blogosphere had an interest in alarm. When violent crime fell 6 per cent in 2009 on the previous year, no media celebration. The *Daily Mail* instead headlined an 11 per cent rise in shoplifting (an offence always likely to rise in recession). Television crime is ubiquitous, and it must colour perception. Hyperventilating Tories said London crime was like that in *The Wire* until Sir Paul

Stephenson, the Metropolitan Police Commissioner, reminded them that homicide was seventeen times more frequent in Baltimore.

It was not just disparity between people's views and the statistics. Most people lived the recorded reality of crime – that is to say, they went out and about to shops, work and leisure without fear. In the cities, 1980s' talk of 'no-go areas' was forgotten (though Jacqui Smith had embarrassing doubts about the danger of collecting a doner kebab in south London). The reasons for prevalent misconceptions about crime included an in-built tendency to generalize the atypical – dreadful murders, bank robberies, child abduction – into the commonplace. Homicide, the best recorded of crimes, shot up in 2002 as the 172 corpses attributable to the murderous GP Harold Shipman were added to the tally – but then fell back into its downwards trend, reaching a twenty-year low in 2009.

The fall in crime was real, the downward trend unmistakable across Europe, North America and Australia. Demography was part of the explanation. Teenage men commit a lot of crime; they were fewer in number. Reasons were also banal. Engine immobilizers made cars harder to steal. The NAO praised the Home Office for collaborating with the motor manufacturers in cutting thefts from and of vehicles by a third between 1999 and 2005 – though that still left 1.3 million thefts from vehicles a year and 241,000 thefts of vehicles. A campaign to harden targets on vulnerable estates saw locks, entry-phones and bars installed: burglaries fell accordingly. The government demanded mobile phones be rendered harder to use once stolen.

On crime, Labour were hyper-active, partly because of a criminal act. As shadow home secretary Blair stole crime from under Tory noses, outbidding them in appeal to the public appetite for punishment, markedly stronger than elsewhere in Europe. Neither Blair nor Brown did avuncular calm; successive home secretaries, even the laid-back Alan Johnson, threatened rather than reassured. It was sometimes as if Labour wanted to feed the fear. 'The purpose,' Blair said in 2004, introducing a new five-year strategy for criminal justice, 'is to rebalance the system radically in favour of the victim.' Later the appointment of Sarah Payne, mother of a murdered child, as the first national victims' champion made the point; she was a doughty fighter in a good cause. But did Labour need to ration sympathy? If victims received it, how much was left for the causes of crime, on which Labour had also once promised to be tough? Programmes and policies dug at causes – children and youth a focus – but spending on preventing offences was minuscule compared with the budgets given to courts, coppers and incarceration.

The government deliberately played up certain crimes, with the aim of mobilizing public opinion – for example, violence against women at home. Labour moved against 'honour' killings. A new forced marriages unit was soon dealing with 5000 inquiries and 300 cases of forced marriage a year, and 2008 legislation gave victims further civil remedies. The BCS found one in four women (and one in six men) experiencing domestic violence at some point in their lives. The Domestic Violence, Crime and Victims Act 2004 made breaching a non-molestation order a criminal offence. The government planned 120 new specialist courts with staff trained to support victims; successful prosecutions increased, and cases collapsing when the victim withdrew evidence through fear fell in number.

Such targeted response to offending would have served the government better than bang 'em up, putting more bobbies on the beat and installing surveillance cameras. Instead of confidence-building, Labour tried to exploit fear.

You often sensed ministers scrabbling but failing to control the monster they had a hand in creating. One reason Blair fell in love with foreign military action may have been its directness. Summon the chiefs of the general staff, and they turned the handle and cranked the machine to put troops into Basra and Helmand. Crime was so much more complex. The tabloids bayed, home secretaries summoned camera crews, but what happened next involved autonomous chief constables, judges and magistrates. Yet some Downing Street initiatives worked, for at least a time. Because the 2002 Street Crime Initiative gave some but not all police forces extra money for taking on robbery, its effect can be measured; and this category of crime was cut. The reason was both the extra bobbies and bureaucratic changes.

Ministers' knees jerked in response to passing panics – for example, over knife crime. We spoke in 2008 to the chief constable of Gloucestershire, Dr Tim Brain, who was being inundated with public demands for action on the slashing horrors of Cheltenham, of all places. The local papers were full of it and he was under pressure. Yet his records revealed only a tiny annual number of incidents involving knives, which had not changed from year to year. That story was repeated up and down the country: over paedophiles after the Soham murders or over gun crime when in Liverpool a passing child on a bike was shot dead in a gang attack. The crimes were dreadful but Labour could not throw off the false belief they were typical.

Labour's response was to expand the crime industry, boosting proportionate UK budgets for crime and security to among the EU's highest. Spending on public order and safety rose 47 per cent in real terms between 1997–8 and 2007–8. Policing costs rose to £17.5 billion a year, which was a fifth more in relation to GDP than in the US, home of all those police dramas. Labour added shelves to the law libraries, believing legislation changed behaviour. (It could, but only with time, and sometimes indirectly.) In 2009 the reassuringly named Lord (Igor) Judge, Lord Chief Justice from 2008, put on his white tie for the Lord Mayor of London's annual judicial dinner then pooped the party by protesting the government had created over 3500 new offences since 1997, and even he found them confusing. Labour put through fifty criminal justice bills – compared with just six between 1929 and 1945. Justice Secretary Jack Straw, also in white tie, rose to rebut Lord Justice Judge, claiming the 40 per cent decrease in crime under Labour 'would suggest all these measures – as well as far better policing and firmer sentencing – have made a significant contribution'.

But this risked confusing cause and correlation. Criminologists reckoned government measures did cut crime, but only by a little.

Much (perhaps four-fifths) of the reduction in crime could be attributed to economic circumstances and demography. Government measures had certainly helped, such as the New Deal, which found work for half a million long-term unemployed young people, though studies worried about the effect of more stringent conditions for unemployment benefit on single younger men. The minimum wage, too. Educational maintenance allowances plus the rapid expansion of college places meant more young people had purpose and cash in their pockets, less need to steal and more to lose if caught. Paul Wiles, the Home Office chief researcher, said crime was 'simply becoming a less fashionable pursuit for high-risk age groups'. What all that subverts is one of Labour's great claims, that by vastly expanding the police force, it was cutting crime.

In 2009, 143,770 officers were serving in England and Wales, 2000 more than in the previous year and 15,000 more than when Labour came to power. The picture was mixed; police numbers were falling from peak levels in some forces, such as South Yorkshire and Humberside. But the scale of the expansion was unmistakable. More bobbies on the beat was what the people wanted, so they kept telling pollsters. But what if bobbies were little better than decorative? No reliable evidence linked increased police numbers and falling crime. Other countries had fewer officers, some more, but all recorded similar crime trends. Police numbers were not irrelevant, because at the very least uniforms assured the public. Certain initiatives worked. For example, the Prolific Offender Strategy hit burglaries, at least for a few years after 2004 – but it is hard to say the effect on crime was permanent. The public itself, having willed the extra numbers, seemed dubious, with only half thinking the police 'would be there when needed'. Perhaps their perceived absence from the streets was because they were 'sitting in the station', as Jack Straw blurted out in a radio interview on New Year's Day 2010, where they 'quite enjoyed being in the warm'. This was a bit rich; was Straw admitting his own failure to change police practice? He was right, the average officer spent only one in seven of his or her duty hours on patrol (community support officers were on patrol three out of four duty hours). Labour failed to modernize the force, and computers, and voice-to-speech software were slow in coming; the police service in England and Wales spent £1 billion a year in 2008 on technology, but out of every ten words written down, seven were being entered into systems more than once.

Labour left the police service bigger and better supported by auxiliaries – 16,000 support officers and 14,500 specials, plus 81,000 staff (up 24,000 since 1997). But it was as if they were poured into an antique vessel. For example, a sensible plan for a countrywide non-emergency 101 number for contacting the police, allowing cost-effective triage between proper crime, disorder and life's little difficulties, foundered, which meant the 999 number continued to be misused.

Labour could not decide about the size of police forces, or how to offer the public bobbies on the beat, home visits and community assurance at the same time as trapping terrorists and mafias operating on a global scale. Globalization brought international criminal organization to urban doorsteps (and households' internet connections) and in March 2004 Blunkett admitted: '[W]e have not yet seen reductions in the overall harm caused by organized crime on the scale of those seen for volume [everyday] crime.' Labour continued down the path towards an embryo national force with the creation of the Serious Organized Crime Agency in 2005, its first chair a former director general of MI5. Inspectors estimated 2800 organized crime gangs were operating in the UK. Yet despite costing £430 million a year and having 3900 staff, the new agency claimed seizures worth only £21 million in the three years after its creation.

Usually Labour liked size. When professionals – for example, fire officers – said that because emergencies were getting bigger, so should their services, the government assented. Fire and rescue moved to regional scale, but the government stopped a long way short of creating a common emergency service, which would have saved money and brought faster and better responses to daily crises. After 9/11, fire and rescue spent £330 million on buying new engines, chemical protection suits and boats, which were then given a generally successful workout at the 2005 Buncefield explosion near Hemel Hempstead and the 2007 summer floods. The NAO was not happy about procurement – it rarely was – but the emergency services did become more capable of dealing with flood and fire. Those the Labour years had in abundance, but no plague (swine flu aside) and only a little pestilence (once foot-and-mouth was over). Without fanfare the government reorganized civil contingencies. After Labour stood up to the Fire Brigades Union when it went on strike in 2002, modernization went ahead. The Fire and Rescue Services Act 2004 established a duty to promote fire safety, but beefy white men better suited to sliding down poles still dominated the service, when women and ethnic minority recruits were more likely to be welcomed into people's homes to install fire detectors. By contrast, the police force did diversify: 27 per cent of officers are now women, with several women chief constables. Labour missed their own 7 per cent target for ethnic-minority officers, but in England and Wales they now number 6290 across the 43 forces.

With prisons, as with police, big extra spending had no clear effect on crime – but did answer a raucous public demand. True to their determination to outgun the Tories, Straw and Blair added yet more prison places to the plans they inherited. Brown's offence was to bankroll this excess, pumping money in. Between 1995 and 2009 the prison population in England and Wales grew by two-thirds, adding another 32,500 inmates, to give a daily average inmate population of 83,887 by 2009. The punitive regime was often commented on abroad: the UK had proportionately more people in jail than China or Burma did.

To choke the rise in prisoners, ministers did make distinct efforts to cut reoffending. Spending on probation increased 70 per cent in real terms in the ten years from 1999; staff increased by 7000. The new National Offender Management Service was meant to coordinate and streamline local probation boards: it was instructed to cut reoffending by 10 per cent by the end of the decade. Workloads rose, as courts used community orders in greater numbers, but they were not that much more effective than jail. Still, community sentences cost £2000–£3000 a year compared with £41,000 for a prison place.

Jails were no more than warehouses. Four-fifths of inmates read and wrote below the level of an eleven-year-old: back on the streets, still illiterate, they remained unemployable and prone to crime. The average number of hours per week per prisoner spent in classes, behaviour programmes, training or workshops rose slightly from 23.8 in 1997 to 25.3 in 2008, but this was still less than the 26.2 hours recorded in 1995. Successive chief inspectors were scathing about conditions. Prison did not work – on release, between 60 and 80 per cent of inmates reoffended.

Eventually lack of space meant Labour had to let more prisoners out early wearing tags. Definitely cheaper than jail, the NAO reported in 2006. Studies commended early-release 'packages', linking probation, job opportunities and supervision, for cutting reoffending; Labour deserve plus marks for allowing experiments. But then, in the run-up to the 2010 election, Old Adam returned. Straw, now Justice Secretary, abandoned the government's own early-exit scheme on the grounds that the prison-building programme had created enough room to re-absorb those who had been released. The prison population hit a record 85,000 in England and Wales in April 2010 after the early-release scheme ended, against a total capacity of 87,000.

The government could claim its investment had made prison more secure, as breakouts fell from thirty-three in 1996–7 to only four in 2007–8. Labour tentatively contracted out more prisons and prisoner transport. Don't blame me, ministers could say, blame Securicor. Escapes from contracted-out escorts also fell. But in the public's view, too many still 'escaped' prison. Focus groups, polls – the vox pops during the 2010 election – all said judges favoured the rights of criminals. It was not true. Under Labour, courts got tougher: the numbers going to jail attested to that. A first-time burglar had a 27 per cent chance of going to prison in 1995, which became a 48 per cent chance by 2000. Between 1997 and 2004, the number of offenders sentenced did not change much but the numbers in prison soared, because average custodial sentence lengths increased. The Criminal Justice Act 2003 strengthened penalties for serious offenders. The right to trial by jury ended for certain categories of offence, to the chagrin of the lawyers. Breaches of licences and orders led more often to jail. More offenders broke the conditions of their licence and were recalled in greater numbers and for longer. But the 2010 recall of Jon Venables showed the waywardness of individual cases.

Venables had been convicted of the killing of the toddler Jamie Bulger – a case that has reverberated down the years. Penal policy pullulates with the anger generated by specific offences.

Labour, well aware that crime and disorder afflicted their electoral heartlands, came up with new policies, many of them bearing the 'community' tag. One was to make justice more visible locally. The North Liverpool Community Justice Centre, in new, open buildings, was meant to be seen by the people of Anfield and Everton as it speeded up hearings and cut postponements – encouraging them to report crime. Visitors flocked to it as it appeared to make justice more credible locally, but like so many Roman candle Labour initiatives, it fizzled out – especially after the government accelerated the closure of magistrates' courts as part of its effort to shrink the legal aid and other justice bills.

Labour sought to stop petty cases coming to magistrates, giving the police more power to caution and impose fines on the spot. But summary justice made lawyers and libertarians twitch. Blair made a speech in June 2000 telling the police to frogmarch young offenders to the nearest cash machine to get the money to pay the on-the-spot fines. When Number Ten gathered together bemused chief constables a few days later they pointed out that yobs were unlikely to possess bank accounts, let alone credit cards; the frogmarch was never mentioned again.

But still Labour teased away at making criminal justice more visible, inventing a new punishment called community payback. Under the probation service, offenders would wear fluorescent yellow jackets when doing their community service, to inspire trust in non-prison sentences by demonstrating they were not a soft option. Civil liberty campaigners blenched, regarding this as redolent of Alabama chain gangs. But in, for example, the High Street South area of Boston, Lincolnshire, stressed by a rapid influx of eastern Europeans, the cash-strapped council used community payback gangs to tidy up, in response to residents' complaints about litter and fly tipping.

Community was trotted out to answer intractable problems of behaviour. Statutory community safety partnerships were established under the 1998 Crime and Disorder Act with the aim of enrolling citizens in Neighbourhood Watch (the quasi-vigilante scheme invented by the Tories) and other local anti-crime schemes. But a later study said they spent too much time on paperwork and soliciting grants. Perhaps people were not sufficiently 'neighbourly' to sustain the scheme; perhaps, in the modern division of labour, they regarded patrolling and observation as the job of the police. Studies credited the partnerships with some impact on domestic violence and drink-related crime. The police tried getting closer to the people, as smaller borough command units gave forces a more personal face: police in Wanstead in East London offered to walk anyone their last mile home if they were afraid.

In the absence of an officer many people put their faith in technology, specifically digital cameras. According to Councillor Vanessa Cole of the London Borough of Redbridge (in the *Epping Forest Guardian*, 1 December 2009): 'I would say that residents have been the driving force for CCTV. All the surveys conducted for the last four years or so have put crime prevention and the fear of crime at the top of residents' lists of priorities.' Her association was clear: cameras made for safety. In Corby, Northants, Judy Caine, chair of the Oakley Vale community association, told the *Mercury and Citizen* (25 March 2010): 'I think cameras are a great deterrent especially when they are linked to the control centre.' Corby Borough Council mounted sixty cameras, five with loudspeakers through which officials could talk to people directly on the street, some of them with lenses able to capture car number plates. If CCTV was Big Brother, he was an arrival welcome enough for Labour to make a right to petition for cameras a selling point in their 2010 election campaign.

CCTV – closed-circuit television – raised questions of political identity and hackles on all sides. Liberty and campaign groups protested that over 4.5 million CCTV cameras monitored the UK, 'making us one of the most watched nations in the world'. No solid evidence supported the number, but the sentiment was widely felt. Labour sided with the majority who liked the idea of ubiquitous cameras. According to an Ipsos MORI survey for the Home Office in 2008, four-fifths favoured the police having access to CCTV recordings. Yet four out of ten in the same survey did not like the council having access to pictures of them. Studies disputed whether CCTV cut total crime, and reported that the effect of cameras at a particular spot was short-lived. The trouble was, people believed the contrary – seven out of ten in the regular Home Office tracking survey looked up to the cameras perched on lampposts and cornices and felt assured. That belief was compelling evidence to a Labour government desperate to prove it was doing something about crime anxiety.

What especially worried communities was youth. In the set of national indicators of satisfaction with place commissioned by the Communities and Local Government Department and published in 2009, perceptions of young people 'hanging around on the streets' determined people's overall sense of safety. What the hangers around did was something else. One of Labour's famous five pledges of 1997 had been to halve the time juvenile offenders spent between arrest and sentencing to seventy-one days, so they did not drift. This target was realized in time for the 2001 election. It turned out to be more of an achievement than Labour cared to claim because the number of hardcore young offenders was rising. The youth crime figures showed a fall to 2002–3 then a 20 per cent rise to 2007–8, but this could have been an artefact of reporting, caused by Labour's own determination to shrink the gap between offences reported and prosecutions by encouraging more reprimands and warnings by the police. Younger children were offending in greater numbers. Those being sentenced for robbery rose 76 per cent by 2007 from 2343 in 1997, often juveniles stealing mobile phones and money from one other. The proportion of girls offending also rose slightly. The Tories, exaggerating, saw 'a depressing decade of yobbery' in these increases in children's convictions for motoring offences, criminal damage and drugs.

Drunken and loutish behaviour and vandalism were real enough in neighbourhoods. But was their volume increasing? Three-quarters of young people never came anywhere near crime, with about one in fourteen habitually offending during their adolescence, and those proportions remained steady over time. We seemed unable to confront hard-wired social facts – such as the likelihood of young people deviating off the straight and narrow. Panic was the wrong response, even if improvement would take time and patience. Ipsos MORI data found anxiety about youth crime diminished the more people knew what the police, probation and Young Offender Teams were doing. And, a regular finding: the higher the average income in a neighbourhood, the more confident its residents; the more deprived, the more fearful.

When the headlines linked Labour and knives, they lacked the rhetoric to respond – gangs and knives have their season and were not jeopardizing the public; young gangs used them on each other in search of elusive 'respect' on estates. From 1996 fatal stabbings had risen sharply before declining from 2003. Knife homicides increased by a dramatic 27 per cent in 2006–7 to reach 270 in 2007–8, the highest total recorded since this way of classifying homicides started in 1977, but then fell away. Convictions of under-eighteens for carrying knives and other weapons doubled in a decade, to 4181 in 2006. But knives seem to have been a fashion. An inquiry by MPs concluded, unsurprisingly, that excessive and lurid media coverage had blown the phenomenon out of proportion.

On the basis of such exaggeration, Britain was 'broken', the Tories cried in the run-up to the 2010 election, and Labour had at one time seemed to agree. In response, they had invented Asbos, anti-social behaviour orders, to answer frustration at the bullying and low-level thuggery that made life hell for residents of the estates usually represented in parliament by Labour. One in six people perceived high levels of anti-social behaviour in their area. Labour councils, led by Manchester, pressed for new powers to take on the hard core of young troublemakers. Drawing on research by the innovative Social Exclusion Unit, the government created these new civil orders to bar people from where they caused trouble, to keep them out of gang turf or away from residents they had been harassing. A tenth of all crime was committed by 5000 sociopaths belonging to a 100,000-strong core of offenders. Many came from jobless, deprived families, dysfunctional for generations, and often targeted by different government departments each dealing with separate symptoms, whether it was drugs, teen pregnancy or school failure. Studies estimated that these families made up 2 per cent of all families. But their effect in certain areas was huge. The horror of the case of Fiona Pilkington brought it into sharp focus, when in 2009 she set fire to herself and her mentally disabled daughter in their car, after years of harassment from local thugs. Labour oscillated between regretting the offensive behaviour that gave rise to the need for Asbos and celebrating them. Brown, in a speech on the digital economy, lauded software developers for inventing an 'asborometer', an application that finds where the user is by means of GPS then calculates how many have been served with an Asbo in the area. When it launched it was the top free app on the iTunes store, with 80,000 downloads.

The public approved of Asbos but police found obtaining and enforcing them difficult. Fewer than 15,000 were taken out in the eight years between 1999 and 2007. Of those taken out, half were breached and a third breached five or more times, according to a report by the NAO. Asbo-breakers often ended up in jail, for offences that would never have earned a custodial sentence. Overall, 65 per cent of those who had received a warning letter (a lot cheaper than an Asbo) or Asbo did not re-engage in anti-social behaviour. Crime and Disorder Reduction Partnerships were supposed to help by pulling together police, social services, probation, health, youth offending and drug teams: they worked well in some places, but in many areas their efforts amounted to not much more than meetings. The 1998 Crime and Disorder Act created orders obliging parents to shape up, and studies showed savings in court and police costs. Four-fifths of the families referred were jobless; the same proportion had educational or learning problems, two-thirds with physical or mental health problems. The government ultimately failed to concentrate spending and gather the multiple initiatives together. Getting professionals to share information and budgets was as hard as changing the habits of the problem families.

When the public talked of 'crime', they often included rowdy girls in high heels vomiting into the gutter on Friday night and raucous alcohol-fuelled gangs of boys on buses. Asked to name the problems facing their areas, one in seven put drugs in their top three, just a shade above 'too much alcohol-related crime' (Ipsos MORI for the Home Office, November 2009). Labour's policy was unabashedly conservative. Smoking was toxic and killed and so did drink, but drugs were banned because they always had been. Radical initiatives – such as decriminalizing and medicalizing drug addiction in the UK – were never on the cards. Crime was higher and prisons fuller because of the government's refusal to rethink.

In 1998, in tough mode, the government appointed as drugs 'tsar' Keith Hellawell, the former chief constable of West Yorkshire. He set himself the impossible task of halving drug-related crime by 2008. In 2002 home secretary David Blunkett had to declare these targets 'not credible'. Downgrading cannabis from Class B to Class C, he declared that he wanted the police to focus on where the worst social dangers lay – in Class A drug use. Instead of arresting 97,000 people a year for possession, police were now required simply to confiscate cannabis and issue on-the-spot warnings. Hellawell resigned in 2002 but the policy worked, with arrests falling by a third, saving 180,000 hours of police time.

Cannabis use continued to fall, perhaps because of better drugs education, or merely a change in fashion. Surveys showed overall illicit drug use falling to its lowest level since the early

1980s. Against that backdrop, Labour reversed and recategorized cannabis to Class B in 2009, amid anxiety about higher sales of stronger and more dangerous skunk. Alan Johnson fired the chair of the drugs advisory council for objecting that the classifications made no scientific sense. Professor David Nutt of Bristol University made the headlines, pointing out that a hundred people a year died horse riding but only thirty from the more widely spread leisure pursuit of taking ecstasy. His successor backed the Home Office in banning a newly discovered source of harm in the drug mephedrone in April 2010, but once again it felt like policy-making as reflex, pushed by newspaper headlines and political panic.

Labour's efforts in rehabilitation were not insignificant. New drug-treatment orders allowed courts to divert offenders if they would accept treatment; waiting times for treatment programmes fell. But the expensive residential clinics that worked best remained scarce. The NHS created local drugs teams, which were treating 133,000 people in 2008. Recidivism ruled: the NAO found only 28 per cent of offenders completed their drug-treatment orders. Hard-drug addicts rose by 7 per cent a year, to a total of between 250,000 and 300,000 — only 5000 had been registered in 1971. The all-in cost of drug addiction was reckoned at £17 billion a year.

Heroin came from Afghanistan, where its production fuelled insurgency, corruption and mass addiction; the government was deaf to radical suggestions it might buy up entire crops and intervene decisively in the supply chain. The 'Home' Office was an anachronism; domestic and foreign, security and 'community' now mixed in a soup of concern about drugs, organized crime and terrorism.

In the first decade of the twenty-first century, regardless of party, ministers would have had to act against the threat of Islamicist terrorism and, because of the Pakistani diaspora from Luton to Leeds, it had a distinctly homespun dimension. Labour ministers never quite explained the foreign–domestic connection, either to themselves or to their constituents. British troops were fighting the Taliban in Helmand province in Afghanistan to make British streets safer, they said. But Al Qaeda bombers were boarding plans in Karachi and Islamabad to fly to Heathrow – so why weren't troops fighting in the Sind?

The Chilcot inquiry established that the Security Service did warn about domestic consequences before the invasion of Iraq, something Blair never acknowledged. Not that Iraq caused domestic terrorism – other assaults, notably the train bomb horror in Madrid, showed none were immune. The London bus and underground bombings on 7 July 2005, killing 56 and injuring 700, were carried out by home-grown amateurs, using shop-bought peroxide explosives – though in 'asymmetric warfare' old pro–am distinctions had lost their point. The government claimed that this outrage proved the need for tougher anti-terror laws, while others claimed it showed how the untreated sores of Pakistan and Palestine added recruits to the Islamicist cause.

As far as can be judged, Labour ministers performed creditably in regrouping domestic security, expanding the Security Service MI5 and improving intelligence, thwarting further attacks. They also went into legislative overdrive, meeting demands for protective action by expanding powers of detention. Anti-terror laws were passed in 2000, 2001, 2003, 2005, 2006 and 2008, making it easier to suspend habeas corpus and imprison suspects without trial. Tightening the screws outraged Muslims, many too ready to deny responsibility for what was happening in their mosques. It also provoked a new libertarian movement straddling right and left. In 2008 David Davis, the rightish Tory shadow home secretary, stood down to fight a by-election over the detention of terrorist suspects for up to forty-two days, and other alleged breaches of fundamental liberties. People in his constituency in the suburbs of Hull and villages of East Yorkshire were as bemused as most of the rest of the country, which broadly backed Labour's assertion of state power.

But its attempt to allow indefinite detention of suspected foreign terrorists became a political and judicial nightmare.

Justice

Ministers sincerely believed they had a duty to protect the public but could not deliver when disapproving judges read from Labour's own Human Rights Act. Labour extended detention without charge to seven days beyond the initial forty-eight hours (Terrorism Act 2000), then to fourteen (Criminal Justice Act 2003), then to twenty-eight days (Terrorism Act 2006) – all these extensions subject to judges or magistrates. Labour then proposed ninety days. Legislation created a new offence of 'glorifying terrorism', endangering freedom of speech. Labour MPs rebelled and defeated the ninety-days proposal.

Terrorist threats were potent enough: deep plots were being hatched across the world, and the police and security services needed time to decipher intercepts and make geographical connections. But somehow Labour ministers positioned themselves beyond even the chief constables and security chiefs, usually reliable allies in scaring the public and wowing the tabloids. A peculiar spectacle unfolded. Civil liberties are in jeopardy, cried Stella Rimington, the ex-head of MI5, which had routinely bugged Labour MPs and trade unionists in the 1970s and 1980s. A conspiracy theorist might have interpreted the flanking fire directed at Labour as further evidence of MI5's political biases. But she did, admittedly, have a book to promote.

Labour's eventual compromise was forty-two days without trial, regarded as repressive not only by David Davis. The public saw mugshots of bearded, swarthy suspects with Arabic names; the reports said they could be neither charged nor released. Suspects could leave the country if they chose, but because some of the suspects were said to face torture or execution they could not be forced out. In response, the government invented a form of house arrest called control orders, provoking extended litigation until, in January 2010, the Supreme Court quashed the orders.

The government pursued a twin track, in Rochdale, Huddersfield and other English towns that were now the front line of global struggle. Counter-terrorism was boosted and intense debate began about how far minority cultures were to be prized or feared and criticized. In 2008 the UK's first National

Security Strategy was supposed to reinvigorate the counter-terrorism plan drawn up after 9/11. Its twin streams were security and 'culture', including English-language learning and control of forced marriage. From 2008 no one could bring in a spouse under the age of twenty-one.

'Counter radicalization', the so-called Prevent strategy, was about encouraging moderate Muslims, introducing locally trained instead of imported imams, bridging the relationship with the police and encouraging universities to report suspect students. Prevent mixed community projects and spying with a rich source of jobs: £140 million was spent in 2008–9 on the security apparatus, specialist police, projects in ninety-four local areas and Prevent advisers. Councillors had to allocate scarce money to suspect groups, risking the ire of BNP-susceptible whites. After the attacks on London in 2005 the number of life-threatening incidents were few. Too many fingers were kept crossed from day to day to allow a definitive answer as to whether the lack of attacks resulted from better intelligence or from the generally pacific nature of settled Muslim communities.

Identity cards were a further Labour response to the twenty-first century's threats; ministers had a vague hope they could at once express social solidarity and enhance security. The puzzle is why Labour proposed them with such dogmatic certainty, despite the known fallibility of the IT on which they would depend – the alacrity with which they were offered up in Labour's brief negotiations with the Liberal Democrats after the 2010 election made previous bloody-mindedness even harder to fathom. The plan was a National Identity Register to keep biometric data, justified variously by catching criminals, then terrorists, then benefit cheats, then immigration illegals. But Charles Clarke as home secretary admitted that the cards would not have prevented the London bombings; in over nine out of ten cases of benefit fraud, people lied about their circumstances, not their identity.

Labour, typically ambiguous, wanted to expand the state on the cheap and tried to offset the £5 billion cost by making citizens pay £30 to acquire or replace a card. Issued at first in 2008 to foreigners, pilots and airport staff were next, but when they protested, the government backed off and the whole thing became voluntary. By July 2009 the Home Office was saying that ID cards would only be a 'choice for British citizens'. Public opinion swung towards the campaigners: by 2009 a YouGov poll found that 68 per cent of those polled thought the state held too much personal information and they were unconvinced by the case for identity cards or a new identity register.

Paranoia mounted, especially among bloggers, who glibly depicted the era as Orwell's *1984*, painting a dark picture of a 'data base state'. A House of Commons inquiry confirmed the UK's DNA database was large by international standards, 4,264,251 individuals or 5.2 per cent of the population, compared with 0.5 per cent in the US. One test of its worth was effectiveness. In 2007–8, 17,614 crimes were detected in which a DNA match was available, including 83 homicides and 184 rapes. Did solving 1 per cent of crimes not justify the intrusion? Before 2001, the police could take DNA samples during investigations but had to destroy the samples and the records derived from them if those concerned were acquitted or charges were not proceeded with. Labour removed this requirement in 2001, then changed the law again in 2004 so that DNA samples could be taken from anyone arrested for a recordable offence and detained in a police station.

The impression of a heavy-handed Labour state was confirmed for some by the handling of demonstrations. The Commons Home Affairs Committee reported in June 2009 that the policing of the G20 protests in London had 'in many ways been a successful operation'. This was true: the vast majority of protesters were allowed to demonstrate peacefully with a minimum of fuss. But lack of training and, the MPs might have added, the inadequacy of the City of London toytown police – part of the anomalous governance of the Square Mile that Labour had mysteriously left alone – produced the indelible video image of a passer-by being pushed to the ground by a burly officer; the man died.

The inquiry into the death passed to the Independent Police Complaints Commission (IPCC), revamped and given a fourfold increase in budget by Labour – mitigating the charge of oppressiveness. In 2007–8 the IPCC opened 100 new investigations, compared with 31 in 2004–5. The increase came in part from Human Rights Act case law and in part because of improved public access to the police complaints system. The release of previously secret reports on an older demonstration death, of Blair Peach in 1978, showed the system opening up; Labour deserved some credit.

Higher police numbers had some effect – on robberies. The police successfully targeted prolific offenders. Tagging helped cut reconviction. But 'there is no clear evidence that the large increase in locking people up has reduced crime', according to the Centre for Economic Performance. No Labour home secretary even momentarily contemplated cutting prison numbers or decriminalizing drugs, with the exception of Blunkett's brief reclassification of cannabis. This would have been unpopular and Labour were determined not to yield an inch to the Tories on criminal justice. The same rationale saw multiple criminal justice Acts, much of the new law ineffective and costly. Asbos were an innovation whose time had come, but community courts might have been more effective. Good programmes included family intervention and parenting schemes, the Youth Justice Board, drug treatment and domestic violence strategies, crime prevention, and better treatments in prison despite the soaring numbers. Beneath the noisy punitive rhetoric, ministers understood the social causes of crime and how to divert the young from a life of offending. They all represented constituencies rife with the problems that give rise to crime, filled with constituents who suffered its effects worst of all. Pursuing populism did not even succeed in persuading people that Labour had been toughest on crime.

The mettle of governments is tested most severely by how they confront the issues thrown up by the Home Office. No ministers could shelter from the tempests of public panic that swept over crime, disorder, drugs, immigration, surveillance and terrorism. Public anxiety cannot and should not be ignored. But it was far from consistent. Governments should be judged on the policy they enact when public opinion is out of kilter with the facts.

Under Labour the Home Office was fated to become more 'ideological', squeezed between foreign threat and domestic response, between security and the protection of liberty. Addressing the causes of crime would – should – have carried ministers deep into society and the economy, querying the distribution of income and life chances. Those were too big and radical for this government to contemplate, leading to palliative spending, fated never to be cost-effective.

Gorton's verdict

Greater Manchester Police was second from the bottom on the inspectors' national scoreboard in spring 2010. Yet crime of all kinds was falling. Gun crime, for which Manchester was briefly notorious, had plummeted. The report card from HM Inspector of Constabulary had only just been published when we visited, and the local neighbourhood team in Gorton and Levenshulme was smarting. In Gorton 75 per cent were confident that police were getting to grips with crime and anti-social behaviour. Here, up close, was the disconnect of the Labour years: more police, better policing, and – in microcosm – shifting public confidence, overlaid by a public perception that crime was rising.

Manchester invested heavily in neighbourhood policing, focused on the toughest zones in the city. Inspector Damian O'Reilly was in charge of three difficult wards, Gorton North, Gorton South and Levenshulme. With a round, ruddy face and a small beard and moustache, the inspector bounded with energy and explanations and the keenest sense of place. He had been on this patch for ten years. When he came, eight officers patrolled the area; now he had forty-eight police and community support officers, including those assigned him from less troubled places. 'Community reassurance' had become the name of the game.

He was feeling pleased about breaking up the Ryder Brow Soldiers, a gang of 15–17-year-olds terrorizing an estate. Two dozen of them had surrounded a lone community support officer on a bike, their hoodies hiding their faces. One shouted, 'Rush him.' But back-up arrived and the gang leaders were charged and convicted. Apart from fines and one jail term, all were given Asbos, restricting where they went and banning them from getting together in groups of more than three.

A member of O'Reilly's Key Individuals Network (KIN) had called the police to the incident. This carefully nurtured group of curtain twitchers met every few months, linked by a newsletter. Some were secret members, not wanting police coming to their doors; other networkers, such as Liz Shaw, held open house for any passing officer, doling out coffee and biscuits.

'It started when my son was fifteen, and he got head butted coming back from school.' He had been bullied over a facial disfigurement. The community support officer who had befriended him had been great. 'She found my Matthew a job, asking around until she found a place at the garden centre. Now he's got his confidence back and he's doing a sports course at college.' It took two years to get the evidence on the bullies and eventually they were Asbo'd. Liz Shaw helped with a scheme mentoring young Gorton boys on the periphery of trouble, taking them on trips, 'teaching them to take their hoods down and smile at people in the street. Makes all the difference.' The police helped youth groups apply for grants and themselves handed out leaflets on the streets to kids who had no idea what projects and schemes were on offer.

Are things better in Gorton? 'There's no comparison,' Liz Shaw declared. 'They were selling drugs on every street corner, great groups of them. I couldn't let my son go down to the shops alone, but I can now.' A month ago Operation Super Vortex had hit the neighbourhood, O'Reilly reported. 'We used 100 bobbies, briefed by me, swamped a small area, put all the doors in where we knew things were going on, using information from all the local KINs. We got a lot of drugs and a shotgun with fifty cartridges.'

A few streets away lived Irene, tiny and frail and in her eighties, but the keenest of KINs. Awarded an MBE for community services, she used to run a residents' association and had always been a street watcher. 'I know everyone round here and they know me, the naughty boys too. I wave at people going by and they wave at me, the bad ones too, and they say, "Are you all right?" If I hear sirens, I want to know what's going on. In my time, I've been shot at and I've had a brick thrown at my head but that was a while ago.' Older generations are naturally inclined to remember golden ages and imagine everything was getting worse, but not Irene. 'Oh, better, definitely. I'm an old Gortonian so I've seen a thing or two, and I've definitely seen worse.' We noted Irene's views about migration earlier.

Neighbourhood policing went to schools. Local secondaries had a Safer Schools Officer as a full-time member of staff. The aim was to get to know neighbourhood children and their parents, to break down barriers, to find out more about what was happening, as well as backing up the teachers. PC Dawn Harrison had been part of the life of Wright Robinson School for five years. A beneficiary of Labour's massive school-building programme, the 1900-strong school gleamed with a sophisticated modernity, looking like the headquarters of a hi-tech company. Inside, three years after opening, all was still remarkably pristine, not a hand-wipe or kick on the walls. PC Harrison was a no-nonsense, tough-as-her-black-boots-and-trousers officer, hair scraped back, zipped uniform vest with walkie-talkie pegged to the lapel. She had been far from pleased to be lumbered with this job, in police canteen culture the lowest of the low. 'I thought it wasn't real policing. I thought when I got here the staff would be dead against having me on the premises and they'd reckon it stig-matized the school.' Now she wouldn't leave and wanted to stay for ever. 'The staff were so welcoming, so pleased to see me, from day one. What I do here was most important, when you realize 50 per cent of the children here are from criminal backgrounds. They've grown up with the police putting people's doors in, taught never ever to speak to police. But now they know me, I sort things out and I know I've helped turn around a lot of kids' lives.' Catching them on the cusp of crime, talking to parents, calming down incidents, knowing information about what they get up to on the streets outside, she's an odd ingredient in their lives – not a teacher, yet with real power and a mother of two children herself.

'I take the year nines, the thirteen-year-olds, and teach them about knives. I show them graphic photos and videos of knifings, real-life cases. They ask a lot of questions, they think about their families. They talk about people they know carrying knives, some of them say they have, and in the end, it does change attitudes.' She talked about going to jail, about how distraught their family and young siblings would be. 'I tell about young men being gang-raped in prison. That's not something they ever knew about, and it gives them a fright. They go away and really think about that. You see the cogs turning and you see them thinking again.'

Parents complained to her about stolen iPods, phones and bikes. 'Nine times out of ten I can sort it out. We have CCTV everywhere in the school except the toilet cubicles.' Angry parents stormed in to protest their children's innocence. 'Sometimes I can show them the film of what their kid did. Sometimes I can just get the kid to admit to his parents what it was, because they always lie when they get home.'

CHAPTER 8

Fairer?

Blair once said if he did not leave behind a fairer Britain, he would have failed. He failed. Brown too, despite using the words fair and fairness forty times in his 2008 conference speech. How much money people have relative to others is the touchstone of equity. Gender, race, disability and class can generate injustice, but income decides, binding children's life chances to their home background. Labour tried but did not quite prevent income inequality getting worse in an already notably unequal country. But they slowed down the rise in inequality. Tax, benefits and spending changes 'significantly redistributed income to the less well off', the Centre for Economic Performance concluded. 'Inequality would have been much higher otherwise.'

The 1997 campaign banned references to poverty as too redolent of Old Labour. So when Blair, having been prime minister for only a month, walked up a disinfected stairway on the Aylesbury estate in Peckham to make his first speech about the plight of the poor, he addressed 'social exclusion' instead. The Aylesbury was only two miles across London from Westminster but a world away in wealth and power. Estates – 'schemes' in Scotland – had over the years become physically degraded, home to concentrations of single parents and the unemployed, a byword for social waste. They were also Labour electoral strongholds. Poverty was too stark a word for their condition – residents had shoes and televisions. Worse, for the New Labour view of the world, the term denoted passivity, a plight not of their making, cueing the dangerous idea that if the state gave them more money they would stop being poor. Social exclusion was something people could pull themselves out of; it avoided the suggestion that there might be something endemically wrong with social structure, labour market or the economy.

Among his audience that morning were women with prams out in the sunshine. Looking at them, the Labour leader might have paused. Their fate is complex. Income cross-cuts family dynamics, the labour market, attitudes. No welfare without work was the message, but what if the available jobs barely paid or were an expensive bus and Tube ride away, or the state was the only likely provider of employment? Who would look after the children? Wouldn't employers find it easier to give a job to a pliable Pole rather than an estate dweller who, at best, would take a while to adapt to employment?

Two years later, the Aylesbury gained notoriety when ten-year-old Damilola Taylor was stabbed to death on his way back home from the library. The media had a fit; young estate dwellers became 'feral'. To Labour the killing showed how nostrums, such as work, could not heal the multiple and overlapping problems of race, family breakdown, failure at school, gangs and knives – all now to be subject of a plethora of initiatives and programmes. Some initiatives were intensely local, such as the first Sure Start projects, restricted to a tightly defined list of addresses. Others set England-wide targets – for example, on school attainment, devised in the hope they would pull up lower-attaining pupils in poorer areas. Most were breathtakingly ambitious and bound to come up short as long as underlying inequality persisted.

But then, suddenly, Labour moved to tackle that as well. In 2000 Blair spoke at Toynbee Hall, one of the East End 'settlements' of the late nineteenth century, where both Clement Attlee and William Beveridge had worked. He promised to abolish child poverty within twenty years, reaching half the target by 2010. No previous speech had hinted at Blair's commitment on child poverty, a promise that, for some, gave Labour's tenure point and purpose.

His audience gasped. The wonks turned to one another to check that they had heard right. How was backward Britain, near the bottom of the EU social scales, to transform itself into Norway, which in 2003 abolished child poverty? Poor, on the definition used by the European Union and United Nations, meant a yearly household income, adjusted for family size, of less than 60 per cent of the national median. The median is the mid-point where half of all households have more income and half have less. It was a better measure than average income, which would shoot up if, say, a Bill Gates came to live in the UK and drop if higher-rate taxpayers were to leave, as they sometimes threatened. But the median was still a moving target, pushed up as general living standards rose.

Later, in 2009, Labour passed the Child Poverty Act formalizing Blair's 2020 target. Aspiration was easier than attainment. Instead of halving the number of poor children by 2010, Labour barely managed to cut it by a sixth. In 1997 Labour inherited 3.4 million poor children – 26 per cent of all children. By 2010 (figures always lagged) there were still 2.8 million. That meant 600,000 children were no longer living in poor households, an achievement. Jane Waldfogel, an American analyst, compared the British record favourably not just with the US, where numbers of poor children rose, but even with such Scandinavian countries as Denmark. Nearly all poor families had seen their standard of living rise, but so had the general standard: theirs failed to rise, enough to take them across the magic line.

No need for 'redistribution', Blair said when pressed. What he meant was no extra taxes, no pain, only gain. Economic growth would funnel income towards poor households, pulling them and their children up nearer the middle. From a revenue stream already creaking under the weight of spending claims, Labour would conjure inner-city programmes and raise child benefit and pay tax credits. But here was Labour's problem. Only the reditribution of extra tax would boost the income of poor households up towards the child poverty target; only extra tax would damp the soar-away incomes of the better-off. And this Labour would not address openly and squarely. Without changing the basic distribution of wealth and income, they could never attain their stated ambition.

Something was pulling incomes apart in all rich countries, except possibly France. Overall income inequality is measured by a standard called the Gini coefficient – the higher it is, the more unequal the society. On a scale of 100 in 2008, the US figure was 46.6. When Labour left office in 1979, the UK stood at 25. It rose during the 1980s, far more than in comparable countries, stabilizing at 34 in the early 1990s. From 1997 it rose two points to 36 – notably higher than Germany, Canada, France and the Scandinavian countries. This amounted to 'some edging up of inequality under Labour', but nothing like the big rise in the 1980s. It was largely accounted for by the richest 1 per cent of the population increasing their share of income. Labour proved a benign government under which to be rich, in that it took very little more from their pockets. The top 1 per cent of income earners paid 21.3 per cent of all income tax in 1999–2000 and 21.9 per cent in 2007–8. Alistair Darling eventually found the courage to ask them to contribute a little more to public revenues in Labour's last month, but it 'is not ideological, you understand', he said reassuringly. Perhaps it should have been. From April 2010 a new top rate of income tax and abolition of allowances meant, for a while at least, that families containing £100,000-plus earners were losing another £1 of every £7 they took home. Suddenly, the Institute for Fiscal Studies said, Labour government was painful: if the tax rates of 1997 had applied in April 2010, high earners would be 15 per cent better off than they actually were now.

Until 2010, 40 per cent was the top rate. It was higher in most other OECD countries. The well-off seemed to lose touch with how far their earnings had departed from the norm, and Labour chose not to remind them. In 2007, for our book *Unjust Rewards*, we conducted focus groups with investment bankers and City lawyers at the peak of the boom: what they displayed was a cast-iron sense of their own entitlement, and they had never heard government ministers say anything discomfiting.

Labour largely ignored the rich and focused on channelling money downwards. Had Labour done nothing, the poorest would have been worse off than they were in 2008–9. In fact, the bottom tenth ended up 12 per cent better off than they would have been. The charge against the government is not lack of intent or passivity: it created a welter of commissions, programmes and policies. What got lost in the maelstrom was politics. Labour came to power in an ungenerous and unneighbourly society, but – so the attitude surveys suggested – one open to persuasion. The practical and moral case for redistribution needed to be made, but never was.

When Labour came to power, a third of all the poor children in the EU 15 countries were born in the UK. The 1980s had seen relative poverty shoot up; the health of the poor was bad and getting relatively worse; the gap in life expectancy between rich and poor was growing. These trends played out intensively where deindustrialization had gone furthest, in places such as Sheffield. Within the city, inequality took physical shape as poorer areas became even more concentrated, while in Hallam and the west of the city people with higher earnings clustered together even more closely. Increasingly, according to the geographer Professor Danny Dorling, 'people in different parts of Britain and people living within different quarters of its cities are living in different worlds with different norms and expectations. This was not the case a few decades ago. This is not the case to the same extent in the majority of affluent nations in the world.'

From the moment Labour ministers came to power, they eagerly commissioned studies on how to remedy the inequality. The Index of Multiple Deprivation was a great Domesday Book of the dispossessed chronicling where the money should go. Blair set up a Social Exclusion Taskforce close to him in the heart of Whitehall; most members were women. Eighteen expert sub-groups examined causes and solutions for truancy, school expulsions, rough sleepers, teenage pregnancy, children leaving care, failed housing estates, juvenile crime, lack of basic banking. The reports were a monument to Labour's efforts, capturing and confronting problems – leading to a quick alleviation of a few of the easier symptoms. For example, the number of families with children put into bed-and-breakfast accommodation as an emergency response to homelessness fell, and the rough sleepers initiative created hostel spaces and 'move on' flats, clearing the night-time streets of their Dickensian cargo. But Number Ten had a limited attention span. It downgraded the exclusion unit; ministers found pulling levers in Whitehall did not lead to immediate action. The intellectual challenge fired Blair but he was bored by the dull mechanisms of local government, which would have to deliver on the ground.

Brown, on the contrary, loved detail. In his final speech to the Labour Party conference in October 2009, he promised to enrol 50,000 'chaotic' families in Family Intervention Projects (FIPs). Run by charities, FIPs offered intensive help to families facing eviction, and to children about to be taken into care, plagued by drugs and drink. Policy had shifted towards case-working with the persistent 2 per cent of difficult families. In Swindon the Family Life Project directed specially trained teams of social workers and police officers at a handful of families, investing now to save later, to ensure they no longer turned up in courts, or dealt drugs, or truanted from school. Such good work often went unreported and unseen by voters, but it also absolved Labour from addressing the relationship between family circumstances and income.

Inspired by Bill Clinton, Labour came to power spouting such maxims as 'a hand up not a handout' and 'work is the best welfare'. Work made people 'deserving'. At 1997's radical dawning, the government slapped a windfall tax on the privatized gas and electricity giants and BT. Sold off too cheaply, they were making super-profits. The tax was a remarkable gesture, never to be repeated, even against the banks, its £5 billion proceeds earmarked for the young unemployed. Tough but tender, the New Deal assigned a personal adviser to 18–25-year-olds to help them over obstacles to finding work – for example, helping with reading and counting. They would be helped to pass job interviews; advisers would pick them up again if things did not work out. If they were still jobless after four months, New Dealers had to take a college course or a subsidized position with an employer (paid £60 a week) or work on an environmental project or help a voluntary organization.

The New Deal was similar to schemes begun a generation ago by the Manpower Services Commission under the Tories, but this time the vibe was positive and budgets satisfactory. Young people heard a positive emancipatory message about work and a firm warning of benefit loss if they failed to take part. A New Deal for the over-fifties and another for disabled people followed, combining sticks and carrots in similar measure. But Labour, desperate to register the effect of their measures, often mis-understood the marginal labour markets in and out of which the poor and unskilled moved, veering between work, semi-work and benefit. Two-thirds of each year's new Jobseeker's Allowance claims were repeats. Posts were often precarious, working for temp agencies, say, offering neither security nor promotion. The moral of the tale was that in Britain's famously flexible labour market well-resourced intervention was needed to keep people in work.

Visitors from abroad admired the 800 Jobcentre Plus offices resurrected from old employment and benefit offices, which forged better links with employers, put vacancies online and 'actively managed' their cases. Their rebuilding cost £314 million less than budget and, so the NAO said, the state did good business in recycling the offices no longer needed. Jobcentre Plus offices showed their worth when they helped keep unemployment down during the recession. They had polite meeters and greeters at the door, plush bright furnishings and computers where anyone was welcome to come in and check available jobs and book appointments. Gone were the bolted-down plastic seats, scuffed lino floors, long queues and interviews conducted from behind protective Perspex screens. Labour had changed the culture for claimants, whose satisfaction ratings hit 86 per cent. But strict penalties remained for non-compliers. All this was easier to do when jobs were getting more plentiful by the year.

By 2005 Labour claimed the 'virtual eradication of youth long-term unemployment'; over 500,000 long-term-unemployed young people had found work. But the Centre for Economic Performance found it was rising, even before the recession. The reasons, surmised because the evidence is thin, could be immigration, school failure or the continuing fall in demand for no-skill employment. People move in and out of work. Two out of five who found jobs through the New Deal were back on the dole within six months. Since they were not claiming benefits either, no one knew if the Neets were into crime, the black economy (15 per cent of GDP on some estimates), sitting at home watching daytime television or drinking White Lightning in the local park.

The New Deal had a late revival, when a recession avalanche of nearly a million young people crashed on the job centres. Under-twenty-fives were guaranteed employment or training if they had been out of work for six months. Labour were alarmed by the ghost of the lost generation of the early 1980s who never found work again. Problem parents of 2010 were often the youthful fallers of 1980 who had never found their feet, and now had children and even grandchildren growing up without seeing anyone work. Labour strove to prevent the children of the 2008 crash starting on that same downward spiral.

Lone parents, whatever the tabloids said, were also working. Thanks to the New Deal, their employment rate rose from 45 per cent in 1997 to 57 per cent twelve years later; Labour had wanted 70 per cent. At first the New Deal only obliged mothers to come for interviews to meet an adviser. It soon applied stiffer sanctions, forcing single mothers with children over the age of seven to leave Income Support and go on Job Seekers Allowance, taking whatever employment was on offer: stern treatment. But in 2009 work and pensions secretary Yvette Cooper eased the rules: single mothers only had to take the job if it suited school hours and if they had childcare.

This was a sore subject, as there were many in Labour ranks who never forgot – or forgave – the government's early blunder when it cut single-parent benefits to keep within Tory spending plans. In a first brutal blooding in 1997 MPs had trooped obediently into the lobby to vote for something they passionately hated, some in tears. Though other benefits soon restored the money, it had been a moment of disillusion.

Looking after children was a plausible excuse for not having a job. To be unemployed yet childless was a cardinal sin. The government put to the test tabloid allegations that able-bodied adults were out of the labour force because benefits were too generous, and cut them. Benefit for a single adult aged over twenty-five was a pitiful £64.30 a week in the year to April 2010, down to 10 per cent from 13 per cent of average earnings in 1997. Cutting benefits did not force people into work, either because there was none or they were unfit for what there was; a huge investment in counselling, training and one-to-one case-working was needed. Alongside the slackers many had serious trouble finding work. They included young people adrift from care, mothers whose children had grown up, former offenders and the hard-to-employ to be seen queuing outside post offices on benefit day. They were to be punished, and the result was a stain on Labour's record. More adults fell into poverty than children escaped from it. Media pressure and focus group findings pushed Labour to pander to 'middle England' sensibilities, but ministers could surely have made more of the sheer indignity of poverty. In 2003–4 poor households made four million applications to the Social Fund, to pay for furniture and clothes – purchases you save for, if you have any money. That figure was shaming. Worse was the NAO finding that only 47 per cent of poor people even knew of the fund's existence, a sign of how so much to do with the poor and poverty had been consigned to the shadowy edges of a consumer society.

Labour inherited 2.6 million claimants of incapacity benefit, many covertly encouraged during the early 1990s to move to 'the sick' to reduce headline unemployment figures. In places without jobs, doctors were happy to sign people off to give them the few extra pounds that incapacity added to their dole money. Now the ebbing tide of unemployment left them a prominent outcrop in the figures. Labour set tougher medical tests for new claimants and their numbers fell. After retesting old claimants, it put many on a new benefit, Employment Support Allowance, signifying that they were fit for work of some kind. Numbers rose to a 2003 peak before falling back. In the recession, the TUC praised the government for not hiding the impact on unemployment by encouraging more to claim incapacity benefit.

Labour accepted that if work were to be 'the best welfare', logic pointed to a minimum wage. Hardly a revolution – Franklin Roosevelt had introduced a minimum wage to the United States in 1936 – but the government still felt the need to go cap in hand to employers. Without any evidence, the CBI predicted that a minimum would kill a million jobs. This was tantamount to admitting that their version of private enterprise could be sustained only by paying staff less than they could live on, something even Victorian mill-owners had found troubling.

The minimum wage was introduced in 1998, a hundred years after Winston Churchill, another well-known revolutionary, had brought in wages councils that set minima for particular industries. Starting at £3.60 an hour for adults, it immediately pushed up the pay of 1.2 million low-paid workers, most of them women. The Tories, having fought its introduction, then said they were in favour, making the national minimum a permanent gain for Labour. By 2010 the rate had risen, but only to £5.91. The minimum could not support a family. First Ken Livingstone and then Boris Johnson as mayors of London agreed a benchmark 'living wage' for their employees and contractors – £7.60 in London, £7 elsewhere in 2010. Ministers hammering on about 'getting the poor off benefits and into work' forgot that many who worked were still living below the poverty line. When pollsters asked about poverty the public thought *Shameless* and scroungers, not hospital cleaners, security guards, street cleaners, old people's care assistants, dinner ladies, check-out staff or nursery assistants.

Turning a blind eye to low pay was one reason why Labour's child poverty promise went unredeemed. The number of poor children who lived in families with a parent who was working, but still earning too little, was 2.1 million in 1998. The number was precisely the same at the peak before the crash in 2007. That represented 55 per cent of all poor children. When tax credits came in, boosting the extra parents could earn in work, most families living on benefits were better off if they took a job. But the figures showed that many were still not earning enough to stop being poor, even with tax credits.

As with the minimum wage, tax credits were both an urgent extension of Labour's own policy and a throwback – all the way back to a benevolent bench of Tory magistrates in Speenhamland in Berkshire in 1795 who admitted farm workers would starve on what they were paid and topped up their pay out of the rates. Brown called this new welfare benefit a 'credit' to avoid putting extra sums in the spending columns of the national accounts; he fooled few.

Tax credits were an administrative nightmare for HM Revenue & Customs, but a hugely successful social policy. They explain why child poverty fell and why inequality did not grow as much as it would have done. They also boosted corporate profits by subsidizing employers who paid too little. Labour might alternatively have pushed up the minimum wage, cutting state spending and the call on taxpayers. Their choice said they believed the state's job was in effect to subsidize business, despite its reluctance to pay the necessary taxes, corporate or individual. Tax credits were sticking plaster. The wound was the failure of successive governments since 1945 properly to support families. Child rearing was a principal cause of poverty. Parents, especially mothers, cannot add to household income by working unless they have reliable and trustworthy care for their children.

Tax credits were supposed to pay 80 per cent of the cost of childcare. But on a low wage the remainder was still beyond many. Working mothers still relied on friends and relatives. A 2007 survey found the poorest working mothers were least able to use the credits, and their children least likely to benefit from good nursery daycare. Labour had the right idea but thought they could solve large problems with far too little money.

Poverty was not the whole story of fairness. Labour had a large equalities agenda. The age of consent for gays was made the same as for heterosexuals, sixteen. The gap between women's and men's pay narrowed, though less than Labour's rhetoric had seemed to promise. Between 1997 and 2009 the gap shrank from 27 per cent to 22 per cent. Average pay per week for full-time women workers in 2008 was £426, compared with men's £531.

Labour's 1997 intake included 101 women MPs. Some had arrived thanks to the party's use of all-women shortlists, given legal backing in the Sex Discrimination (Election Candidates) Act in 2002. They pushed pro-woman policies. Much of the new assistance to the low-paid, including the minimum wage, benefited women. Seven out of ten of the lowest-paid employees were women. Child tax credits boosted women's incomes, especially single mothers. Women who had been low earners all their lives were disproportionately poor in old age, and Labour's new pension credit helped them. Women, who were almost always long-term financial losers after divorce, won the right to a fair share of their former husband's occupational pension. But Labour were reluctant to challenge what happened in labour markets and firms' pay settlements, so the pay gap narrowed only slowly.

School results for ethnic minorities improved relative to the average. But boys from poor white families trailed. Pakistani and Bangladeshi households were still two and a half times more likely to be living in poverty than the average. Ethnic minority groups were still twice as likely to be in-patients on mental health wards than others; and children living in deprived areas were twice as likely to have mental health disorders than those in better-off areas. Yet what was striking was the sheer volume of activity in pursuit of – what? Under Labour, diversity had become the object of policy but ministers had avoided the philosophical conundrum of why 'difference' should be prized but 'inequality' fended off. The vogue term was 'equality and diversity', though related policies were potentially contradictory: in the treatment of girls in Muslim communities, or of mothers at work. Rights to equal treatment were formalized in the Human Rights Act but they often remained inactive till tested in the courts. Case law built up only slowly and to give rights a push, Labour felt obliged to rework the quango landscape and merged the separate disability, race and gender bodies into a single Commission for Equality and Human Rights Commission. It did not prove a happy birth, amid arguments about costing and staffing. Perhaps that did not matter when, in social reality, integration was happening. Mixed-race births (white–black and white–Indian at least) rose.

But segregation was also a fact. Fewer than one in a hundred Manchester Pakistanis went to schools with mostly white pupils; half went to schools where most pupils were non-white, like them. A report from Bristol University suggested that segregation was not intensifying. Four out of five primary-age pupils in Oldham went to majority non-white schools, but that ratio had not changed over the years. Ministers' reluctance to force public bodies to pay living wages or employ New Deal youngsters contrasts with their enthusiasm to impose disability and other duties on the same organizations. Labour pushed the shift that the Tories had resisted, away from individual acts of prejudice or discrimination, towards remedying the way organizations and 'cultures' put people at a disadvantage. Sir William Macpherson's inquiry into the murder of Stephen Lawrence in 1993 popularized the term 'institutional racism'. In the follow-up the Home Office gave the Metropolitan Police targets for recruitment of ethnic minorities. Labour amended race relations legislation to impose duties on public bodies to promote race equality. Having created a Disability Rights Commission to parallel the other equalities quangos (the Disability Discrimination Act was passed by the Tories), Labour used it to police new duties. Labour established a separate Whitehall sub-department for disability, an accolade not accorded gender or race. New regulations gave rights to people who changed gender and European Union directives pushed the government to bring into employment law discrimination on grounds of sexual orientation and age.

What is hard to measure is how far Labour's attentiveness to equality and diversity extended 'awareness'. Organizations amassed more data than before. Take Rugby Borough Council – though it could have been any public body. It now published 'equality assessments' of the local labour market and its own workforce. In 2009 the district had a black and ethnic minority population of 8.8 per cent, while the council's workforce was 5.7 per cent black and minority ethnic. But while 16.1 per cent of the population had a 'limiting long term illness', the council registered 21.2 per cent of its employees with a disability, defined as an impairment, physical or mental, 'that has a substantial and long term adverse effect on his or her ability to carry out normal day to day activities' as defined by the person themselves. As for gender, the council employed more women (54 per cent) than the proportion of women in the Rugby population (50 per cent). How far were such calculations a sign of bureaucratic inwardness and dispensable in the eyes of the government that succeeded Labour?

Towards the end, equalities – the era preferred the plural – came together as the party's deputy leader Harriet Harman brought in an omnibus Act putting inequality based on class and material deprivation on the same footing as that related to gender and race. It imposed new duties on public bodies over pregnancy and maternity, sexual orientation, gender reassignment and religion and belief. In a contested move, it required big private-sector employers (a tiny proportion of firms) to audit their gender pay gap. As if to acknowledge all that Labour had failed to do and say, the Act required all public authorities to act to reduce class inequality. Passed in Labour's last week, the Act was a mocking afterthought, a ghost of all that might have been.

The inequality that hardly dared speak its name was social class. On their deathbed Labour recognized that society was closed: 45 per cent of senior civil servants, 70 per cent of finance directors and 75 per cent of judges were privately educated – as were the victorious Tory prime minister and his Liberal Democrat deputy after the election. Jon Cruddas, who stood as Labour deputy leader in 2007, said class had been 'disinvented ideologically' and people who worked in factories, shops and offices had ceased to have much of a political existence.

Class was old-speak; Labour preferred to talk social mobility. The Blairite Alan Milburn announced in early 2009 that he had returned to the colours to 'break the middle class monopoly on professional jobs'. He wanted to open out the informal contacts middle-class parents used to get their children work experience and internships. This was inflammatory. Soft power – culture and networking – was precisely the basis of class, in alliance with education, inheritance and money. Milburn retreated, saying what state-school children needed was better careers advice. A major general on his committee thought scouting, the Duke of Edinburgh's Awards and cadet forces in comprehensives would do the trick.

Yet even Blair had talked of the day when two babies born on the same day in the same hospital would have the same chance in life, though one was from a well-off and one from a poor family. Raising aspirations was the answer, declared Milburn. If only the poor would try harder, strive, reach for the stars. It was all in tune with pervading individualism – with talent and determination you too could be Damon Buffini or Alan Sugar, and get a peerage from a Labour government. Historically Labour had simultaneously respected background – it was the party of the working class – and despised it, by encouraging young men and women to move on, up and out. The paradox had informed left-of-centre fiction and biography from Raymond Williams through Richard Hoggart; the sentiment ensured Labour attitudes towards grammar, later academy, schools were pained and ambiguous.

Since the 1950s, Britain had been more mobile as middle-class and service jobs, including posts in the public sector, increased in number: sons and daughters ended higher up the incomes and jobs ladder. But the jobs machine had slowed. Since the 1980s birth had again become destiny. Labour devised schemes to expose children from poor areas to the possibility of higher education. But they found it too hard to make the big point: background means less in a more equal society. If the distribution of income is fairer, the ladder between poor and affluent homes will have fewer rungs. Where the ladder is shorter, people move up with relative ease – and stepping down becomes a lot less painful. Labour did not want to think about the size of the ladder. Instead, ministers scouted for ways to give children at the bottom crampons and ropes for the daunting upward climb. Sure Start was to be their first rung upwards, but middle-class children were benefiting from the programme as much as the deprived, so the gap remained the same.

Born of a novel think-tank idea, the Child Trust Fund was another attempt to level the playing field without making anyone worse off. Poor children lacked financial backing and were often unable to borrow to pay towards college or university, or put down a deposit or ride out a rough patch. Now every baby born after 2002 qualified for a state endowment of £250, with those from low-income families given £500 – sums that would be doubled when the child was seven years old. Parents could add another £1000 a year. At eighteen, young people could take out the money to use as they liked. Yet many poor parents chose to look this gift horse squarely in the mouth. A third of parents in deprived areas were not claiming, perhaps because of lack of knowledge or a consumerist society's suspicion of something for nothing. The fund became a target for budget cutters after the 2010 election.

Imagine a highly paid QC arguing Labour's case. He might plead mitigation. ('He' because women had still to penetrate the upper reaches of the legal profession.) Income inequality had risen dramatically before 1997. To make a difference, Labour would have needed a much clearer understanding of trends than ministers could muster, especially the spread of rewards within private companies.

Yet under Labour child poverty showed its sharpest fall for decades, and the UK showed the biggest drop in the EU. For the first time since the mid 1970s the figures were moving in the right direction. Labour certainly stopped things getting worse. Professor John Hills of the London School of Economics, an expert witness, even put a number on Labour's impact. Child poverty would have been between 6 and 9 per cent higher if not for Labour's measures. The Gini coefficient would have gone up three points rather than the two points it actually rose under Labour. A one-point mitigation – that was Labour's record.

Labour's barrister would claim A for effort: the emphasis on equality in school attainment, public health, programmes for deprived communities, early years interventions, the New Deal for unemployed youth, adults and the disabled, a minimum wage, tax credits. An equalities review compiled by Trevor Phillips, who became chair of the new Equalities and Human Rights Commission, talked of 'the huge potential benefit of this work to the most disadvantaged groups'. But even this friend of the government continued: 'some kinds of inequality remain at levels that can only be described as intolerable, particularly in education and employment', adding that new economic and social trends – globalization, for example – will either freeze those inequality gaps or widen them. 'Progress is fragile and uneven. In too many areas we have stopped the clock; in some it is starting to turn backwards.' It sounded like a hung verdict.

The verdict from Brighton Jobcentre Plus

Junior was a skinny boy with a black woolly hat pulled down to his ears, his pasty elfin face a bit pinched – no, not a boy; it turned out he was nineteen. He had done nothing since drifting away from school without a qualification to his name. He had only been signing on at the Brighton Jobcentre Plus for the previous six months and who knows how he survived before that. 'Living at home,' was all he would say. If he had claimed the dole he would have been channelled smartly into work or training, which is probably why he did not sign on and collect his £50.95 a week, the under-twenty-fives' rate. Instead he had been one of the 15–19-year-olds who vanish into statistical thin air, Not in Education, Employment or Training. This was Labour at their best. Give a problem a name, try to measure it, throw effort and resources in – for the sake of preventing another cycle of deprivation and disadvantage. Memories were still green of what happened in the 1980s: even when the economy picked up, it was the new school leavers who found work in preference to those who had been unemployed for several years. 'Never again,'

Labour said, but nearly one million young people were out of work when they left office.

Junior had now been claiming Jobseeker's Allowance for six months, and pressure was mounting on him to find work. Extra opportunities opened up as the £2 billion Young Person's Guarantee kicked in, with its promises of work or training. 'My dad drives a cab and when I'm twenty-one I can get a cab licence. I'll be earning £250 a week, easy. He'll drive it nights, I'll drive days. I've got the Knowledge,' he added with a grin. 'You get asked seventy questions on seventy roads in Brighton and Hove – and I can do that.' 'Yes, but . . .' said his personal adviser Jane, who had seen him regularly and knew him quite well. 'That's a year and a half away before you can sit for your licence.' You got the impression they had had this conversation before. So, meanwhile, what else?

He leant across the desk to peer at the computer screen where Jane was trawling possibilities. He qualified for the Future Jobs Fund, which started to come on-line in the autumn of 2009, an anti-recession measure, aiming at 170,000 new jobs for young people; employers were paid £6500 to take on a 16–24-year-old for six months doing a proper job with training attached, paid the minimum wage. Half the employers coming forward were offering to match the grant and pay for a second six months, making the job last a full year. It had to be a new job, not substituting for an existing one, and it had to pay the minimum wage, which made the programme unlike any work experience, job training or internship before it. This week, Jane told Junior, a jobs fair in the Funky Fish nightclub (in the daytime) would offer jobs in the NHS: apprenticeships in healthcare, as ward clerks, in human resources and clinical support. Junior perked up. 'Definitely,' he said. 'I'll definitely go look and see.' She explained that NHS employers would give preliminary interviews there and then and three people would be chosen for a further interview for each job. 'It's proper pay, a real job?' 'Yes, you'd be getting £4.83 an hour, the young person's rate.' He beamed. The NHS as employer of last resort? It was deep into the recession by the time employers could be rallied and organized to make these offers.

Most are public-sector or charity jobs because they had to be 'of benefit to the local community'.

She swivelled the screen towards him, showing a list of Future Jobs Fund offers. A maintenance apprenticeship at the Dome, Brighton's magnificent old concert hall; a creative apprenticeship with an arts group, nursery nursing, trainee cooks and a jeweller's assistant. There were office jobs in the council, work at a wood recycling charity. To be sure, they would only last a year and few would convert into permanent posts, but a year's work that included training and qualifications could be life-transforming for a Junior. Something seemed to have clicked with him that day and he went off folding up his Action Plan and the forms for the jobs fair into his pocket, with a bounce in his sneakers.

Micky had a Future Job already. 'Brilliant,' he declared, though he has had hard winter months with snow, rain and ice, chopping trees into firewood. With a pink Mohican he did not look like a typical forestry worker – but now he was saying it was what he wanted to do for ever. He liked working outside and he would be getting his chainsaw certificate soon, plus a health and safety certificate to go with it; two others had been taken on permanently from the scheme. His supervisor said he was brilliant too. The difference with Future Jobs was in the pay, that universal measure of worth. Someone who gets paid feels they are worth something and an employer makes sure they do something worthwhile. Was this expensive at £1 billion for 170,000 jobs? Yes, if they would have got jobs anyway; no, if it found jobs for young people who otherwise might be a drag on the state for most of their lives.

Jobcentre Plus offices such as this one in Brighton were unrecognizable from the state employment and benefits service of the late 1990s. Labour inherited bleak and punitive offices as grim as the one in *The Full Monty* and precious little dancing went on in them. But beneath the gloss the Brighton office was ever watchful for scammers or skivers.

Joanne remembered the old days well, after thirty years. She started out with the weary old Employment Service in 1979. During the 1980s recession, 'We had 17,000 unemployed here, and very little to offer them. We let them phone in because we couldn't cope. But this time, although the recession is said to be worse, we've only got 5600 on Job Seekers Allowance and we do have a lot to offer.' Even so, the workload here had doubled since the crash.

She had seen schemes come and go since the old youth training. 'Everything really did all change after 1997 with the New Deal,' she recalled. 'Our job improved no end. We had special training and we were able to offer people so much more.' She talked of hard cases that she helped over the years, people who started out angry and ended up in work they liked, their life chances improved. She reeled off the schemes, to give new self-employed people £50 a week on top of whatever they can earn for their first thirteen weeks, to get them on their feet. She began to sound like a Soviet-era farm worker praising the beetroot crop while in the hearing of the commissar, but was not untypical in her enthusiasm for her job. Personal advisers we have talked to over the last decade often had this zeal. Jobcentre Plus was one of the few places you could go to hear authentic enthusiasm from people working in the public sector. Drop in on school staffrooms, a GP surgery or a hospital, and the default mode is a long low rumble of grumble and complaint – about Sats, targets, form-filling, paperwork and chivvying from on high.

Gerald, a personal adviser for a year, was often looking for work for graduates from Brighton's two universities and many colleges. Once, student work was plentiful in the bars and hotels. Dinah had been looking for anything, cleaning, caring; but now after six months she was eligible for one of the Future Jobs. She had a degree in library and information studies, but lived on her dole. She also had something less welcome – a student loan of £20,000. Only one library assistant job had come up, a job with West Sussex libraries, but 140 people had applied, most of them with experience, and she never stood a chance. She doubted she would ever get what used to be called a 'graduate' job and had got used to the idea: looking down the list of new temporary Future Jobs, she said, 'I'd just be thrilled to get any of them – just anything, please.'

Lord Freud, the Tory peer who had helped draw up the government's welfare-to-work plans, acknowledged 500,000 fewer people were out of work during the recession because of government action. 'Active Labour policy' could shift people into work, or at least keep churning them in and out of jobs. But however optimistic the personal advisers were, 10 per cent of the labour force were in precarious positions, moving in and out of unemployment and insecure jobs, rarely moving up to something better.

CHAPTER 9

Climate and environment

'Celebrities will arrive in cars powered by cooking oil. The projector will be powered by batteries charged from solar panels and the tent lit by gas from London landfill sites, and heated with stoves using recycled free London newspapers, and possibly also horse manure.' So promised the flyer for the premiere of *Age of Stupid* in Leicester Square in February 2009. The celebrity audience stamped and cheered when the lights came up and Pete Postlethwaite – narrator of an awkward and preachy quasi-documentary – declared he would renounce his Labour-era OBE in green protest. He had once wowed Labour sentimentalists with his denunciation of Mrs Thatcher in the film *Brassed Off*. Now he would vote for anyone other than Labour . . . unless they vetoed new coal-burning generating capacity at Kingsnorth power station in Kent.

Ed Miliband, the energy and climate change secretary, supported Kingsnorth but the German owners of the plant did not go ahead, so Pete kept his gong and Labour got his vote. The government carbon record was like that: a mixture of accident and design, and undistinguished in the main. Overall, greenhouse gas emissions fell at about the same rate after 1997 as they had between 1990 and the start of Labour's tenure. But Labour's pusillanimity mirrored the public's. It left office with a decent plan for cutting emissions and that reflected the people's Augustinian wish: take these carbohydrons away, O minister, but not just yet.

Justice

Celebs exiting the premiere of *Age of Stupid* might have been hesitating before flying off for a screen test in California; some would self-righteously return to expensive eco-homes in the hills. The film was little more than a green group-hug. Within months the climate deniers were on the march. Northern Europe's severe winter of 2009–10 deepened the disbelief of millions in global warming. Neither the government nor its green critics fathomed the depths of public ignorance and scepticism. Would we ever connect trivial daily carbon emission – the standby light on the television in the sitting room – with the struggle for agreement at, say, the UN Copenhagen summit that took place in December 2009? Labour ministers generally did well at such conferences, within agreed EU positions; pity they could not point to exemplary UK performance to back up their enthusiasm.

Did Labour do enough to educate, explain and sharpen public perceptions? Meteorologists could not attribute any single storm to emissions, but disturbed weather might have given ministers their cue. At last, in 2009, there stood the environment secretary Hilary Benn, the angry river Derwent foaming at his back, making a connection in Cockermouth. A 'one-in-a-thousand-year event' was happening soon after an 'unprecedented' one-in-a-hundred-year flood: 'the scientists do say we are going to see more extreme weather events'. The reference was mild enough, reflecting the fact that Labour never managed to translate the environmental analysis into policy, especially tax. To sum up, between 1997 and 2009, green taxes fell from 9.5 to 7.9 per cent of total receipts, with three-quarters of that made up of fuel duty.

That was the tax that tested the government when in 2000 lorry drivers protested at how the automatic adjustment in duty put in place by the Conservatives was pushing up prices at the pumps. Hauliers and farmers suddenly combined with Poujadist force and ministers took fright. Cabinet secretary Sir Richard Wilson later told us how the government had rocked. At the same time torrential rains fell: Labour's was a watery decade, as the inhabitants of Lewes, Hull and Gloucester discovered. But as irate lorry drivers struggled through the flooded streets of York

218

in November that year, was a great educational opportunity missed? What should Labour have done: risked civil disorder to make the point?

Polling indicated that by 1997 the public had not registered climate change as a fundamental threat. Labour, however, arrived in office convinced by the science and aware of the implications of climate change. A few months after the election, environment secretary John Prescott left for the Kyoto summit in a blaze of publicity. There he signed Labour up to a 2012 target of cutting by 12.5 per cent the greenhouse gases emitted in 1990. Easy, ministers knew: during the 1990s the UK had dashed for gas, converting power plants from more expensive coal, and gas-fired power plants emit about half the carbon of coal power stations. Hubristically, Labour set themselves a higher target based on back-of-an-envelope calculations by a researcher while the party was still in opposition. They promised that by 2010 the UK would cut carbon emissions by 20 per cent from their 1990 levels. Three successive manifestos repeated the pledge, to no effect.

Total carbon did fall from its 1997 levels but by paltry amounts, about 0.3 per cent a year. Labour's 2010 pledge was missed by miles. Add in carbon emitted in producing the goods we import, especially from China, and from ships and planes leaving the UK, and the deficit was even worse. Some estimates said greenhouse gas emissions had risen on the 1990s baseline by 19 per cent. Even in the government's own backyard, it failed. The Carbon Trust had placed newspaper ads urging us to turn lights out, but night-time strollers past government offices might doubt whether the message had reached civil servants. The NAO was contemptuous of permanent secretaries who allowed Whitehall's emissions to rise.

Kyoto seemed to promise concerted action but Labour's attention soon wandered; it is hard to trace a green line through their policies on road, rail, housing and urban living. Later on, in a rare example of Blair–Brown harmony at the Gleneagles summit in 2005, the government sounded a fanfare over Sir Nicholas

Stern's powerful report. In it, the Treasury official argued that small cuts in GDP growth now could lessen climate change in the future. Save now for your grandchildren's sake. Polls showed 60 per cent of adults felt climate change would have little or no effect on them personally, but 85 per cent reckoned the effect on future generations 'would be a great deal or quite a lot'. The Stern report was influential abroad but Labour, devoted to economic growth, found his message too tough.

'By exaggerating the trade off between economic dynamism and environmental protection, between human welfare and nature,' David Miliband observed, 'the politics of the environment failed to gain the legitimacy needed to make it a governing idea for a majority party.' Which was an elegant way of saying: too hard for us, guv. And yet the government had pushed expectations. Individuals and some public bodies picked up the momentum. After Copenhagen, the City of Birmingham pledged to buy only electric or gas-powered vehicles. Half its electricity would be generated from renewable sources by 2015.

Labour were good at promises, too. A 2003 energy white paper said the UK would cut carbon emissions by 60 per cent by 2050. Then, as interest in climate change revived under Brown, the Climate Change Act 2008 upped the ante, promising an 80 per cent cut by 2050. This was heavyweight legislation, massing intellectual firepower behind calculations of what needed to be done. But that was the problem: how to connect targets with the daily lives of citizens, and especially the way they travelled?

If Jeremy Clarkson was one of the decade's climate gargoyles, another was Michael O'Leary, the Mr Nasty of bog-standard flying. The boom years produced record business for Ryanair, and emissions from aviation soared. Flying contributed only a small part of total emissions but aviation carbon was growing fast. Labour's conscience was tweaked by claims that the less affluent would be hit hardest if a shortage of runways raised the price of cheap holidays. They should have noted the Civil Aviation Authority's estimate that people in the top half of the income distribution took 70 per cent of all UK leisure flights. The most frequent flyers also had the loudest voices.

Labour had nothing like a 'policy' for air, beyond letting rip. They had insisted that private capital take over air traffic control, but whittled this down to a part-sale of the National Air Traffic System, bringing the state £800 million. Fine, but when Icelandic ash plumed over northern Europe in April 2010, lines of interest and responsibility got worryingly crossed.

The government heroically proposed UK aviation emissions should be no higher in 2050 than in 2005 – heroic because even tentative moves to keep pushing Air Passenger Duty up produced a snarling backlash. Put it in right-wing media speak: the 2009 increase would add £240 to the cost of a family of four flying economy to Egypt; 'Why is this government against holiday-makers?' asked a headline in the *Daily Telegraph*.

Labour might have sought to plan airport access and capacity, but interference with markets was anathema, even though competition was often slim, because of restricted airspace and landing slots. In pro-business mode, the Cabinet approved Heathrow expansion again in early 2009 after a mighty row. Climateer Ed Miliband gave way.

In exchange he was allowed to publish a map showing an emissions cut of 34 per cent by 2020. The committee set up to check progress, chaired by Adair Turner, calculated what would have to happen. To cut the carbon intensity of energy by 2020 the UK would have to build four clean coal plants, two new nuclear plants and 8000 wind turbines. To stand a chance of reaching Miliband's targets, emissions from residential buildings had to fall by a third by 2020. This implied insulating 10 million lofts and 2.3 million walls, installing 12 million new boilers and phasing out washing machines and dishwashers without an A+ rating.

By the end, Labour had a reasonable-sounding policy, based on the first climate change target legally binding on a government and a new, post-recession enthusiasm for green employment in manufacturing turbines and solar panels, pushed by subsidies. But internationally the UK was johnny-come-lately. The Centre for Economic Performance put the UK sixth in the league table of patents for 'clean technologies', with German, Japanese and

American innovators holding three times as many as UK researchers. Even so, Labour found themselves in the place where, if it had been the starting point, great things could have been done.

Domestic under-achievement contrasts with the UK's disproportionate and largely benign influence on the global stage. Britain helped set up the European Union Emission Trading Scheme in 2002, covering the large companies that accounted for around 40 per cent of EU greenhouse gas emissions, and from 2012 it would also include aviation. The Institute for Fiscal Studies sniffed that its targets were not set 'in a very coherent way' and by 2007 had produced no cuts. But the scheme offered rich pickings: in 2009 it emerged that organized crime had moved in and siphoned off €5 billion in tax credits. The Commons Environmental Audit Committee said the collapse in carbon prices in the recession had done for the scheme, leaving big firms with more carbon allowances than they need.

Blair's alliance with an all-but-climate-change-denying American president sat oddly with the UK's international activism. The best he could do was flap weakly at the US refusal to adopt the Kyoto protocols. But condemn his good friend George, or even raise an eyebrow at the oil industry connections of vice-president Dick Cheney – never. Yet Blair had pushed for a climate agreement at the G8 Gleneagles summit, and at Copenhagen Brown also worked hard, if in vain. First American then Chinese intransigence meant no deals, no timetables, only the usual expressions of good intent for some unspecified time in the future.

Labour left the UK as dependent on carbon as ever. And even more dependent on foreign energy supply. In 2009 gas generated 45 per cent of UK electricity, coal 32 per cent. Long gone were the rich flows of home-drilled North Sea oil and gas, whose revenues had helped pay for mass unemployment in the Thatcher years. The North Sea was running down. In 2006 the UK became a net importer of natural gas, foreign supplies meeting 38 per cent of UK electricity demand. The geopolitics of carbon shifted east and the EU became sensitive to its dependency after Russia started using its gas and oil as a diplomatic tool: why manoeuvre tanks when you can turn off the taps? By 2015 the UK would depend on imports of gas for 75 per cent of supply, and the regulator Ofgem said the UK gas market faced a cliff edge in 2015.

To secure supply and cut carbon, Ofgem said the UK should invest £200 billion by 2020 in smart meters, transmission, renewable heating, wind and nuclear. The challenge was ideological as much as practical because cutting carbon meant more state action. Liberalized gas markets simply did not give firms enough incentive to invest – even the CBI agreed with that.

Of course the UK still sat on top of millions of tonnes of potentially usable carbon. Coal was a sore subject for Labour. They wanted to mine it, as a gesture to their heartlands, but only 'cleanly'. Ministers paid for experimental schemes at Tilbury in Essex and Longannet in Fife. Meanwhile they tidied up coal's residues. Between 1981 and 2004, 190,000 people had lost coal-related jobs in England. The conviction of two young boys from Edlington near Doncaster in 2009 for near-murderous assault provoked exaggerated 'broken Britain' talk, but no one could deny that pit closures had ruptured such grim but formerly cohesive estates and villages. Labour ramped up the ungenerous programme bequeathed by the Tories, and by 2009 had spent £464 million on regenerating 107 sites. Flattened slagheaps, newly sown grass, warehousing and distribution centres were signs of the 'impressive' physical regeneration recorded by the Audit Commission. People were the problem, many inheriting their parents' dependence on invalidity benefit.

Turn on the lights in Pimlico and French taxpayers obliged; turn them on in Portobello in Edinburgh and you had Spanish shareholders to thank. Only two of the UK's household energy suppliers were still British in ownership. Why worry, Labour said, globalization is benign. Besides, electricity producers were all obliged to source 10 per cent from wind, solar, hydro, biomass and other renewable sources (excluding nuclear) by 2010 and 15 per cent by 2015. The government praised itself for having trebled the supply of electricity from renewable sources. Their share in electricity generation rose from 3.6 per cent in

1997 to 5.5 per cent in 2008 – well short of the target. In Scotland, thanks to hydro, 22 per cent of electricity came from renewables.

Progress was slow partly because of Nimbys. Isle of Wight councillors rejected a test site for turbine trials by Vestas, one of the few companies with a stake in turbine construction in the UK; it promptly closed its main plant. Yet a breeze was blowing. Nine consortia signed agreements with the Crown Estate over offshore wind, but only five included UK companies. Off the Thames Estuary, turbines were installed, but of the £1.7 billion worth of plant in the London Array wind farm, 90 per cent would come from outside the UK. E.ON and the other developers complained about the lack of UK suppliers. Unlike other countries, the UK did not require developers to source turbines or parts from home-based manufacturers. Labour's hyper-ambitious target for energy production from renewables by 2020 implied building one new turbine every eleven days. After years of green lobbying, in early 2010 Miliband announced a new tariff which would make it worthwhile for even householders to generate electricity from solar panels on their roofs or mini-windmills in the garden.

In energy, as with the railways, markets were not like those described in economics textbooks; without state subsidy, shareholders would receive no dividends. Nuclear power was unprofitable unless government underwrote returns. The Tories had privatized British Energy, the company set up to run civil nuclear power. But gas was temporarily cheap and the cost of electricity fell, causing the company to fail. The government had no choice but to step in. Nuclear installations were dangerous and decommissioning was expensive; without nuclear capacity the national grid could not keep the lights on, and nuclear was carbon-free. But at what cost? Successive energy ministers swore they would pay no subsidy so that nuclear, wind and the rest would compete fairly. But as with the banks, the hidden subsidies to nuclear included insurance: the taxpayer was liable for accidents and the long-term cost of storing nuclear waste, which no private insurer would ever cover. Enter

the Nuclear Decommissioning Authority, a giant new nationalized industry. Created in 2005, it owned nineteen sites: the
Magnox reactors still producing much of the UK's stand-by
electricity, research stations and the fuel handling and recycling
plant at Sellafield on Cumbria's glowing coast.

In 2007 the new authority reckoned it would need to spend
£73 billion over a century: decommissioning alone was going to
cost £61 billion at 2007 prices. The more realistic its assessment
of the decaying rods and the isolation pools, the higher the estimates went. Nuclear arithmetic was staggering: the authority cost
£1.4 billion a year. For the public it was out of sight, out of mind,
as long as something happened when they flicked the switch.

Labour had once been nuclear enthusiasts and so they became
again, but this time the magic of private capital would do the
trick. Companies would build ten new stations, the government
announced in 2009. Not in your backyard either. All were going
to be sited next to existing plants or in nuclear-friendly Cumbria.
The new stations would still meet only half the projected growth
in electricity demand. Labour left a large gap in the energy
accounts.

We would need less fuel if only we used less energy. Households
produced 15 per cent of UK carbon emissions. To discourage
them, ministers dreamt up initiatives, some imaginative, but too
many in penny packets, lacking a political thread to tie them
together. In his first budget Brown cut VAT on domestic fuel, to
redeem a manifesto pledge and soothe backbenchers demanding
help for the old and cold. The decision was joined to no wider
thinking about energy fairness or climate. But there were incentives to emit less carbon at home. The government cut VAT on
energy-saving materials, gave grants to landlords to improve efficiency, and built savings into its upgrading of social housing. It
invented the Warm Front scheme, paying up to £3500 to older
and poorer owner-occupiers in England, with variants in the
devolved administrations, to cut their use of energy. When we visited Beryl and Tom Comer in Gorton they were delighted at their
energy-saving conversion. 'I could hardly believe it. They came in
here, all paid by the government, and they lagged the loft and they

put in a new boiler too.' Schemes helped 635,000 households, cutting 40,000 tonnes of carbon in 2008–9 alone.

Road travel accounted for 22 per cent of carbon emissions. In the first flush of victory Prescott promised to get people out of cars and into buses and trains. He even had a long-term plan and brazenly claimed Treasury backing worth £140 billion for local buses, railways and roads. But his foreword to the grand plan failed to mention climate change at all.

The £140 billion was not forthcoming. It is hard, even in retrospect, to see where Labour's sundry plans for road and rail joined up. Transport policy and behaviour went on as usual. Road traffic increased by 87 per cent in Great Britain between 1980 and 2007. Most of this growth occurred between 1980 and 1990; Labour oversaw a rise of 67 billion vehicle kilometres in the ten years after 1997.

Blair was bored: in his briefing to MPs after a decade in power, he gave transport less space than the arts or Africa. His interest, chilled to zero after the 2000 lorry blockade, was defensive. In opposition Blair had sought to make Labour the driver's pal, a party white van man might vote for. In March 2007 the prime minister invited Richard Hammond of *Top Gear* to Number Ten. 'The amazing thing is that there are six million more cars on the road since we came to office, and over the next 20 years there are going to be I don't know how many millions more.' It sounded like breathless wish fulfilment.

Car users knew the carbon score: in 2009, 42 per cent of the public said cars were a principal cause of climate-changing emissions. But the government, like its predecessors, accommodated them by building roads, including an extra lane on the most heavily used section of the M1. Traffic started rolling on a new stretch of toll road looping round Birmingham, started under John Major, in December 2003. In 2009 the government stepped in when private financing of the £1.25 billion widening of the M25 fell apart. Fuel duty did rise over Labour's tenure, despite the lorry protests – by 11 per cent in real terms. But factoring in other taxes, insurance and the rest, the cost of motoring fell by 13 per cent.

Climate and environment

It might have risen if Labour nationally had followed Labour locally on pricing the use of roads. The 2000 Transport Act gave councils the same power to charge for road use that London's new government had: any revenues produced had to be spent on public transport. But when pro-charging Ken Livingstone declared himself a candidate for London mayor, the official Labour candidate Frank Dobson (following the Number Ten line) did a swerving volte-face and took against congestion charging. Blair emphasized the risks of using the very powers his government had introduced. Once the London congestion charge worked, he changed his mind. By then precious momentum had been lost. Votes on charging schemes came and went in Manchester and Edinburgh where, in a welter of local circumstances, residents rejected opportunities to reconcile urban living with reduced emissions.

At least roads were safer. The downward trend in accidents continued. One thousand fewer people died on the roads each year when Labour left office compared with the mid 1990s. UK roads were, with Sweden's, among the safest in the world – though 572 pedestrians still died on them in 2008, a quarter of all road deaths and a growing proportion of road casualties as the safety of drivers and passengers in cars improved. Roads remained the biggest cause of death of 12–16-year-olds, thanks in part to a campaign against speed cameras by the *Daily Mail*. Government banned driving while using a mobile phone in December 2003. Much grumbling, much evasion, but here, like seatbelts, was a law that enforced something most people knew was right.

Car journeys might be rising in number but Labour tried to make them greener. They manipulated vehicle excise duty to favour lorries and buses with cleaner engines, and from 2002 linked company-car tax to carbon output. Petrol companies were to source 5 per cent of forecourt sales from renewables from 2010 onwards. Towards the end, the government mustered enthusiasm for ultra-low and non-hydrocarbon vehicles, subsidizing manufacturers of electric cars and hybrids. Wrecked cars, meanwhile, were less visible. Responding to council complaints and public anger at wrecks on the streets, the government tightened the law on dumping.

Labour had said they wanted to see 10,000 miles of cycleways by 2005. Two-thirds of them would be tracks on existing roads, cheaper but unenticing for nervous new cyclists as traffic thundered close. Transport for London reported the number of cyclists up by 107 per cent on the capital's main roads since 2000. Six cycling 'demonstration towns', including Aylesbury, Brighton, Exeter and Derby, saw increases akin to London. But cycling's share of all trips was the same in 2008 as twelve years before, according to the Department of Transport, even if total distance travelled by bike did rise. The number of cyclists killed or seriously injured fell between 2000 and 2004, but rose again by 11 per cent between 2004 and 2007, prompting the 'Think!' advertising campaign to remind drivers to look out for bikes on their off-side.

Policy was thin. Ministers laughed at David Cameron's bike antics but since Blair had briefly mounted a bike for the cameras at the Amsterdam summit in 1997, he had rarely been seen on two wheels. The difficulty of getting bikes on trains showed the bane of transport policy was disconnections. Under Labour integration got nowhere, with buses, trains and planes separately owned and often competing. Nor could bikes accompany their owners on Eurostar, whose tunnel debacle just before Christmas 2009 illustrated the disproportionate attention media paid to rail travel for the relatively few. A triumph of the era was the redesigned St Pancras International station, but the huge public subsidy of railways was hard to justify on social equity grounds, or even as a push to growth or productivity.

Under Labour train journeys rose 40 per cent on the back of subsidies worth £4.5 billion a year. Yet outside London only small numbers used the railways for daily travel. Journeys were no more punctual: in 1996–7, 89 per cent of rail network trains arrived on time, falling to 78 per cent five years later, but climbing back to 90 per cent in 2008–9. Accidents fell to their lowest recorded level.

Labour came to power with no wish to unpick rail privatization.

Renationalization was too costly and, new ministers feared, too retro. Their faint-heartedness cost them and the public dear. Instead of public ownership we got a mish-mash of subsidies and arm's-length state involvement. A bad crash at Ladbroke Grove on the Paddington line in 1999, followed a year later by a derailment near Hatfield in October 2000, caused a safety panic. It offered a great opportunity, which Labour failed to seize. The private owner of the infrastructure, Railtrack, had brazenly boasted of driving down the costs of maintenance, and stories emerged of how those economies had led to untrained and unsupervised track engineers, shoddy repairs and missing nuts and bolts. In its place the Transport Department put another arm's-length body, Network Rail, supervised by a further arm's-length body, the Strategic Rail Authority (SRA). Within four years Labour changed their mind again and the Railways Act 2005 divided the SRA's work between Network Rail and the Department for Transport.

The tangle Labour inherited included 7–15-year franchises. Some worked, notably Chiltern, owned by the German nationalized railway Deutsche Bahn; notionally German taxpayers had responsibility for the trains arriving at St Marylebone. In autumn 2009 the government said a publicly owned company was to take over the East Coast rail franchise held by National Express. What this proved was that the state and the railways were indissolubly bound together. The government, with Network Rail, successfully modernized the West Coast Main Line. State subsidy (at least £8.6 billion) kept Virgin afloat. One result was to cut the fastest journey between Manchester and London by thirty-six minutes and from London to Glasgow by forty-two minutes.

But no sooner were the improvements made than experts muttered gloomily that even the upgraded West Coast line could not carry the traffic they were projecting for 2015 onwards. That was before the recession. The government had earlier pulled another big piece of UK infrastructure from the ashes of a collapsed Tory funding model and completed the fast link to Folkestone. Improved journey times gave Eurostar – even with its poor management – a fighting chance of commercial success. Labour bailed out London and Continental Railways, putting enough money in to secure completion of the second section of the fast link. The government set up High Speed Two to work out a new route northward, from London to Birmingham. That meant going through or under the Chilterns, posing the question to the homeowners and mainly Conservative-inclined councillors and MPs: were local or national interests foremost?

Like so much else, had Brown really put an end to bust, the sums might have come right. A taxpayer subsidy to the train operators of £811 million in 2006–7 was meant soon to become a repayment to the state of £326 million. The recession squashed that hope. Later, in the form of the nerdish Andrew Adonis – one of the few ministers who convinced the public of their passion for the job they had – a Labour transport secretary displayed strategic grasp, but got no nearer to settling what the scale of subsidy was going to be. What was the benefit of knocking an hour off journey times? And who benefited? Government thinking was shaped by the CBI. Business demanded easier journeys to Heathrow, and Labour agreed a huge gift of public money to waft the panjandrums from the City and Canary Wharf under the London traffic. In 2007, 307,000 people worked in the City of London and 103,000 at Canary Wharf: an extraordinary amount of construction was devoted to meeting their travel requirements over the years, the Docklands Light Railway included. Now the government projected a new railway line, Crossrail, at a cost of £16 billion.

If the City slickers did not get Crossrail, they would have to rub shoulders with the hordes on the Central Line. The Treasury praised London as the motor of UK economic growth but put tight limits on the corollary: the investment needed to sustain transport in the capital. Labour gave London its own government but then Brown refused London's transport authority any involvement in upgrading the Tube. Here, Professor Stephen Glaister of Imperial College noted, was 'a major policy developed not by the prime minister, not by the secretary of state for transport, not by the civil service, not by management consultants but by an ad hoc group of businessmen selected by a minister and against the considered policy of the board responsible for running the Underground'.

The government said a public–private partnership (PPP) would deliver munificently; in the 1998 spending review Brown even claimed it would remove the need for public subsidy from 2001 onwards. The scale of that delusion is still hard to comprehend. Perhaps ministers did not understand complex procurements. Brown had a banker to advise him, which may be part of the explanation: later we saw how little bankers understood their own business, let alone anyone else's. Blair called for the contracts, spreading them out on a table at Chequers, drawing on his barrister's training to figure out the clauses himself.

He gave up. The scheme went ahead, the Tube works divided between two consortia. In 2007 the inevitable happened. One of them, Metronet, announced it could not go ahead on the contracted terms and demanded more money. Its collapse cost the taxpayer between £170 million and £410 million, the NAO said. And, to make the original Brown foot-stamping even more ridiculous, Transport for London had to finance its half of the refurbishment by borrowing on the security of ticket income and grants from the government. The underground PPP was a disaster born of dogma and personal animosity towards Ken Livingstone.

Above ground, a bright light shone from the front of an old vehicle become fashionable, the tram. Long in gestation but boosted under Labour, tramways opened in Nottingham and from Birmingham to Wolverhampton, and were expanded in Manchester, with £600 million invested on new lines to Oldham and Rochdale. Late on, the government gave the council-owned Tyneside Metro a big funding boost, £580 million over eleven years. That was the plan at least. If the Magpies were to meet the Black Cats up or down their respective promotions and relegations, Geordies could travel from St James's Park to the Stadium of Light in Sunderland in upgraded rolling stock, run by a subsidiary of German state railways. But auditors worried about passenger numbers, well short of targets on the Midland Metro and the Sheffield Supertram, deflating revenues. Getting going took too long — four and half years for approval of an extension to the Leeds Supertram.

Labour extended concessions for older citizens on bus and train fares. In April 2003 men over sixty became entitled to local concessionary fare schemes, the same age as women. London's generous freedom pass was hugely popular. Poor Preston complained bitterly that, with one of Europe's largest bus stations where passengers transferred between routes in their thousands, it had to pick up large bills for concessionary fares calculated on where journeys began and ended. Cost-benefit analysis said buses deserved more public subsidy than rail. Four times more journeys were taken by bus, the less affluent used them and they were cheaper than trains, if less glamorous. But over the three years from 2005 bus subsidies amounted to a seventh of Network Rail's budget.

Still, buses and trains had this in common: the Tories had botched the job. Labour inherited chaotic deregulation of municipal buses. In the name of competition in towns outside London, buses queued up to poach customers. Some companies even put up rival stops. Privatization had deprived councils of the capacity to plan and coordinate. Labour responded timidly, as if their greatest fear was to be accused of state control even in an arena where regulation was essential and most services depended on municipal subsidies. Labour promised to cut the average age of buses to eight years and linked support payments to improved fuel efficiency. Councils got extra leverage to negotiate more 'quality contracts' with the bus companies, meaning they did not have to go with the cheapest. So much for competition: the bigger coach companies started eating up franchises and monopolizing services. The Office of Fair Trading later found that the big five operators, including Stagecoach and Arriva, were overcharging as they carved up territories. Such cities as Leeds, Aberdeen and Cardiff became the fiefdoms of a single company. The cost of bus and coach fares rose 17 per cent above inflation between 1997 and 2010.

London showed how successful an overarching public transport authority with power and money could be. Mayor Livingstone expanded the bus network and improved frequencies, spending the proceeds from his new congestion charge and then some. In the capital, Margaret Thatcher's silly adage about anyone over twenty-six using a bus being a failure was disproved: many more people of all social groups took to the bus. Use rose by a third in the five years from 2000. Labour was on course to meet its target of achieving 12 per cent growth in bus and light rail use in England by 2010, but only because the number of bus journeys was increasing in London (which accounted for 44 per cent of bus use in England). Elsewhere, bus use kept falling.

A 'carbon-conscious' government would have joined buses, cars and trains to land use, planning and housing, both the existing stock and homes yet to be built. Instead, Labour made only desultory efforts to decarbonize new housing. From 2007 stamp duty would not be payable on new dwellings worth up to half a million that had a zero carbon rating – a standard for the building materials and use of solar panels. Two years later only twenty-four homes hitting that target were sold.

On what households threw out, Labour made some progress. Here, again, it is too easy to blame the politicians. Households did not need government to tell them to recycle; consumers could insist on less packaging. Councils were often amenable: they could be lobbied and pressured, and the public told pollsters they believed they had much more influence locally than over national policy-makers. But environmental awareness remained patchy. The UK continued to send a higher proportion of municipal waste to landfill – 75 per cent – than most other EU member states, risking fines. Meeting EU targets implied a cut of 3.5 million tonnes in biodegradable waste sent to landfill by 2010, and a further 3.7 million tonnes by 2013. Councils were on course to miss the 2010 target by 270,000 tonnes, the waste produced by some 225,000 households. Labour increased the Tories' landfill tax, prompting anguished local debates about incinerators (one alternative) and outraged newspaper articles about pressure to recycle (the other alternative). The public typically wanted neither.

The government threatened to ban supermarket carrier bags, but the grocers claimed to have exceeded their own voluntary targets with a 40 per cent reduction in their environmental impact from 2007 to 2009.

Labour introduced a new tax on aggregates – the sand and gravel used in building – diverting some of the proceeds into a sustainability fund to pay for research on alternatives and recycling. Streets became a bit tidier. Keep Britain Tidy reckoned litter levels fell about 3 per cent from 2000 to 2010, with evidence that pavements were less polluted by both dog poo and gum. But it found more cigarette butts and increases in fast-food and drink litter. Against a general picture of 'overall improvement', with cleaner railway and bus stations, there was more rubbish on the roads.

Refuse and recycling were standard examples of why the twenty-first century should have been Labour's to command: they demanded not just close cooperation between the state and private interests, but substantial social investment which government alone would think of making. The model was not necessarily public ownership, but certainly close public supervision and regulation. Take water. Labour missed the political chance to make the case for closer state supervision and made no changes to the privatized regime inherited from the Tories. Water bills started to rise, to allow the companies to invest in reservoirs and pipes, but water companies still let many lavatories flush directly into the sea. Surfers off the Cornish coast took their health in their hands.

History demanded of Labour, as the legatee of years of under-investment in the public realm, that it make good and mend below ground as well as above. In 2000 in England and Wales, three million cubic metres of water leaked away every day, equivalent to half the average flow rate of the river Thames in London. Ofwat, the Office of Water Services, should have pressed the private suppliers to cut the amount, but it lacked data, auditors said. Companies had work to do on sewers, too. Private companies were unlikely to collaborate on a national grid for water, moving it between the haves and the dries, or to build the reservoirs needed if the government's own housing and expansion plans were to be feasible, especially in the South East.

Lack of water often sounded implausible. The Environment Agency improved its handling of floods and had plenty of practice. It managed rivers and, pushing up protection standards, offered reassurance to owners of the 2.4 million properties at risk of flooding. Auditors worried that the general condition of defences had not improved much after the 2000 floods, and spending did not reflect the flooding risks. In the downpours of summer 2007, the floodwaters rose, costing some £3.2 billion.

The Environment Agency was the giant quango belonging to the Department of Environment, Food and Rural Affairs, which in turn was descended from Maff, the Ministry of Agriculture, Fisheries and Food. Whitehall juggling said something about Labour's discomfort with the countryside, which often seemed a continuous source of trouble, from its landowners to its animal epidemics. Labour's instincts were those of the concerned townie, as they sought to civilize farms and improve the welfare of animals by setting minimum standards for housing and feeding hens, pigs and calves. They banned fur farming, and shooting in sensitive wetlands. In 2009, Helen Philips of Natural England said three-quarters of priority wildlife species were on track to recover, against half when the agency was formed from English Nature, the Countryside Agency and the Rural Development Service in 2006. Among recovering species were the polecat, large blue butterfly, sand lizard and bittern. No one blamed Labour, but the kittiwake, grey plover and red squirrel were nearing extinction and reports said the degradation of salt marshes continued and their bird populations declined.

In their braver early days, Labour did set out to confront landowners with their long-promised ban on hunting with dogs and an enactment of an equally long-standing right to ramble. The Countryside Alliance, formed to protect foxhunting, managed to persuade press and politicians that it stood for the mystical soul of England. In September 2004, 400,000 marchers filled London with green wellies and Barbour jackets, unnerving the government. The hunting ban paraded Old Labour atavism, some said. It also exposed New Labour's failure to complete the reform of the Lords by leaving a rump of reactionary aristocrats in place. Yet after the ban, the baying hounds went oddly quiet. Perhaps the pink-coats were finding ways around it, as they still turned up on the village green in their finery to down a stirrup cup or two.

Labour's own quango, the Commission for Rural Communities, struggled against such stereotyping, trying to make the case for more housing, better public transport and opportunities for young people. Its case was undermined by consistent polling (for example, the *Rural Insights* survey, published in March 2010) finding 'a contented and optimistic tone' predominant among rural residents.

Labour sincerely wanted more townies to enjoy the countryside and backed a new national trail through the Cotswolds. On coming into force in September 2004, the Countryside and Rights of Way Act made it legal to walk across 3200 square miles of open countryside. Like the minimum wage, this was an old commitment, a right to roam across upland England. These were good years for hikers. After fifty years of campaigning they were awarded what Tom Franklin, chief executive of the Ramblers, called 'a victory for everyone who walks in this island nation', in the Marine and Coastal Access Act 2009. The Act underwrote a path to run round England's coastland, and granted new powers to combat erosion, where, for example, in North Yorkshire the Cleveland Way was sliding into the sea. Delineating the path would rest on cooperation between Natural England, councils and landowners. Another quango, English Heritage, would have to agree to allow walkers in front of Osborne House on the Isle of Wight rather than shunting them off on a detour. If voluntary agreement failed after five years, then ministers could compel. Not to be outdone, the devolved governments of Scotland and Wales discussed coastal walking, too.

People did not have to go to the countryside or seaside to put one foot in front of another. One of the government's green strategies said all residents should have at least two hectares of 'quality green space' within 500 metres of where they lived. Public health would become pleasure. People who lived more than a mile from a park or green space were less active and more likely to be overweight or obese. In response, the Walking for Health Initiative enrolled 37,000 volunteer walk leaders and *Walk* magazine reported in late 2009 that 32,000 people were taking part each week.

Farmers now accepted that walkers were not just a commercial opportunity but truer friends of the countryside than the industrial magnates in their midst. Subsidies traditionally went to the big arable farmers rather than to tenants on the hillsides whose dry-stone walling, hedging and ditching preserved the countryside that urban dwellers wanted for their recreation. Labour kept to the long-term UK script in Brussels negotiations on the Common Agricultural Policy and the EU inched away from subsidizing food towards paying to protect rural ways of life. Farmers got their dole through the Rural Payments Agency, set up to run the new grants introduced in 2005. In a notorious sequence, it successively underpaid them, then overpaid them, then failed to reclaim the excess. No civil service heads rolled.

Labour created new national parks for the New Forest and part of the South Downs, with an extra 30,000 hectares classified as green belt. Tracts of the Midlands were mapped out as the future National Forest. Urban hedges became a source of rows between neighbours, so the Anti-Social Behaviour Act 2003 empowered local authorities to take strimmers to fast-growing high hedges and monster leylandii.

The NAO praised the environment department for its work in eradicating pests of the animal kind although outbreaks were rising: from an average of 150 a year over the period 1993 to 2000 to more than 370 in 2002. Many were imported. Mad cow disease, a legacy of the Major years, petered out. When a committee of inquiry under Lord Phillips reported in October 2000, Labour's response was a new regulator, the Food Standards Agency. Food simmered away during these years: its price, quality, sustainability, security of supply and questions about the human cost of food production. After migrant Chinese cockle pickers drowned in Morecambe Bay in 2004, the government moved to regulate agricultural gangmasters through a new licensing authority. As with energy, the needs of the planet and anxiety about national vulnerability came together. The government urged farmers and householders to grow more produce at home and allotments became fashionable. One in three people in the UK purportedly grew fruit and vegetables and if more did it would 'foster community spirit'. This was naive. Food was an industry where giant retailers were robber barons. In Boston in Lincolnshire, huge packing sheds daily received lorry-loads of world produce to be packed and trans-shipped inside and outside the UK, eating up millions of carbon miles.

Vets confirmed foot-and-mouth at an Essex abattoir in February 2001, but not until fifty-seven farms had already been infected. Only by September that year was the last case destroyed, on an Appleby farm, after six million animals had been slaughtered and burned on stinking pyres. The outbreak cost the public £3 billion and private firms, including bed and breakfasts in areas forsaken by tourists, over £5 billion. Mobilization was impressive and by mid-April 2001, at the height of the crisis, more than 10,000 vets, soldiers and field and support staff, assisted by thousands more contractors, were fighting the disease. The NAO complimented Maff for containing the disease, keeping it out of much of East Anglia, the East Midlands, southern England, west Wales and central and northern Scotland, protecting big tracts of dairy and pig rearing.

The government approved field trials of genetically modified crops, and on cloning and at the new frontiers of bioethics, Labour ministers underpinned the UK's reputation as a place to perform properly regulated experiments. While urging the use of fewer animals in laboratory testing, the government took strong action against animal activist raiders.

So, we can give Labour credit for making Britain a bit tidier and greener, easier to walk over. Voluntary bodies such as the Royal Society for the Protection of Birds were vital, but protecting species depended ultimately on regulation and the work of such quangos as Natural England. But the fate of species depends on climate change, and so Labour's reputation has to stand or fall on carbon. The government's priority was to keep the home fires burning and pray that future miracles of coal carbon capture might work. And yet progress was made: the Centre for Economic Performance said the Climate Change Act had 'created a sensible overarching framework'.

The charge is that ministers did not confront people with the hard choices still to come, such as fewer jets, dim lights, less consumption and higher taxes. The mitigation is that people could work all those out for themselves, and their responses to pollsters suggested they were mostly in denial, in their behaviour, if not about climate science. If Labour gravely disappointed such prophets as Franny Armstrong, the director of *Age of Stupid*, and the *Guardian*'s George Monbiot, they in turn had no convincing politics, no strategy to move opinion, let alone popular behaviour. Labour's green garment was a thing of shreds and patches, but this was still a government a little way ahead of the people. Polls showed people were concerned (76 per cent in 2009) but not that concerned, and climate change was one of the top three issues facing the country for only 24 per cent. Compare the few news-bulletin clips of climate activists scaling power-station chimneys with the attention paid to British Airways strikes.

For climate change activists, for ministers and for those British people who did believe the scientific consensus, the popular politics of climate change were frustratingly 'not just yet'. Growth, jobs, freedom of the road and the fun of flying all took precedence. The sound of Jeremy Clarkson at full throttle and a nation of drivers behind him echoed through Labour's years. Summit heroics at Gleneagles and Copenhagen aside, the government offered faint domestic leadership, neither in rhetoric nor in ministerial lifestyles. No symbolic wind turbine on the hills overlooked Chequers; instead, Labour leaders indulged in a version of denial. When in 2004 the chief scientist, Sir David King, declared that climate change was a more serious threat than terrorism, Downing Street forced him back to the *Today* programme to recant. A nasty, immediate but small-scale risk from fundamentalist bombers trumped the distant, invisible but total global threat of temperature rise.

Woking's verdict

Nothing about Woking would suggest it was on the green front line. In *The Deeper Meaning of Liff* Douglas Adams defined 'Woking' as 'standing in the kitchen wondering what you came in here for'. But the Surrey dormitory town, twenty-three miles from Charing Cross, put itself in the environmental vanguard. It stands as an example of what was possible, given the political will – in Woking's case, the will of a coalition of Tory and Liberal Democrat councillors.

'Thinking Globally, Acting Locally' had been the town slogan for several years. Step out of the train station and you saw it right away. Above it, a vast new glass canopy covered in solar panels channelled energy into Woking's independent energy grid. Cycling round the town on its exceptional 'cycle motorway', you could see the panels on council-owned buildings, rainwater collected into butts for recycling.

By 2010 Woking Borough Council had cut its energy bill by 28 per cent, on the Kyoto 1990 baseline, and carbon emissions by 55 per cent. It was drawing 60 per cent of its energy from its own sustainable generation company and 11 per cent from renewables. (This had temporarily dipped to 2 per cent in 2009 when a solar system installed by outside contractors failed.) The council supported Cycle Woking, handing out breakfast baps to cyclists on their way to work and school as an incentive. Woking was one of Labour's six national cycling demonstration projects, one aim of which was to see every child pass a cycling test. Separately, a Woking car club aimed to cut car ownership. The town's streetlights are renewable-powered.

Woking is far from being a green paradise, but the sense of collective commitment is infectious. The town started down the green path before Labour came to power, after the Rio Earth summit of 1992. First concerns were about saving money by cutting civic energy bills. Things took off in 1999 with the creation of Thameswey, an energy company owned by the council but free to operate at arm's length. It was the vision of a dynamic council chief executive, supported by a group of Tory and Liberal Democrat councillors.

It in turn part owns Thameswey Energy, in a joint venture with a Danish company, which launched a combined heat and power (CHP) station on commercial lines. Its electricity output is distributed by its own private wires, with heat and chilled water delivered by its own pipes to all the council's buildings. It sells energy to the Holiday Inn, shops and a conference centre. Thameswey Energy went on to open other CHP plants to provide energy to housing estates, care homes and private firms and had won commissions from other councils, such as Milton Keynes.

Asked about Labour, Thameswey's director John Thorp was scathing. A burly, cigarette-smoking environmental enthusiast, he started life as a marine engineer. He had been a prime mover in Woking's green policies. Watching commercial building in the borough, he got indignant at the government allowing such poor energy standards. Why so few obligations on developers? 'They should be paying towards the extra cost of joining up to local CHP systems, selling their new homes as cheaper on energy.' He wanted more 'polluter pays' fees added to all new development to give an incentive to build in energy efficiency. 'District heating systems could have been encouraged,' he said. He saw the government caving in to the construction industry. Regulate us and we won't build, the housebuilders threatened, but they didn't build anyway. Instead of preparing for climate change, Labour relaxed building regulations in 2002 and allowed jerry-built low-specification homes without basic insulation and energy saving – no cavity walls, no loft insulation. Home extensions were exempt altogether. 'People could add on rooms and conservatories with absolutely no double glazing or energy efficiency,' he complained. As for energy policy, 'the government did five u-turns on installing smart electric meters in all homes, although they make a real difference when people can see their energy use. Finally they are coming in, but far too late. That was pressure from the energy companies that didn't want to bear the cost.'

Thameswey supported an initiative called Actio2n Woking which promoted more efficient domestic energy use, and which had been running an advice shop in the town centre. In the first six months of a scheme launched in September 2009, 3 per cent of Woking's 34,000 households committed to follow fifty energy-saving steps. Kenton Keys, the project manager, said: 'These are mostly rich people in Woking, so we don't need to give grants. It's the rich who put out the most CO_2, so it makes sense to target them. We persuade them of the savings they can make as well as the CO_2 cuts, if they install things in a logical order. Lofts and walls first – though often they've spent a fortune on double-glazing that does less. They are afraid of cowboys, so we have recommended installers.'

He unlocked the door to Oak Tree House with obvious pride. This show house in the Knaphill district of Woking was a typical 1940s square box, a red-brick detached house with garden. But everything conceivable had been done to save energy and water. It had cost £30,000 to modify, 'But that's a price many Woking people can afford, if they do it over a few years, one thing at a time,' Keys observed. Over the back garden wall was a new estate. Most homes, at affordable rents, had been built by the council's arm's-length company, which paid for them by building and selling some grand executive homes, also built to zero-carbon standards.

Keys showed off the LED lights in the kitchen, examples of the bright but expensive new generation of bulbs costing £20 each, cold to the touch, using just seven watts of electricity but shining like 150. In the sitting room the flat-screen television was not plasma – outrageously high energy use – but again LED technology. The water was metered and the taps adapted to use less without losing pressure; water saved from the roof flushed the toilet and filled the washing machine. On the roof was an array of solar panels: 'The good news is that at last the government is setting a feed-in tariff that makes solar panels worthwhile, generating around 30 per cent for a typical home. It used to take twenty-five years to get back the money you spent, now it will be ten to twelve years. If energy prices rise, it'll be less. You feed energy in during the day when the sun's out and everyone's out so the house is using no electricity, cutting the bills on what you use at night.'

Permeable paving in the garden and on the front drive allowed rainwater to seep through, since heavily paved urban Woking has been subject to flash flooding when torrential rain cascaded into overflowing drains. Climate change means there may be more of that. The garden had a lawn planted with special grass that needed little cutting or water, and with sustainable drought plants that like the dry. Preparing for worse to come is part of Woking's climate message.

The project is impressive. Keys and Actio2n Woking are part of the Sustainable Energy Academy, which promotes energy-efficient methods and links pioneers. But it is slow going. And how much of a bridgehead to the future is a comfortable Surrey town? Probably 20 per cent of the electorate were passionately in favour of the green policy, 60 per cent passively accepting and 20 per cent noisily against. Innovations had faced opposition, scepticism and downright climate denial. In 2010 the Tories had a majority on the council and some of their members were sceptical, one resigning from the party to become an anti-climate-change independent. Council-owned car parks were fitted with technology that could charge gas-guzzling vehicles more, but vociferous opposition prevented its use. The local paper, typically desperate for dwindling readers, looked for angles to create sensation. The solar canopy over the Woking railway station entrance was a 'scandal' when costs overran. The programme's political supporters had toughed it out so far. But if Woking put Labour to shame with its dynamism, it also illustrated both political pitfalls and the sheer slog of mobilizing the public. Is '60 per cent passively accepting' ever going to be enough?

PART FOUR

Home and Abroad

CHAPTER 10

Constituting Britain

Despite being the party of strong, interventionist government, Labour had never been entirely comfortable with the state and its powers. They went into the 2010 election accused of oppression and the subversion of liberty and good order. But Labour also modernized and innovated, creating a supreme court and bringing in freedom of information and statutory human rights. The record is not coherent; Labour had no 'philosophy'. They made permanent changes to the constitution, such as devolution. They also worried at but came nowhere near resolving such long-standing questions as people's alienation from civic life and non-participation. Labour left a legacy of unfinished business over the House of Lords, England's place within the UK and unfair voting for the House of Commons.

By the end of Labour's term, politics was in a rumbling and grumbling state. The reason was partly just having been in power for so long. The May 2010 election calmed nerves. Outrage about the duck islands, moats and bath plugs was real enough but much of the fuss over MPs' expenses was evanescent panic and media hoopla. Polls showed people retained confidence though only 65 per cent of registered voters cast a ballot, and 3.5 million adults were not even on the register.

In 1997, 71 per cent of electors had turned out. Labour won 43 per cent of their votes, which meant they gained two-thirds of

Commons seats from the support of less than a third of the electorate. In 2001, only a quarter of those eligible to vote chose Labour and by 2005 that had shrunk to just over a fifth. A far bigger scandal than expenses was the lack of popular support for the all-powerful governments that whipped MPs through the lobbies.

For all Blair's early personal popularity, May 1997's enthusiasm soon collapsed into sour disaffection. The climate had started turning against politics in the 1980s. The media, newspapers themselves caught up in a circulation and advertising revenues hurricane, tried to ingratiate themselves by sporting ever louder contempt of politicians. Fair-weather members of the Labour Party who joined in the run-up to 1997 soon departed. Iraq dispatched many who had gladly weathered rain and storm. By 2005 only 1.3 per cent of the population belonged to any political party, one of the lowest rates in the EU.

Fair voting at Westminster would not have cured apathy, but it would have made politics more honest by ensuring that the number of MPs elected was proportionate to votes cast. Labour grasped the principle, insisting on fairer voting for the new parliament in Edinburgh, for the assemblies in Cardiff and Belfast, for the Greater London Authority and for their own abortive regional assemblies in England. But Blair flinched at the one reform that would stop a party ever again getting twice as many Commons seats as the next party, despite winning only three percentage points more of the popular vote, as Labour did in 2005. Blair the colossus, the man whose personal conviction carried party and country to wage war on Baghdad, bottled when confronted with his own tribalists. How meekly he killed the workable scheme for voting reform he had commissioned from Roy Jenkins – an alternative vote, choosing candidates in order of preference, topped up by a party list that would make the result considerably more proportional while keeping a constituency link. Breathing their last gasp, Labour finally proposed a referendum on the alternative vote – electors putting one, two or three against a list of parliamentary candidates. Announced with a flourish by Gordon Brown in his final party conference speech in 2009, he gave this most timid of reforms so little priority that it never completed its passage through parliament before his time was up. At least, in the unforeseen circumstances of the post-election negotiations between the parties, fairer voting loomed larger than it might otherwise have done.

Labour created an elections quango, the Electoral Commission, which failed to do much more than bleat about antiquated voting methods, failed to push reform of party funding and added little to hand-wringing debate about declining participation. The government lowered the minimum age for standing as a candidate to eighteen and made postal voting easier; electoral fraud increased, notably in Asian areas. People did like to vote, at least in *Britain's Got Talent* and *Big Brother* plebiscites. But the question was how to confront our yes–no button-punching temperament with the complexities of twenty-first-century decision-making.

Labour believed in giving people more opportunities to vote, but people were not sure they wanted to. Londoners half-heartedly said yes to a mayor and assembly. Geordies disengaged, disappointing John Prescott by voting down his plan for elected regional assemblies: the North East was regarded as the most likely to seize a chance to define its regional identity, but contempt for yet more bureaucracy and a new cadre of politicians won the day. Elsewhere public indifference was deafening. What were these 'regions' anyway, when Tewkesbury, at the tip of the South-West, was nearer York than Penzance? If ministers were accused of control freakery, they also showed absurd enthusiasm for democracy. Brown, despite his earlier opposition to NHS foundation trusts, talked up the opportunity for participation awaiting the three million who would in theory be allowed to vote for their governors, if – as he hoped – the number of foundation trusts were to double. Voting was seen as a solution to deeper problems, or sometimes as a displacement activity.

Neither foundation trusts nor the private finance initiative had anything to do with the 'constitution' as conventionally defined but Labour, unwittingly, stumbled into a wider debate about power, public services and procedure – and left office with most of the questions unanswered. Was there an unslaked popular thirst for less formal participation, as Blears and David Miliband believed? How consciously did Labour foment mistrust in representative politics as the forum for resolving disputes between interest groups, and sanction a shift to the courts for redress and retribution? The Supreme Court may come to tilt the balance further from parliament, for faith in the law grew stronger, amid demands for judicial reviews of government action and independent inquiries.

Labour's formal changes to the constitution prodded Professor Peter Hennessy to compare their scope with what happened after 1688. From Bank of England independence to devolution and the Human Rights Act, the government reconfigured the landscape, even if it 'could never quite weave a convincing tale. It knitted no pattern to its patchwork. You have to ask,' Hennessy wondered, 'why this extraordinary enterprise lacked the central position it deserved in the self-image of this most image-conscious of administrations.' Labour had, without stating it as a purpose, given the UK a written constitution.

The Human Rights Act (HRA) stiffened the senior judiciary's sense of its own worth. Lord Steyn said the new Supreme Court, sitting at the revamped Middlesex Guildhall from 2009, might now 'consider a constitutional fundamental which even a sovereign parliament acting at the behest of a complaisant House of Commons cannot abolish' – the judges' duty to strike down parliamentary statutes that affronted basic rights. But such a constitutional 'moment of truth' did not dawn on Labour's watch. Another distinguished judge, Stephen Sedley, said the old British empiricism that had muddled through since 1688 still ruled OK. The judges behaved with restraint in their constitutional pronouncements and forsook the opportunity given them by parliament's decrepit state.

Enshrining the European Convention on Human Rights in UK law in 1998 fulfilled a long-standing promise. Over the years more and more litigants dissatisfied with national courts made the legal pilgrimage to Strasbourg and the European Court of Human Rights. Jurisprudence and public sentiment were moving in the same direction across the West, and many in the east and south caught the wind: humans have inalienable freedoms and rights. Tibetans, Iraqi civilians, UK asylum-seekers were all potential beneficiaries of the new wave; it was bound to break over twenty-first-century UK government whichever party was in power.

But was the new wave philosophically individualist, putting the interests of the collective and the state second? The Court of Appeal rejected a claim by Northern Rock shareholders, nationalized in February 2008, that their human rights had been injured, but even mounting the case was indicative. We interviewed Jack Straw, then Home Secretary, as the Act passed. He was aware of the problem, but did not think through the consequences. When the judges later bit them over terrorism and asylum, ministers seemed surprised. Critics said suspending habeas corpus betrayed the government's carelessness about the most fundamental rights that the UK was simultaneously so eager to promote in Afghanistan and Iraq. The judges, usually cautious, also used the HRA to fix a right to privacy in cases involving Naomi Campbell and Max Mosley. Government and public had black-and-white notions of security yet were uncertain when a right to protection against something became an entitlement to a service or benefit. The HRA and the judges were confused too. How could the statute give a Somali migrant a right to a council house? Could you have a claim on something that elected representatives had built, after complex decisions about tax, spending and need? The public, egged on by the media, were aghast: 'rights' offended embedded ideas of fairness. But the public were also dead keen on their own rights in context.

Labour mishandled the politics, reacting petulantly to adverse judicial decisions under the HRA and blankly refusing to explain to an increasingly hostile public the teasing ambiguities at the heart of the enterprise. The Equalities and Human Rights Commission's purposes were vaguely specified, disappointing those who hoped for more enlightenment over the balance between competing rights (gender vs. religion) and between fundamentals and contingent claims on spending (such as disabled access ramps).

Looking around at the signs and symbols of British statehood, you could hardly call Labour radical and reforming. Elizabeth R slept safely in her bed. Once Tony had saved the day, the monarchy relapsed into its pre-Diana torpor. Labour were loyally monarchist, even when (as a Freedom of Information request showed) ministers were bombarded by letters from an eccentric heir to the throne with too little to do.

Labour barely disturbed the old English establishment; but they did view one of its buttresses with indifference bordering on disdain. The three cabinet secretaries departing during Labour's tenure were critical of their ministers. Andrew Turnbull, cabinet secretary from 2001 to 2005, even abused convention by calling Gordon Brown a Stalinist (his attack coming only after he was safely possessed of peerage and pension); he then demonstrated his political neutrality by becoming an adviser to David Cameron. With the civil service, ministers were in general correct and relations functional. Some worked enthusiastically together – for example, Blunkett with his permanent secretary Sir Michael Bichard. But in general Labour were unimpressed by Whitehall, so the feeling was mutual. Labour did pass legislation giving the civil service statutory protections, and issued the first code setting out ethical obligations for ministers.

Yet Labour office-holders were amateur. A bid to give ministers training flopped. Retired mandarins launched broadsides against Labour's binge style of government, vomiting out legislation and, so they claimed, failing to listen to sage advice. Blair and Brown treated government as a playground. Trade and industry had a dozen secretaries of state and changed its name three times. Nine different secretaries of state ran social security and pensions in thirteen years.

'Prerogative' gave the executive wide discretion unbound by rules or parliamentary inspection and Labour revelled in it. Blair's control centre was the sofa in his den, relying on small groups of advisers; Brown was even more hermetic. But style mattered only if it excluded expertise or advice, which, if listened to, would have set Labour on a better course. The civil service covers up the quality and pertinence of its advice, so we do not know how big a part officials played in Labour missteps. The world had grown more complex. The Phillips report on BSE exposed the limits of the civil service mindset. Whitehall had too few experts, only one psychologist and a handful of engineers, and locked its scientists in a ghetto. Departments had to be dragged into appointing professional finance directors. Turnbull could boast unashamedly that he had never had a day's training in his career.

That picture changed, but less than it should have done. The government added performance and strategy units to fill the gaps. Their thinking was often first-rate, but implementation was something else. In new 'public service agreement' contracts the Treasury and Number Ten pushed departments, agencies and local authorities to reach specified targets. Attacked for being over-precise, PSAs made government more transparent even if the public never had much idea what they covered. Ministers were often naive, thinking that a Whitehall edict would translate seamlessly into improved services on the public doorstep.

Blair invented the Number Ten Delivery Unit. From the account by its head, Sir Michael Barber, its favoured method of delivering was to phone up chief constables and berate them because muggings were up in their area; Labour never seemed to realize the far-flung nature of public services, bobbies and nurses and teachers working at the end of a complex 'delivery chain'. In fact it was more a leaky Thames Water pipe, out of which money leached on its way to the front line. Labour discovered mandarins did not do delivery, the tricky business of joining together centre and periphery. Thwarted, they resorted to envoys and tsars to deliver on drugs, e-government, homelessness and cancer. Running the rough sleepers' unit and later the respect agenda, a former charity worker turned civil servant, Louise Casey, behaved like Ivan the Terrible, her critics said. He was the kind of tsar Blair had in mind.

Labour over-governed. Unwilling to confront civil service inadequacy (which in turn would have meant asking searching questions about parliament and ministers, their role and capacity) and plan long-lasting changes, Labour resorted to quick fixes, more targets, quangos and arm's-length bodies devoted to special tasks. Their ranks included such big spenders as Network Rail, the Olympic Delivery Authority and the Environment Agency. At arm's length, they became less accountable and some started paying their chief executives huge sums. But some of Labour's creations represented a valid attempt to use arm's-length bodies to handle sensitive matters. They created an autonomous commission to oversee the ONS, as ministers relinquished control of when, or in what form, numbers were presented. Before the 2010 election, the Tories also discovered the UK Statistics Authority would not tolerate abuse when its chair, Sir Michael Scholar, reprimanded them for using misleading figures to claim that violent crime had risen.

At the end of 2009 the Cabinet Office said public bodies were 10 per cent fewer than in 1997, but its census was selective and missed the multitude of quasi-autonomous committees Labour had created. At one stage, Newcastle upon Tyne had bagged a health action zone, an education action zone, a project under the Better Government for Older People, a New Deal for Communities and a Sure Start pilot. They were not cheap: for every £6.73 spent on schools in education action zones £1 went on administration. It suited Labour's enemies to exaggerate 'bureaucracy', but managerial excess was unquestionably part of its package.

Another result of Labour's dusty view of the civil service as unimaginative and unknowing, as well as error-prone, was to employ sympathetic advisers. Spending on a gaggle in Downing Street and a couple for each secretary of state rose from £1.9 million under the Tories before 1997 to £4 million a year. The media sneered at the special advisers, but a new code of practice soon regulated what they did. If their contribution to policy was unclear and the role of Brown's character assassins unwelcome, in general special advisers made government more open, giving journalists and others far more access to ministerial thinking than official press officers ever could. Yet press officer numbers grew too, along with government advertising through the Central Office of Information, where spending rose from £59 million in 1998 to £232 million in 2009 on messages about swine flu, obesity and cutting smoking.

A good guide to a government's reforming intent in matters of state is how far it lays its hands on the law. Margaret Thatcher had talked big, but delivered little. Labour's first Lord Chancellor was the equivocal figure of Lord Irvine of Lairg, formerly barrister Blair's boss. He was a reformer but also had a soft spot for the hats, garters, breeches and – to the newspaper diarists' delight – wallpaper of his ancient office. One of his first reforms had unseen consequences. In 1999 the government abolished legal aid for personal injury cases and instead allowed 'no win no fee' suits. Lawyers started chasing ambulances, bringing trivial but hard to defend slip-and-trip suits against councils, forcing youth adventure centres, riding and canoe schools to become over-cautious. The Health and Safety Executive was unfairly blamed for local authorities' hyper-anxiety not to be sued by these new freebooting lawyers.

Irvine and Lord Woolf, Lord Chief Justice from 2000, welcomed the impact of the Human Rights Act on judges' training and culture, but the legal profession remained immune to modernization and as expensive as ever. Although worried by the rising cost of legal aid, the government stopped short of examining lawyers' training and restrictive practices, such as the preferment of certain barristers as QCs, access to training and discrimination against solicitors. The UK spent more on legal aid than other EU countries and rates were frozen for a decade, leading to complaints by the Law Society that its members would be less willing to do benefits and mental health cases.

Long-overdue modernization got going, as computers started appearing (at vast cost) in magistrates' courts. In 2004, the first woman law lord, Baroness Brenda Hale, joined more ethnic-minority JPs in a slightly more diverse legal system. Despised solicitors got to argue cases in the higher courts and the first of that crossbreed was appointed to the Court of Appeal. But the government did not pursue more radical ideas about giving non-lawyers a bigger role in adjudication and home sales.

When Blair and Blunkett wanted to unclog courts and speed up asylum processing, Irvine stood in the way, arguing rights and procedure. What followed was an example of allowing pressing but temporary political problems to dictate big institutional reforms that might have benefited from cautious appraisal. To get rid of Irvine, Blair decided overnight to abolish the post of Lord Chancellor. To be sure, it was a bizarre anomaly; he had a silver-buckled foot in each of the three ostensibly separate branches of government: Cabinet, courts and the Lords. But on appointing his old Scottish flatmate and fellow barrister, Charlie Falconer, as secretary of state for a new Department of Constitutional Affairs, Blair discovered the post could not be deleted without primary legislation. Hastily, for lack of a Speaker in the Lords, he sent the hapless Falconer off in garters to sit on the Woolsack. It took the Constitutional Reform Act 2006 to sort it all out. Peers got a new chair for debates (Lord Speaker with costume and upholstered seat); the Lord Chief Justice sat atop the judiciary with an independent commission to appoint judges; and a cabinet minister (still occasionally wearing the Lord Chancellor's gear) was responsible for courts and prisons, probation and sentencing in the new Ministry of Justice. Labour's uncompleted business was personified by the new Tory justice secretary, Ken Clarke, parading to the courts in 2010 in the same silver buckles and a full-bottomed wig.

Labour's impatience with ancient ways was commendable, but spasmodic. Where was the narrative when the government expressed its lack of faith in juries? The Criminal Justice Act 2003 allowed trial by a judge sitting alone where jury tampering was feared and in complex fraud cases, but it was not conjoined – in the tale Labour might have told – with, for example, the new rules it introduced, from April 1999, to make civil courts quicker and more proportionate in how they allocated their time and energies to cases. Coroners' courts, a medieval hold-over, bit back against Labour reforms, and coroners led protracted investigations into deaths that occurred abroad, including those of the Princess of Wales and service personnel killed in Afghanistan.

Any story Labour might have told about ridding the ancient building of its crenellations and porticos and making over the habitation in twenty-first-century style lost whatever plausibility it might have had at Black Rod's gate. Its parliamentary reforms were partial, incomplete and too late to head off the storm over MPs' expenses.

After thirteen years Labour more or less rid the UK of government by ermine-clad aristos, even if ninety-two clung on, like zombies terrorizing democracy from beyond the grave. In the Lords, Labour created an extraordinary franchise: after one of the remaining hereditaries died, the others refilled the vacancy by picking someone from Burke's Peerage. Labour created an independent appointments commission to nominate new unaffiliated cross-bench peers – 'people's peers' — most of whom were eminent establishmentarians who disappeared straight into anonymity in those gloomy corridors, never to surface again. The man chosen to chair this commission exemplified its in-group status – Lord (Dennis) Stevenson, chair of one of the mighty banks, HBOS, which overpaid its executives, contracted unpayable debt then went bust. One of the first peers selected under this new arrangement was Elspeth Howe, married to a knight (the former Tory chancellor Geoffrey Howe) who himself had been elevated to the Lords . . . once, twice, three times a lady. Twenty-six bishops sat on in what became a more bolshie second chamber, tending the Tory way on social issues.

February 2003 saw the nadir of reforming efforts when – instead of focusing on the forthcoming war in Iraq – MPs marched in and out of division lobbies on a string of mutually contradictory plans for the upper house, elected, part-elected, non-elected. The Lords, not inclined to be turkeys, voted of course for the all-appointed option, believing themselves to be the wisest and best of all possible second chambers. 'It is important to decide what the Lords is for,' said Falconer, 'and what it should contribute to the parliamentary process.' Indeed. The

Labour government never did and in 2010 walked away like a bankrupt construction company from a half-finished building site.

Labour's reforms of the House of Commons were superficial and dodged the 'existential question'. Ministers and MPs were unsure what the principal task of the 646 MPs was – to inspect and chivvy the executive, pass good law or take up constituents' complaints? Over four-fifths of the 1997 intake had said their priority was 'being a good constituency member', and half the 2005 intake spent half their time as MPs on constituency work. Labour were reluctant to probe the consequences, such as giving MPs more support for their surgeries, or what this attitude meant for MPs' capacity to scrutinize complex legislation. Overall, Labour were conservative when it came to parliamentary procedure. A huge effort, led by women MPs, secured small changes in absurd voting hours and some were later reversed. A modernization effort of sorts produced better timetabling of bills, and prime minister's questions was repackaged from twice a week into one longer session. From July 2002 Blair agreed to allow the liaison committee of chairs of the select committees to grill him. Earlier scrutiny was possible now bills appeared in draft. The idiocy of having to raise a top hat to make a point of order during voting was abolished.

But MPs could not even control who sat on and chaired their own select committees. Only in February 2010, after the expenses scandal, did MPs propose they should have the right to select by secret ballot the chairs and members of committees and control at least 40 per cent of the Commons timetable. Patronage and punishment by the whips kept them in thrall. The Public Accounts Committee, with the brainpower of the NAO at its service, behaved more like a clique than a powerful agency for scrutiny. The Commons speaker elected from Labour ranks in 2000 to replace Betty Boothroyd displayed their dog-in-the-manger attitude. The charge against Michael Martin was not his Glasgow accent but his self-referential conservatism. Blair was a technophobe and his indifference to both the Commons and modern communications ensured that MPs did not adopt email and websites with alacrity. As for electronic voting in the chamber, God forbid the twentieth let alone the twenty-first century should obtrude into hallowed precincts. Emblematic was the passage in 2007 of a private member's bill promoted by a Tory MP, David Maclean, exempting parliament from the Freedom of Information Act. Either Labour MPs had not understood what they were doing in approving that legislation or they were making a case for the Commons to be literally above the law.

The political scientist Philip Cowley counters the charge that under Labour the Commons became more supine. He says the picture was in fact one of growing activism and rebelliousness by backbenchers. MPs got several full-dress debates on Iraq; Blair could have lost the votes. In March 2003, 139 Labour MPs did vote against the war, which Cowley said was the largest rebellion seen under any party on any issue since the repeal of the Corn Laws under Sir Robert Peel. Big commitments on schools or on Trident only passed thanks to Tory support. His research found the class of 2005 Labour MPs the most rebellious of any since the war, but in truth, few rebellions threatened government business.

Labour were also conservative about how to pay for politics. Reform was never going to be easy because the antidote to plutocracy was state funding. But Blair's inaction was all the more puzzling since emancipation from the unions, who still kept the party financially afloat, was part of his 'new Labour' project. The Political Parties, Elections and Referendum Act did put parties on a legal footing for the first time. It capped election spending and shone a light on donations, though not brightly enough to prevent a non-domiciled businessman from Belize sitting in the Lords while spending huge sums on Tory campaigns in marginal seats. In 2006, the House of Lords Appointments Commission blocked Labour nominations amid allegations that places on the leather benches were for sale. Wealthy men had secretly loaned Labour nearly £14 million. This was against the spirit if not the letter – they were loans, not gifts – of Labour's own earlier legislation. The public wrongly imagined ministers were personally on the take; in fact they were striving to pay for democracy, even if in a disreputable way. Blair commissioned a report on party funding but failed to make the public case for an obvious conclusion: parties are necessary for government and to decontaminate them from private interest, taxpayers should bear their basic costs.

Yet, if Labour left Westminster in a half-rebuilt state, devolution did not just move power away. It created fresh, functional parliaments in Cardiff and Edinburgh, making the edifice by the Thames look even more antique. Their voting systems, devised after international comparison, were made proportional – an extraordinary implicit acknowledgement by Labour of Westminster's decrepitude.

This was 'constitutional change', if that implies permanence: devolution is now irreversible in Scotland, permanent in some form in Wales. Yet it was the opposite of innovative. 'Home rule' was a central tenet of late Victorian liberalism, though Gladstone, like Blair, never quite worked out what its consequences should be for England. Perhaps his indifference to what looked at one stage like Labour's solution – self-government for the regions of England – suggests that devolution was another example of policy-making without much thought about consequences. In November 2003 Labour's majority for creating foundation hospital trusts rested on 44 Scottish Labour MPs and 24 Welsh – though the semi-commercial hospitals would exist in England only. The result of the funding formula applied to Edinburgh and Cardiff was that the Scots enjoyed more public spending per head and the Welsh less than they deserved on the basis of population and need. Labour obfuscated and got away with it, since the much-talked-about English backlash proved hard to spot beyond the election of a member of a fruitcake party, the English Democrats, to be mayor of Doncaster.

In 1997 devolution was a legacy of the former Labour leader John Smith and the party's Scottish chieftain Donald Dewar. Dewar, who died before accomplishing his work, was devolution's midwife, cajoling a far from enthusiastic Blair in collaboration with Lord Irvine of Lairg, the man who had gone off with Dewar's wife. A referendum vote was not overwhelming, but Scotland's will was clear enough: of the 62 per cent who bothered to vote, 74 per cent were in favour. It was hardly legislative love at first sight – the inward-looking Scottish press saw to that. But with fair voting, a third of its members women, a civilized tone to proceedings and a splendid if costly building, this parliament had lessons for Westminster.

Devolution was a milestone event for the 8.5 per cent of the UK people who lived in Scotland, and if it arrived with extraordinary absence of fuss it also had little to show in subsequent creative outpourings, in culture, politics or the economy. Edinburgh's parlous dependence on bubble banks later stood exposed; where was the indigenous industry to build the wind turbines and tidal barrages needed to exploit Scotland's winds and coastline?

Still, devolution offered a test bed for different policies. Or should have. The government made no effort to pull together lessons from differing approaches to hospitals, social care, school league tables, Sats tests, youth crime and universities in the different parts of the UK. These real-world social experiments went unused. Down south Labour, embarrassed at the poor quality of their people at Holyrood, studiously ignored Scotland.

Wales, with 3 per cent of the UK population, was less than enthusiastic about its devolution package: a half of those eligible turned out to vote on an assembly and only a fraction over half of them approved. The Cardiff assembly acquired fewer powers than Edinburgh, sowing doubts about the value of an extra tier of politicians and a new parliamentary building – the centrepiece of a tremendous physical regeneration of Cardiff docks. Blair's control freakery marred its birth as he insisted on Alun Michael as Labour leader of the new Welsh assembly over Rhodri Morgan. It wasn't even ideology; Blair had taken against the shambling Welshman because his house was so untidy. Morgan's retirement nine years after he took office as first minister in 2000, garlanded with praise and popular affection, showed how wrong Blair had been.

Home and Abroad

Morgan tried to make the 'Welsh state' more coherent by introducing common training for all public servants and by abolishing quangos the assembly thought had grown too big and grand, including the Welsh Development Agency and Tourist Board. In Wrexham and other border areas, residents could choose GP surgeries: on the Welsh side of the border prescriptions were free. In 2009 a Labour–Plaid Cymru convention said Wales should have full legislative powers, pending a referendum. Opinion polls showed broad levels of support for such a move: the assembly had proved itself. But devolution did not resolve who paid. The National Union of Teachers Cymru lobbied the assembly on discovering a disparity of £500 in spending for each pupil in Wales compared with England. Unfair, or the appropriate result of the way that priorities had diverged since devolution? The *TES* (27 November 2009) quoted a Welsh Assembly government spokeswoman: '[W]e take decisions on the basis of what we believe is right for Wales, not by reference to developments in England.'

Gladstone, on being called to the prime ministership, had said his mission was to pacify Ireland; wits said Blair's first priority was to pacify Isleworth – middle England was where his heart and Labour's new majority lay. Yet he succeeded where Gladstone failed. The Good Friday agreement in March 1998 started normalizing life in Northern Ireland – though after her death the biographers of the Northern Ireland secretary Mo Mowlam claimed that Blair stole her thunder. The American negotiator Senator George Mitchell (and behind him Bill Clinton) helped, as did the respective republican and loyalist leaders who agreed to suspend history and talk. The subsequent reputation of the other vital midwife, Irish prime minister Bertie Ahern, was stained by charges of personal corruption and economic mismanagement. He did, however, remove offensive clauses from the Republic's constitution, claiming sovereignty over the north.

Ulster, home to 3 per cent of the UK population, surrendered – to exhaustion, the ageing of the conflict generation and the failure of violent republicanism. The withdrawal of American support helped, especially after 9/11 made foreign terrorism less fashionable among the Guinness drinkers of Boston and New

York. John Major had begun the process and subsidies from UK taxpayers lubricated the deal. History soon resumed. A concession to the republicans was an inquiry led by Lord Saville into the Bloody Sunday events in 1972. It dragged on, public hearings lasting till November 2004. The final report, delayed till after the 2010 election, cost £200 million, half of which went on fees for lawyers.

An elected assembly, its voting system fully proportional, sat, was suspended, sat again. For a while you glimpsed normality, with Sinn Fein pronouncing on eleven-plus exams and Unionists on climate change. During suspension, Westminster ministers were able to take tougher decisions on local rates and hospital closures than the devolved assembly. Meanwhile Northern Ireland got a share of the backwash from the UK boom in housing, leisure and financial services – and from sterling depreciation against the euro, encouraging cross-border shopping. Decommissioning of weapons rested on a theology of firing pins, blindfolds and cloak-and-dagger proof. Blair indulged the republicans as they dragged their feet over weapons: 'conceding and capitulating' was Peter Mandelson's phrase. But with more peace, troop numbers fell and a new police service was set up.

Labour's achievement was de-escalation, but the larger goal of a functioning devolved government embracing nationalists and former terrorists looks fragile still. Fringe remnants of Continuity IRA could still stage attacks, but a Sinn Fein minister in a Northern Ireland government condemning the attempted bombing of the Policing Board had to be progress.

A Labour vision for the UK shimmered, then dissipated. In it devolution was accompanied by relegitimization of government inside England; Labour delivered, but only partially. The manifesto had talked about directly elected regional assemblies 'where clear popular consent is established'. It was not, except in London. Brief Blairite enthusiasm for powerful elected mayors for cities coincided with a promise to rectify the abolition of the Greater London Council by the Tories in 1986. (A standing rebuttal of charges that Labour were unique in monkeying around

with the 'constitution' is the Thatcher government's suppression
of local democracy because voters had voted for Labour councillors.)

Labour did not seem to know what they wanted the administration of the metropolis to look like. The idea of a mayor was
vaguely American; Blair, typically, fancied a millionaire entre-
preneur for the job, like New York's Michael Bloomberg. But
Richard Branson did not step forward and Downing Street was
left with an old leftie, the former leader of the GLC. Rejected
by the party machine, Ken Livingstone stood as an independent
and won the first London elections in May 2000. His vote, just
15 per cent of the London electorate's first-choice preferences,
with barely a third of eligible Londoners bothering to vote at
all, showed the public's lack of enthusiasm. And this for a new
office with huge potential. Livingstone won again, standing for
Labour, only to lose to the clownish Boris Johnson in 2008.
Conventional wisdom said lowish turnout and lack of public
interest – especially in the assembly created alongside the mayor –
resulted from the Greater London Authority's lack of powers.
Alternatively, too many people were uninterested in local self-
government.

That seemed to explain the tepid response to Labour's
attempt to push mayors in towns and cities outside London.
Dorothy Thornhill, a local teacher and Liberal Democrat councillor, became full-time mayor of Watford. The Hartlepool
football team's mascot, dressed up as a monkey, stood and won.
The London boroughs of Newham, Lewisham and Hackney
opted for elected mayors and creditable figures emerged, but
elsewhere, especially in the big cities, no enthusiasm. As a substitute, the government pressed councils to set up 'cabinets' of
leading councillors to focus on services, instead of committees,
prompting questions about what the rest of the elected members
were for.

After the failure of regional assemblies, Labour espoused 'city-
regions', which looked like a move back to the metropolitan
counties abolished by the Tories in 1986. Greater Manchester
councils collaborated, except for Stockport. In the West Midlands,

with no love lost between Coventry, Solihull and Sandwell, the idea went nowhere.

The government dodged the biggest question left over from the last time Labour held office, one that became more pressing under the Tories and the failure of their poll tax: how to pay for councils. Nothing was done about the growing anomalies of the hated council tax, neither a full-blown property tax of the kind most other countries had, nor a local tax on income. If Whitehall provided 80 per cent of local funding, councils' autonomy was necessarily going to be limited. Further inquiries only repeated the question.

Labour gave councils freedom to spend funds from housing sales under the Right to Buy and to borrow 'prudentially'. The Local Government Act 2000 ended personal surcharges for councillors, fining them for decisions taken in office, unlike anything that applied to MPs or ministers. Instead, councillors were to answer for their conduct to a new quango, the Standards Board for England. It promptly pursued a Cornish councillor for making disparaging remarks about a constituent's home baking. Under a new 'comprehensive performance assessment', inspectors gave councils scores, and these showed a distinct improvement in local governance, regardless of the party in charge locally.

But the public remained ambiguous about local democracy. The 'new localism' in favour of devolution and extra powers for councils made an attractive subject for speeches and think-tank seminars, and Labour ministers signed up. In practice, the public demanded uniform standards and sharp intervention if services failed, as in Haringey and Doncaster. The public were not too bothered by who provided the services, and they rejected the 'post code lottery' more fiercely than they cared about local democratic variation. A watchword became 'partnership', bringing councils closer to the NHS, police and other services. But Labour's own decisions often flew in the face of joined-upness, notably concerning foundation trusts and part-privately run academies outside council control.

On the one hand Labour liked tsars, edicts and targets; on the other, they talked of liberated communities, empowered, with their own budgets. One example: the 2002 Soham murders of two girls provoked the home secretary into demanding that the chief constable of Humberside resign. He refused, with the full backing of his police authority. Blunkett insisted he would take legal action, but localism stood its ground, ending in a messy stand-off and the chief constable agreeing to take dignified early retirement.

During the noughties the mood shifted. Resentment at interference chimed with a general turn in the tide against 'over-regulation'. The public demanded repressive action one day and freedom the next; ministers were in a bind. It would have helped if Labour had overarching principles on the duty of the state to intervene and interfere and on the boundary of individual liberties and personal risk.

If people grew to mistrust government, the reason was not just Iraq or MPs' expenses. Labour themselves encouraged it. Margaret Thatcher campaigned against the state, pretending to be an outsider cutting government down to size, calling its employees parasites. But she had an ideological commitment to shrinking it. Surely Labour would champion the value and virtue of government? Instead, led by Blair, they copied the Tories: he made a remarkable speech about 'the scars on my back' from his dealings with public servants. Tax and regulation were 'burdens'; nobody did it better than business; firms, social enterprises, they said, anything but bureaucracy. 'There was a time,' said Blair in 1999, 'when we could assume the brightest and best of each generation would want to join the public sector. But that is an assumption that we can no longer make, particularly when the financial rewards at the top of the private sector are so great, and too often public sector workers are weighed down by bureaucracy and silly rules.'

But where was the programme to remove the bureaucracy and silly rules? Blair answered with 'reform', a nebulous mix of proposals and phraseology which characterized Labour's second term and was still being echoed by Brown in the run-up to the 2010 election. Reform was a mixed bag: contracting out, American theories of 'the new public management', more choice among services. The state was a shop and the citizen was a consumer, not a participant in a collective endeavour. The public said they wanted more 'choice', but they also wanted reliability and equity, and usually preferred services to be close to home. Parents might choose among schools, and patients, or at least their GPs, among hospitals. But citizens could never select police, planners or food safety regulators; they were never really going to choose among mental health trusts; subsidized housing was in such short supply choice could never amount to much.

Choice became a flag for Blairites who believed the mantra connected them to aspirational voters in middle England. Alan Milburn made speeches deploring how in the 'era of paternalism' the council, not his family, had chosen the colour of their County Durham front door. 'The choices of patients, parents and tenants should determine the resources that individual providers receive.' This was nonsense. Labour, like all governments, shared out available money on the basis of need; Labour, like all governments, were quick to withdraw services when policy or finance dictated, regardless of the public's appetite for 'choice'. For example, on the 'NHS Choices' website, you can find GPs near your home, but a tick box narrows the search to surgeries 'accepting new patients'. Or post offices. The network had 25,000 offices in 1964 and 14,200 in 2007. The internet and direct debit payments were to blame. In May 2007 the government said 2500 branch offices were to close, as each footfall was costing £17. Many were under-used; the public liked the idea of a post office more than the reality of buying stamps or banking there; the Post Office was losing £500,000 a day. In a huge response, 2.7 million people gave their views, most deploring the cuts, so the government withdrew 350 planned closures.

Choice was a curious episode in Labour's history, an epiphenomenon of the bulge years of extra spending. It was largely bereft of evidence, except for superficial polling; indeed, a government that had come in demanding evidence of 'what works' was curiously incurious about the underpinnings of its own reform prospectus. A Blairite proponent, the trade secretary John Hutton, commissioned a review from the business economist

DeAnne Julius; she found no convincing evidence that private contracts were more economical or effective, but still concluded strongly in their favour.

However, Labour decreed that councils no longer had to seek competitive bids for bins, ground maintenance and parking. Instead, they were encouraged to look for 'best value' – not necessarily the cheapest bid – which suited contracting firms. Labour legislated to ensure staff transferred to private contractors on more or less equal terms. In most services, healthy pragmatism ruled, with public bodies encouraged to test the market, but stay mindful of how they might lose leverage (and face price gouging) if a service were contracted out permanently. Still, the era was a bonanza for outsourcing companies such as the Indian Infosys, Tata Consulting and Wipro, Accenture (headquarters in the Bahamas) and IBM. Home-grown firms, among them Tribal and Serco, grew fat from running public services.

Inexplicably, Labour turned the use of private capital in public-sector building into a dogma. They could have insisted the NHS or councils consider different ways of borrowing, or sale and leaseback or contracting, letting them decide on the best deal in the light of local circumstances. Instead the Treasury imposed rigid formulae. Brown as chancellor instructed public authorities they could not build unless under the Private Finance Initiative.

PFI had been born of deceit or, put more gently, an accounting trick. If a firm or private consortium built a school or road or waste-treatment plant, it could appear on a balance sheet as a tradeable asset to be sold or used as collateral in borrowing – even though it had no other use. The early attraction of PFI for Labour ministers was that because projects were privately accounted for, they did not register on the national accounts, at least until the state started paying interest or a revenue charge. Deals could be sweetened by getting the private contractors not only building a school or hospital but also maintaining it, with the state effectively renting the space.

Not just hospitals. A consortium made up of Thales, the French engineering firm, Sikorsky, the helicopter-makers and the Royal Bank of Scotland proposed entering a £6 billion, 25-year deal with the Ministry of Defence to build and maintain search and rescue aircraft – manned by the RAF.

PFI figures are hard to pin down. The Treasury estimated the lifetime cost of Labour-era deals at £215 billion – paying for deals with a capital value of between £55 billion and £65 billion. Contracts could be rigid and expensive. A surgeon complained to us that his instruments had to be sent out of the PFI hospital for sterilization. The first hospitals had insufficient beds, to bring down costs; the Department of Health then rigged patient flows to ensure PFI hospitals had enough patients to pay their mounting charges. Some Tory-era and early Labour deals were shockingly generous. Private consortia wrote borrowing costs into the contract but often, after signing, managed to cut them: this was, after all, the era of easy money. A lucrative secondary market in PFI contracts arose, and as they were traded, it was unclear who really owned these state facilities. The return to the shareholders of Octagon, a hospital PFI consortium, increased from 16 per cent to 60 per cent following refinancing; the NHS trust got back £34 million out of refinancing gains worth £115 million.

Some were outstanding failures. The NAO censured the twenty-year deal by which Mapeley ran HMRC offices: 'not value for money'. In contrast to a similar property deal struck by the Department for Work and Pensions, HMRC had no long-term plan when it handed over its estate to the firm in 2001. It paid £312 million more than planned – a figure that could rise to £570 million, the NAO said. Potential savings under the deal shrank and it even impeded plans to quit offices HMRC no longer needed. To HMRC's undying shame Mapeley registered its original deal with the taxman offshore in a tax-avoidance scheme.

Other deals worked. The Treasury refurbished its own building in a PFI, saving 7 per cent of the cost of the 2001 deal by running a competition. In a £635 million deal Siemens Business Services took over National Savings, including 4000 of its staff, 'transferring the risk' of modernizing the business. National Savings had wisely hired independent advisers to help it become an 'intelligent customer'. But Siemens' deal with the Passport Office was less happy; the technology did not work and delays peaked in 1999, with 565,000 applications awaiting processing. The NAO totted up the costs of what were largely the firm's errors to be £13 million, 10 per cent of the contract value, including the £16,000 cost of umbrellas for people forced to queue in the rain. The NAO was also scathing about a Siemens IT PFI in the Immigration Office, but that did not stop the firm being awarded an £18 million contract by the Office for National Statistics to digitize birth, marriage and death certificates from 1837 to the present day and a £120 million contract with Transport for London for a bus information system for buses in the capital. For the Highways Agency, Siemens Traffic Controls replaced motorway matrix indicators, and Siemens Medical Solutions secured a £300 million contract to supply and service medical equipment at the new Royal London and St Barts Hospitals for thirty-five years from 2009.

Recession cut PFI off at its roots; the market for corporate bonds collapsed, putting projects at the mercy of banks that would not lend. But cutting new investment did not absolve the state from PFI payments, which in some hospital trusts started to become an immovable annual commitment. Labour bequeathed a poison pill, which may distort service patterns for a generation. In twenty years schools and hospital buildings may be redundant, yet PFI payments on them will still be due.

The zeitgeist said the state should be more 'citizen-centric', and technology certainly made transactions a lot easier. Under the Tories the UK had been ahead of other European governments and much of private business in pioneering use of the internet. After 1997 the baroque-sounding Office of the e-Envoy spent £1 billion to help the government realize its promise that by 2005 citizens and government could in theory transact all forms and payments electronically. By 2008–9 the government could claim that all 'citizen-based' services were fully online, compared with an EU average of 70 per cent. The portal www.directgov.uk allowed citizens to renew road tax and licences or see flood warnings.

Labour took a giant step in opening up the state to public inspection. But like human rights, freedom of information was a reform lacking a thread. Ministers simply did not think it through, including its impact on them as MPs. The more profound question was whether FOI was needed because the state was fundamentally untrustworthy. Journalists' use was sporadic and often focused on trivia. Firms and interest groups used FOI requests to further their causes; opposition MPs trawled for material to denigrate incumbents. More relevant to the public, who were largely indifferent, was the new culture of openness (which FOI may have pushed along) in which public organizations routinely published on their websites vast amounts of documents. Greater transparency had to be progress, but in its infant years FOI often left a sour taste and left unresolved the question whether the state should, in part, be opaque and whether organizations necessarily had to have a private life. Views were contradictory. Why shouldn't openness apply to all public information, including tax returns?

On data, Labour were ambiguous. Blair put his weight behind the Regulation of Interception of Communications Act 2000, which gave the state new powers of e-intrusion – but it included new rights for individuals to prevent the gathering of personal data for commercial gain. Another first-term milestone was the Data Protection Act 1998, in force from 2000, giving individuals rights of inspection over what organizations knew about them. A commissioner's office and tribunals were established and principles of data handling defined, to do with relevance, accuracy and length of holding. HMRC was only one of the government departments that needed more and more intimate data about income, earnings and capital gains for the sake of effective and fair policy – but Labour's advocacy of state data collection for benign public purposes was muted or non-existent.

Like all governments, Labour soon fell in love with state power and secrecy but not until they had rescinded a Tory-era ban on trade-union membership at GCHQ, the intelligence communications centre. Labour's handling of the 'secret state' was uncomfortable. Thanks to Islamicist terror, the Security Service bounced from decline – as the IRA threat faded – to boom, its manpower and money much expanded. The service even felt confident enough to commission an official history from a Cambridge historian. He noted how in a globalized world where Luton and Leeds were front lines, a single national security agency (first mooted in 1925) might work better than two some-times competing groups – MI5 and MI6. The idea, however, was 'more frightening to the spooks than a plot that Osama bin Laden might dream up'.

But then MI5's ex-head warned darkly of a Labour police state, which sounded like a plot-line from *Spooks* with the gallant operatives defending national virtues against the depre-dations of Jack Straw. Besides, you needed only to inspect the organogram supposedly linking the security and intelligence services, counter-terrorism command in the Metropolitan Police, the Defence Intelligence Staff, Whitehall departments and the Office of Security and Counter Terrorism (created in 2007) to have faith that bureaucratic rivalry would ensure pluralism. OSCT was meant to be a version of the American Department of Homeland Security, reporting to the home secretary. MPs observed: 'the UK government's apparatus can at first seem fragmented and confused.'

Much depended on the vigilance of MPs themselves. The par-liamentary intelligence and security committee, made up of MPs and peers, was subject to strong criticism by judges in the case of Binyam Mohamed, who alleged torture in Pakistan with British complicity. This was a classic twenty-first-century case. Mohamed was not a British citizen; his continuing residence in the UK illustrated the non-functioning of the asylum regime. Whether MI5 lied (something that had formerly been its job), its undenied presence halfway round the world showed the unsatisfactory division of labour between agencies. Alleged torture illustrated the blowback from the government's rights agenda: it could not both be the upholder and the destroyer of a basic right of protection.

The media said Labour were obsessed with rights, but news-papers and bloggers themselves fomented a culture of entitlement.

The public had an appetite to blame someone, usually a politician or public official, and proclaimed: 'I have rights and the state has duties.' Who ensured reciprocity? Labour realized the problem and talked about a bill to complete the Human Rights Act, encasing people's responsibilities, but it went nowhere. The reason was Labour's ambiguity about the state. This was a government that simultaneously extended the state's reach – in the growth of public services, in the anti-terror campaign – and diminished the state, through FOI, through its own pro-market rhetoric. The result was confusion, and yet more public mistrust, despite the new opportunities for participation that Labour were also offering.

CHAPTER 11

Labour abroad

Iraq barely registered in the May 2010 election campaign, even though the invasion had once threatened to stamp Labour indelibly. We have been punished enough on Iraq, the foreign secretary David Miliband said during the election. Had they been punished at all? Blair took the blame and once he went, and his evidence to the Chilcot inquiry in February 2010 had sealed the episode, Iraq ceased to be a Labour event. It had never wholly been Labour anyway, because the Tories and a majority of public opinion supported the invasion. Militarily it was only possible because the UK maintained disproportionately large armed forces and hankered after a world role, and no one queried that posture, certainly not the victors of 1997. Labour could and should have rethought foreign and defence affairs in the subsequent thirteen years. They should have called into question affordability – where was big debate needed to put defence spending, principles and realism about UK capacity together? What made government and the public think the UK could afford to spend £8 billion on Iraq, on top of an already exceptional defence budget? Maybe neither the public nor the British political class were ready for self-examination. After all, Labour talked a lot about globalization and adapting to the rise of China and India; they also talked about universal rights and how to enforce them. But as with their efforts on 'Britishness', Labour lacked big themes and overarching vision. Government, like people, faced two ways at once. Many UK citizens had relatives in other countries, but for all the mixing of peoples, consciousness of other lives and other countries was dim. As the Sri Lankan civil war heaved to an end in 2008–9, Tamils marched in London streets, to the resounding indifference of the society around them.

The same streets had thronged with anti-Iraq war protesters in 2003. Then and until British troops pulled out in 2007–8, Labour struggled and failed to convince both themselves and the nation on why this war, now? The measure of any government is how it responds to events thrust upon it. Any incumbent would have had to deal with 9/11 and the Bush White House. The auguries for a measured response were good. Labour had responded coolly in 2000 to the rapid worsening of security in Sierra Leone. Operation Palliser was a textbook example of inter-service rapid reaction, heading off worse conflict. When 9/11 happened, Labour had to respond, and Blair was not wrong in seeing a choice between the continuing influence of the UK, especially in Washington, or diminution in its international profile. In January 2003 he declared that influence meant joining the US in facing the tricky issues. 'By tricky I mean the ones which people wish weren't there, don't want to deal with and, if I can put it a little pejoratively, know the US should confront, but want the luxury of criticising them for it.'

Labour never stopped for a moment to gauge whether diminution in the UK profile might have been the better course. Blair opted for 'influence', but its fruits proved hard to spot. Nor was the US 'confronting' what should happen in Iraq after Saddam, let alone the knock-on consequences of the invasion for Iran, Afghanistan and the rest of central Asia. Michael Clarke of the International Institute for Strategic Studies even wondered if Labour's uncritical stance made policy drift under Bush worse than it might otherwise have been.

Blair's bended knee on Pennsylvania Avenue was a genuflexion made by successive prime ministers, back to Harold Wilson and Macmillan. Brown's dealings with a different president, Barack Obama, differed in style not substance; Obama's indifference to the UK was obvious except when, after the Gulf of Mexico oil spill, anger replaced it. Labour encouraged no wider debate about alternatives to the traditional Anglo-American relationship, especially in military and security matters. Of course the US continued to bulk large. American share of global income, 22 per cent, was the same in 2010 as in 1975; the Pentagon's budget was and remained bigger than those of the next seven powers combined. If not the American, whose umbrella offered any shelter?

Instead of a rigorous appraisal of the UK's available choices, Blair drew upon rhetoric and emotion. At the annual Labour conference in October 2001, not many days after the attack, he exaggerated the strength of Al Qaeda, talking of scores of training camps in Afghanistan. He condemned the Taliban in biblical terms: 'there is no diplomacy with them'. Eight years later his protégé David Miliband was urging the Taliban to take seats in the Afghan parliament.

We have the benefit of hindsight. But greater coolness in autumn 2001 would have served better. The UK, with its history in the Hindu Kush, might have taken its own, inflected view of the why and wherefore of armed intervention. Al Qaeda was a regional more than a global problem; Asian powers, among them Iran and China, would eventually have to be part of the solution. So would India and Pakistan – even if, for the moment, those twin progeny of British imperialism in South Asia were fighting a surrogate war with each other for Kabul.

Blair's promises to the people of Afghanistan became the justification for British military involvement, and after the Iraq war ended for the UK, it became the armed forces' major commitment. The jury is out on whether Labour planned adequately and were prepared to meet the necessary costs.

All along the British were participating in an American operation, dressed up in NATO clothes. The Americans followed the Rumsfeld doctrine rather than Osama Bin Laden: big bangs, pull out and declare peace. Maybe Blair had already turned his attention to Baghdad, and Afghanistan for him was a sideshow, left unattended in the critical years from 2001 to 2006, perhaps wasting what chance there was to secure peace. The Taliban regrouped and resumed war.

The story around UK intervention in Afghanistan was never clearly told then or later, when military casualties mounted. We assumed there was an Afghan people who could build a nation and do democracy, rather than a collection of tribes. Afghanistan's problems were compounded by the nature of Pakistani state and society and so, indirectly, by the Pakistani diaspora in Bradford and Oldham. As troops were killed in Helmand, ministers rarely spelled out the horrible complexity surrounding their deaths.

After British forces left Iraq, Brown's promised inquiry got going, chaired by the former civil servant Sir John Chilcot. It was an Establishment affair, of course, but when Chilcot summoned Brown in March 2010 its constitutional novelty became clear: here were a bumbling bunch of ex-bureaucrats bypassing parliament and questioning sitting ministers. When Blair appeared, he barely bothered to cloak what he had so often denied in the run-up to invasion in March 2003. His view of the world was grossly simplified. In the Lords in September 2002 Roy Jenkins said Blair was far from lacking conviction – the early charge against him. He had too much. 'A little Manichean for my perhaps now jaded taste, seeing matters in stark terms of good and evil, black-and-white, contending with each other.' Saddam was black; he was white. He committed the UK to support military action to depose Saddam Hussein, probably at his April 2002 meeting with George Bush at his ranch in Crawford, Texas. Weapons of mass destruction (WMD) were a shadow play. Labour MPs deceived themselves that WMD were the pretext for invasion and deceived Britain. Blair manoeuvred the enquiry to make the central question his sincerity in believing Saddam owned them. A better question was: if inspectors had definitely reported against the existence of WMD and the Americans had still gone ahead, what would the Labour government have done?

In July 2002 Blair told MPs he had not decided on military action, the same month the Cabinet Office told ministers that occupying Iraq could lead to a protracted and costly nation-building exercise. Blair's purported dismay at what happened in Iraq after the invasion is not credible.

Yet to focus on Blair is to miss Labour's wider complicity. The prime minister wore his commitment to Bush openly. Years later Labour MPs and ministers were swearing that the existence of WMD in Iraq had alone been the trigger. That convicts them not so much of naivety or excessive credulity but of failing to grasp the nature of the US–UK relationship. The Iraq invasion could have been a pivot, an upside-down Suez moment, when the UK kicked its post-war habit of clinging to Washington's skirts.

But Labour would have had to go well beyond received opinion. British people were shocked at 9/11; they broadly backed extirpating the Taliban and Al Qaeda from Afghanistan and then – so the polls showed – followed the government in believing that Saddam presented a clear and present danger. To what, people were less clear about – missiles landing on Cyprus or even London? Their vagueness later reinforced the charge that Blair practised deception.

At Chilcot Blair said many times that the 'calculus of risk' had changed after 9/11, and the West could not tolerate the spread of WMD. In fact he used the vaguely convenient term 'the international community'. But this included China and India, which had all sorts of connections with proliferation, notably in North Korea and Iran. Chilcot did not push Blair on why the Iranian nuclear threat had not figured in 2002, nor whether the removal of Saddam had bolstered the regime in Teheran. If, as Blair and the neoconservatives had believed, invasion would teach a lesson, president Ahmadinejad had failed to get it.

A government that had thought longer and harder than Labour about the UK's place in the international community would have responded differently to 9/11. It might have encouraged the public to confront unpalatable choices, such as non-American partners in defence. But the public's appetite for radical reorientation, especially towards Europe, was slight. Besides, to all intents and purposes Labour policy was Blair policy, messianic and idiosyncratic.

Labour abroad

At a Nato summit in Chicago in 2000 Blair launched the idea of 'liberal intervention'. Did Iraq expose the fatal flaw in the concept or was the operation so badly conceived that you could draw no generic conclusions? After interventions in Kosovo, Afghanistan and Iraq but non-intervention in Congo, Sudan and Zimbabwe, the doctrine remained confused. Blair said, you intervened where you could, but the thread of Labour's thinking was hard to follow. Could action be justified whatever the state of the UN Security Council? Yes in Kosovo, no in Iraq? A Blair guru, Robert Cooper, said lasting intervention by postmodern nations in premodern Kosovo and sub-Saharan Africa was questionable in effectiveness and difficult to justify to a sceptical public. In Darfur and Sudan you got round the problem by not bothering.

Labour were tempted by the belief that projecting our values was both in the UK national interest and the right thing to do because they were also universal values. In a globalizing world, human rights had to be the same, home and abroad, and from that arose a duty to protect them when Ba'athists or Taliban infringed them. The view was not too far from the American neoconservatives' belief that the way things were done in Denver was how they should be done everywhere else; it was the opposite of an older conservative view that we could never know enough about the culture, values and ways of life of another state to be able to interfere with them with any confidence. Blair was no philosopher but the doctrine picked up on contemporary thinking, which led at home to the passage of the Human Rights Act.

Blair and Brown were typically Labour in seeing foreign affairs as a place where the UK could be morally upright. Labour flirted with an 'ethical' foreign policy, especially under their first foreign secretary, Robin Cook. Cynics said that was because New Labour had few clear principles around which it could organize domestic policy. Poverty in Africa was easier to tilt against than poverty at home. Still, if foreign affairs under Labour had a theme, it was the assertion of human rights in the post–Cold War world. But rights turned out to be far from straightforward. Protecting human rights in Afghanistan cost human lives, and minimizing military deaths started to depend on sending armed drones to assassinate the leaders of Al Qaeda in their pick-up trucks. Such remote-control weapons were so cruel that they were beyond the pale of human tolerance, said Lord Bingham, the former Lord Chief Justice.

In July 1997 Cook declared Britain was at the front of the drive to raise standards of human rights. How did these sentiments apply in Israel–Palestine, which Blair had declared to be his great cause? In October 2000 Cook stood helpless on a dusty road, Yasser Arafat at his side, as Israeli shells fell in Gaza. Blair, now the representative of the quartet powers, was as impotent when in January 2009 Israeli shells fell in Gaza, responding to Hamas rockets.

Cook quickly came a cropper over trade in weapons, a British export staple. The UK's military–industrial complex employed 415,000, stretched across plenty of Labour-held seats. At the end of 1996, the UK had been the world's second biggest arms exporter, with 22 per cent of the global export market. The global arms market increased by 50 per cent in value between 2000 and 2008. The UK sold $53 billion worth of arms in the five years to 2008, contending with the $63 billion sold by the US. The US imported more weapons from the UK than from any other country. No wonder the government was so willing to tolerate bribery and corruption in international arms sales. Trading nations cannot afford rigour in foreign policy and precious little principle, which soon makes them liable to the charge of hypocrisy. Labour ministers quickly got the hang of it and whistled up public interest immunity certificates – gagging orders – to mask intelligence services' involvement in supplying arms to Iraq under the Tories. Cook had singled out Iraq and Nigeria, but not Tibet, China or Indian security forces in Kashmir.

Talk of rights inflated the sense of their cross-border applicability. A visit to London by the former Chilean caudillo Augusto Pinochet opened a window for executing a Spanish magistrate's arrest warrant. Lengthy court proceedings followed, but after law lords fumbled their judgment, Jack Straw let Pinochet go in an early instance of Labour 'realism'.

Perhaps, looked at in the round, the decision was unimportant. Chile was on the road to becoming a functioning democracy; its economy was progressing and British people were buying its Merlot in vats. Yet the episode exposed the gap between what Labour said and what ministers did. It fed an underlying suspicion around Straw's later declarations of innocence – he was now justice secretary – when the Scottish government released the Lockerbie bomber from prison in August 2009 and he then failed to succumb to an allegedly fatal illness. And if Pinochet, why not arrest the former Israeli foreign minister Tzipi Livni? Ministers had a fit of vapours when in 2009 London magistrates were about to grant an arrest warrant over her complicity in bombing Gaza, foreign secretary David Miliband at their head vowing to legislate to stop such interventions in the 'normal workings' of diplomacy.

What should diplomacy look like in the twenty-first century? The Foreign & Commonwealth Office went on resisting modernization. Visitors to ambassadors' residences in Delhi, Rome and Paris in autumn 2009 came away without much sense of diplomatic parsimony. The NAO complained in 2010 that ministers had no strategy for the Foreign Office's £1.6 billion estate, including 4000 embassies and houses for diplomats. Their calling was as confused as ever. Mark Malloch Brown, briefly imported as a Foreign Office minister after a career in the UN, said on resigning that it needed more economists and more Pakistan specialists.

Foreign Office grandiosity belonged to the UK's past, yet for Labour, history would not go away. Blair apologized for the Irish famine, later for slavery. Brown apologized for sending surplus children to Australia in the 1940s and 1950s. The Queen apologized (during a 1998 visit to India) for the Amritsar massacre in 1919. But no apologies to the Greeks: the Elgin marbles stayed in Bloomsbury and ministers passed a decision on an Egyptian bid for the Rosetta Stone over to the trustees of the British Museum, and they were never likely to agree.

Empire lived on in claims by the Gurkhas, orchestrated by

Joanna Lumley. She made their case with skill, but what was a twenty-first-century war machine doing employing Nepalese mercenaries? Labour ministers ducked other, more profound questions about UK defence. In one sense, it was remarkable that UK armed forces had been able to invade Iraq, even as subalterns to the Americans. The UK could still project power, and forces and equipment 'performed impressively', the NAO said. It was 'a major achievement' to deploy UK units within ten weeks. The Challenger tank and the principal infantry rifle performed well. But nuclear and chemical warfare protection equipment was scarce.

The question of affordability would not go away, however, and as soldier numbers rose in Afghanistan immediately after exit from Iraq the gap between Labour's ambitions and capacity widened. Defence secretary Bob Ainsworth announced cuts in the RAF's Harrier strength in 2009, not as a strategic decision but because his budget could not support both helicopters and fighters. This was hand-to-mouth war-making. Strategy was lacking and Labour would not hold the long-overdue defence review that was begun by the coalition government in June 2010. Among questions: was dusty Helmand a template for future army and RAF operations? And where next might the forces apply their accumulated experience? UK forces, some said, had become 'most adaptable' thanks to counter-insurgency experience from Malaya to Belfast to Basra. But on whose behalf would these super-police officers be sent out – as mercenaries or adjuncts to another great power? Labour passed the questions to their successors.

The charge that Blair and Brown sent troops into combat without themselves having combat experience is nonsense. Prime ministers with experience of war have proved disastrous as generals. A valid accusation is that Labour did not do enough planning for conflict. The NAO said that the gap between UK commitments and spending was anywhere between £6 billion and £36 billion – in other words, big. Labour ministers were never casual about putting the armed services in harm's way; they just had not thought clearly about which harm, where and why.

Army recruitment prospered – up 14 per cent in the six months to April 2009, on the way to reaching full strength in 2011. But the fuss over Brown's scribbled letters to bereaved relatives, exploited by Rupert Murdoch's editors, suggested that the deference to authority once shown by military families had dropped away. The social bases of the British fighting class remained narrow, drawing disproportionately from the public schools for officers and from poor districts for young recruits.

Lawsuits started over the adequacy of dead soldiers' equipment and decisions made on the battlefield, pointing to changing attitudes. Perhaps security guru Philip Bobbitt was right to warn that 'market states' would find it increasingly hard to persuade a sceptical public to support war and intervention. Especially, he might have added, in Afghanistan, where the domestic threat was hard to understand. The crowds that flocked to honour the cortèges through Wootton Bassett had once accepted military deaths with patriotic phlegm. Now their questions alarmed commanders. 'We must be wary of talking ourselves into a defeat back home,' said Lieutenant General Sir Graeme Lamb. Media coverage and public doubt drained what Captain Doug Beattie called the necessary belief of troops that they were a 'force for good' (*The Independent*, 30 November 2009). They had a mission, building schools, securing the bases of civilization. What was missing was advocacy, observed Sir Richard Dearlove, former head of the Secret Intelligence Service, blaming half-hearted ministers.

Advocates would need a story to tell. The 1998 defence review had said the UK should equip to support peace missions and deal with regional conflicts inside and outside the NATO area. Two new aircraft-carriers were needed to 'deploy more rapidly to trouble spots around the globe' (but not landlocked Afghanistan, presumably). The optimistic plan was for forces able to take part in a Gulf War plus one other small deployment.

What proportion of national income did such aspirations imply for the defence budget, which had to stretch to cover Trident and the Eurofighter, the new aircraft intended to replace the Tornado? In 2006 the government said it would upgrade the

Vanguard submarines carrying Trident nuclear missiles, costing between £15 billion and £20 billion at 2007 prices, the new boats to come into service from 2024. Trident was an instrument of diplomacy rather than warfare, as Brown showed when he offered to cut the number of warheads to ease a global disarmament deal. If opponents of Trident were dumb about what international profile a non-nuclear Britain would cut, Labour were equally inaudible over the reasons for renewal.

Labour never publicly justified defence spending because such spending maintained a military–industrial complex providing jobs and stimulating research; yet it obviously did. And ministers touted for defence business. Jobs and research were reasons why, instead of buying off the (American) shelf, the UK developed its own reconnaissance aircraft, the Nimrod. Not that buying American was necessarily cheaper, as the soaring cost of the proposed joint strike fighters intended to fly off the Scottish-built aircraft-carriers showed. Such ships were expensive and, to shave costs, the government downgraded one of the aircraft-carriers on order to become an amphibious commando ship, with helicopters. What price strategy as long as jobs at Rosyth and in other precious constituencies were preserved? When the UK's existing carrier, HMS *Queen Elizabeth*, went for refit, the UK would have none in service, unless it 'borrowed' one from the French, as president Sarkozy suggested.

The defence state was hugely generous to private firms. In 2003 it sold what had been the crown jewels of defence research in the shape of QinetiQ, making ex-civil servants rich: at flotation the ten top managers received shares worth £107 million, for an investment of half a million. This was a privatization that only made commercial sense if the government continued plying the firm with contracts, which – the NAO said – should have discounted the £576 million sale price. Other ex-civil servants paid a price when in 2010 the privatized company, struggling to find orders, attacked the pension rights of workers transferred from the Ministry of Defence.

The question put to Brown by the Chilcot inquiry was whether, as chancellor, he had starved the Ministry of Defence.

A better one would have been: where did Iraq and Afghanistan fit, and could the UK afford a separate navy, air force and army, let alone the £18 billion spent on Iraq on top of planned defence budgets? High-tech weapons – commentators said the RAF should scrap fighters and buy drones – were not much good at stabilizing states. 'Too few helicopters', was the complaint when insurgents killed soldiers in Helmand, but the UK had the largest helicopter fleet in Europe. As the Iraq commitment wound down in 2006, the Commons defence committee noted that ministers' 'confidence UK Armed Forces are not overstretched contrasts with what we heard from service personnel on the ground'. The MPs worried about dependence on reservists. In a public display of competitiveness among the three armed services, the First Sea Lord and the head of the army argued with one other, with the air chief marshal chipping in. The First Sea Lord faced choppy water. Why support a navy in the Persian Gulf if in 2007 British sailors could not prevent themselves falling into the hands of Iranian revolutionary guards? Somali pirates exposed naval impotence, teaching not just the limits of sea power but how security in the twenty-first century was bound up with the fate of some societies that had regressed to the eighteenth century or earlier.

Globalization had a dark side: other people's climate, financial meltdown, exported terror, syndicated crime, airborne disease, the disruptive migration of people and the weakness of 'the globe' as a source of good regulation. The same planes that took people off to foreign holidays carried back young Britons of Pakistani descent to prepare bombs to explode on Tube trains. From 'the globe' came a wave of asylum seekers, preoccupying ministers and distorting Labour's plans.

The Cabinet Office National Security Strategy (2008) declared that no state threatened the UK directly. Instead, it was at risk from globalization's stepchildren – international terror, WMD, implosion of failed states, pandemics and transnational crime. Labour tried to give the 'international community' some bite. The trials of Slobodan Milošević and Radovan Karadžić at the

International Criminal Court offered a sense that justice might prevail, however long and tortuous the road. Ministers signed the Ottawa Convention to outlaw anti-personnel landmines. The UK tried to stop commerce in diamonds from areas of conflict in Africa. It offered to house a proposed UN military staff college. The UK signed a UNESCO convention on the illegal export of archaeological artefacts. Then there was Brown at the G20 in 2009, bestriding the world like a colossus over better financial regulation.

Labour had once been passionate supporters of the UN. Critics of the Iraq invasion maintained the war was illegal without UN approval. Yet Blair – to applause – had pursued intervention in Kosovo without it. As for permament membership of the Security Council, the UK had nothing to say about including emerging powers such as India or Brazil, let alone such old contenders as Germany and Japan. The UN's stewardship of measures to combat climate change, both before and at the Copenhagen summit, was incompetent. Brown aspired to some new architecture 'to counter financial crises, deal with new priorities such as climate change and recognize the rise of new powers such as India', he declared during a visit there in 2008. But 'radical reform' of the UN, let alone of the International Monetary Fund or the World Bank, was hard to spot.

Labour set up Whitehall's first fully fledged international aid department and wrote the first white paper on aid policy since Harold Wilson in 1975. The UK proved to be one of the most pro-poor and least protectionist of OECD donors. By 2005, Labour claimed to have lifted two million people permanently out of poverty each year around the world and, in one view, 'the UK's international profile on development has probably not been higher since Keynes was negotiating the World Bank in 1944'. Perhaps aid showed what might have happened with climate change – a marriage of policy, diplomacy and extensive popular campaigning, such as Jubilee 2000 and Make Poverty History. The mutual effectiveness of Blair, Brown and such ministers as Clare Short and later Hilary Benn also showed how rare during Labour's tenure was the wholehearted cooperation

286

of prime minister, chancellor and individual secretary of state.

Under Labour the UK pushed to recognize African needs and to make poverty alleviation the touchstone of development. Aid spending rose from 2000 onwards to levels comparable with France and Germany and, by 2005, exceeded them. The UK pledged the UN target of 0.7 per cent of GDP, and pushed well above the budget for aid inherited from the Tories worth 0.26 per cent. But if, by 2005, the UK aid budget had doubled, it was still short of the UN target and would not get there till 2013. At the Gleneagles summit in 2005 Blair had secured promises to increase aid, especially to Africa.

Such countries as Ghana, Mozambique, Rwanda, Tanzania and Uganda, where the UK was a big donor, saw growth and less poverty. The UK was largely a bystander as Zimbabwe collapsed, pushing millions across the Limpopo into South Africa, whose ANC government refused to put pressure on its former comrade-in-arms, Robert Mugabe. Blair established an Africa Commission, Bob Geldof among its members, which underpinned declarations at the Gleneagles summit. But it had little effect in the horn of Africa, or the Sudan or the Ivory Coast, where war and dictatorship – and misaligned French and UK policies – thwarted development. Humanitarian disasters became more common; in 2001–2, with the Department for International Development providing £279 million in aid, the UK was the second largest donor of humanitarian aid for disasters.

The public's wider consciousness of the world was displayed in aid campaigns such as Jubilee 2000 and demonstrations for justice and rights in countries such as Burma. In a demotic age, foreign policy and popular sentiment ought to get closer; might policy be made more intelligible, perhaps even 'co-owned' by the people? Development aid says this is not impossible. By December 2009 the number of self-declared 'fairtrade' towns had grown to 500 since the movement started eight years previously – with schools, shops and churches promising to use Fairtrade products. Yet at the same time many people burrowed deeper into a reactionary, isolated British identity. The Labour years got no nearer to cracking the puzzle of how extraordinary openness in Britain could coexist with xenophobia, how young French people and Germans could come to live and work in Britain in striking numbers, yet core British attitudes to their countries, as to 'Europe', remain uninformed and prejudiced. Holiday homes in the Vendée and the Costa Smeralda did not infuse the UK mind with European consciousness or lead to any more interest in the lives of others; nor did Ryanair flights to Gothenburg nor Erasmus programmes for students. Spanish companies could buy up Heathrow, the London Tube and Abbey bank. Lithuanians could start crowding out the Poles in low-wage fieldwork in Fenland. But under Labour the UK became more marginal in the councils of Brussels, even as the EU itself floundered as a diplomatic and historical actor.

Blair, French-speaking, was well made for a role he seemed to crave – the young, energetic leader of Europe. How he looked the part at the Amsterdam summit in 1997. He remained oddly credible twelve years later amid the jockeying for the new post of president of the EU. But he failed to deliver any shift in British public opinion and was in turn failed by a scheming chancellor with Eurosceptic instincts. Blair then chose to align the UK closely with the interests of the US.

Labour's engagement with the EU merits no more than a few pages. That is partly because the EU itself failed to become the world actor it might have been and its internal solidarity was severely tested over Greek debt. This was not an era when the EU stood tall – it lacked diplomatic unity over Spain's Ceuta or Cyprus, its Middle East influence was slight, invisible in Teheran, absent in Copenhagen. Franco-German differences hampered a joint response to the banking crisis, recession and state debt. And yet absorbing the former Soviet satellites into a peaceful and largely passport-free club counted as a triumph, though the UK was marginal in making it happen. In the debate over the accession of Turkey, the UK hardly counted.

Labour's problem had, from the start, been the way that Blair and Brown conceived themselves as apostles of the neoliberal way, preaching to unbelievers in Berlin and Paris, whether social democrats, conservatives or Gaullists. The respective perform- ances of the French and German regulatory and financial systems during the 2008–9 recession exposed British pretension, with speedier recovery from recession (in France) and relative fiscal soundness (in Germany). Ironically, the Lisbon Treaty (2000) pushed the EU in the 'British' direction of freer trade, capital and labour movement. But such was the quality of European debate in the UK, the only Lisbon issue was alleged cuts in UK sover- eignty; the government did nothing to raise the tone. The result was years of sterile agitation about a UK referendum.

Under Labour the UK got on with completing the single market, but unlike the Tories before them, they were willing to accept the employee and social rights the EU wanted to run alongside greater freedom for trade and capital investment. When it came to people, Labour were mixed up. There was no possibility the UK would join the Schengen countries and abandon passports and border controls. But Polish workers were free to come to the UK almost as soon as Poland joined the EU. Bulgarian and Romanian workers were different, though minis- ters never quite admitted why: the UK did not give them access when their countries joined in January 2007. The UK secured little or no movement on the Common Agricultural Policy despite having given up some of the UK rebate in exchange. Ironically, many thousands of the farmers and countryside adherents who marched with the foxhunters in the Countryside Alliance – also often noisily anti-European – depended on flows of cash from the CAP. Outcry at the administrative failings of the Rural Payments Agency proved just how much the 'British countryside' was made in Brussels. After twelve years, the EU was more to UK liking, policy analysts concluded – but you would be forgiven for mis- taking that amid the prevalent scepticism.

Britain's position crystallized when, eventually, the Lisbon Treaty entered into force in 2009 and member states chose a president of Europe. On the one hand the fact that Blair stood for the post and the EU took him seriously exposed the weakness of the field. On the other hand, the summary fashion in which the

French and Germans made a final decision, British diplomats' noses pressed against the glass, showed how marginal the UK had become. Blair's prospective presidency of Europe was richly ironic. In retrospect, it was unclear whether he had a joined-up view of the EU or of the UK's membership. His 1997 column in *The Sun* – 'no surrender' over sterling – was either an object lesson in Campbell-inspired cynicism or showed his belief in the primacy of nation states (which, if so, made his globalization rhetoric hard to follow). In 2000 in Ghent he said hesitation over Europe had been the UK's 'greatest miscalculation' since 1945. But in the same year, in an oration in Warsaw, he praised a Europe of nations, not so different in tone from Thatcher in Bruges in 1988. What then of collaborating on defence – something Kosovo had shown to be necessary – and why complain about lack of cooperation by the Jospin government over asylum seekers massing at the Calais railhead? The vast 24-country zone created in 2007 to allow free movement across borders excluded the UK. Officials would go on herding Brits through the non-Schengen doors at airports in Madrid, Florence and Tallinn. Here was a prime minister prepared to go to war thousands of miles away for the sake of fundamental rights, in Sierra Leone, in Iraq, who folded when the CBI attacked the European constitution created by the Lisbon Treaty for trying to lodge in the UK social and employment rights understood across the rest of Europe to be fundamental.

Despite Iraq and Afghanistan, Labour changed little, not the UK's global position nor the public's views of the world. Iraq, in retrospect, was as much about the persisting belief that the UK remained a world player, a belief unquestioned by Labour or the public. Blair's missionary zeal may paradoxically have saved the UK from facing the facts of its financial and defence capacity or the possibilities of life decoupled from the US.

Strain showing in the defence budget, under Labour the UK continued to punch above its weight as shown on the GDP scales. But the vigils in Wootton Bassett were a sign that the old British military sangfroid was melting, even if, compared with elsewhere, people were still more prepared to accept governments sending forces to fight and die in far-off lands. Foreign affairs remained a field of dreams: both Blair and Brown bestrode the stage as if they, and the UK, had not given up the role of world arbiters. Brown, even more than Blair, enjoyed international regard disproportionate to his domestic reputation. Presidents and prime ministers still flocked to London for summits and confabs as if Downing Street mattered. And it did. Blair at Gleneagles then Brown through the G20 reaped credit for pushing the aid agenda; Brown arguing for a tax on financial transactions was successfully playing world politics.

But despite a commendable record on aid, the UK did not adopt an 'ethical' line of any consistency; from arms sales came too many jobs. In sum, Labour's tenure shows in absences. Over Europe: because it failed to make the case for engagement, the UK, or at least England, became noticeably more Eurosceptic. And over Afghanistan: few had a clear idea what UK forces were doing and even fewer understood the connection between involvement there and Labour's policies and purposes as the UK government.

The reservists' verdict

The next day the lieutenant and the lance corporal would be on their way to Afghanistan. Or at least they would in all probability be sitting on their kit bags at RAF Brize Norton waiting for the next empty flight, because the military doesn't do scheduled. Brize Norton became a morbid place, only seen on television when planes unloaded coffins draped with the union flag. People started to make the association when they saw young men in uniform.

'It can be embarrassing,' said Lieutenant Pete Quentin. He had been travelling to Warwick a couple of days previously to say goodbye to his parents. Showing his travel warrant for an armed forces discount at the station ticket kiosk, the clerk asked if he was going to Afghanistan. When he said he was, she swivelled open the window and grabbed his hand. 'She said, "I'm a preacher and I'm going to pray for you." She held tightly for half a minute, muttering. That sort of thing can be intimidating.'

He had an odd experience another day, walking down Victoria Street in London carrying his camouflage sack, passing a demonstration outside the Department of Business. Protesters were shouting and waving placards against the arms industry in front of a cardboard tank. 'I tried not to be noticed but they rushed up to me, pointing at the sack, one of them saying, "My God, you're in the army, aren't you?" I thought there was going to be a big argument, but they gave me some flyers and asked if I was going to Afghanistan. When I said I was they were really friendly, gave me some flowers off their tank and said, "Hope you're OK."'

The sight of young men and women setting off to risk their lives while the rest of us sit at home and debate the rights and wrongs is chastening. Even more so when the soldiers are Territorial Army volunteers, who, unlike the regulars, could just say no when their weekend soldiering games in the Brecon Beacons suddenly turn uncomfortably serious and they are ordered to fight in a real conflict. Half the TA's 36,000 strength went to war in the eight years from 2002.

This strand of the UK's military forces reaches deep into local communities. Lt Quentin, based in the Camberwell TA, South London, was often out recruiting in Brixton and Peckham or manning a stall on the Walworth Road. Turnover is high and the unit had to keep its own numbers up. 'Old ladies come up and chat about relatives they've had in the army. Young men are drawn to your uniform: it can be a problem when too many well-wishers pull you into the pub to offer you a drink.' It's not like the days of grizzled recruiting sergeants and the Queen's shilling. 'It would be dubious to hoodwink anyone about what it's like. For one thing, it's me that will be training the people I recruit, me that will be leading them and maybe me taking them off on operations in Afghanistan. We don't want the wrong ones.' What was he looking for? 'Enthusiasm, that's all. Not intelligence, not fitness.'

But they will get fit. The benchmarks are forty push-ups in two minutes and fifty sit-ups in two minutes; combat fitness specifies eight miles in two hours carrying twenty-five kilos. They need to patrol ten miles a day wearing body armour (which 'feels like wearing two paving stones') and water and ammunition. Training includes all night non-stop war-gaming with no sleep. 'Once you've done it, then you don't worry about losing sleep again. You know you can.' The TA paid £35 a day, £55 for officers. For the real thing, a year out of their day job to go on a tour of duty, the army met their regular earnings, and by law their job must be held open for them, like maternity leave. One man heading for Afghanistan was a Barclays investment banker, and the army replaced his £80,000 a year, making him an expensive soldier.

Lt Quentin, twenty-seven, was ready to go in his keenly pressed desert uniform and desert boots. An intense and serious man, his South African parents came to the UK in the 1970s and his father ran a factory in the Midlands making army rations – 5000 calories every twenty-four hours. 'I don't tell anyone that when they are cursing about eating the same thing over and over on exercises.' He joined the regular army at eighteen straight from school in Solihull. His two brothers joined up too, both now out, one a lawyer, one a boarding-school teacher. After six-week officer training at Sandhurst, he was sent to Germany. On a fateful day. While he was in the air, the planes smashed into the twin towers. 'Until then it was Bosnia or Ireland. But on that first day, our company commander jumped on a Warrior and had his *Henry V*, Tim Collins moment. "This is war," he said, "everything will change from now on," and we asked ourselves how the hell America would react. We knew we would be there with them.' But not him, as it happened.

Instead, after eighteen months, the army persuaded him to go to university, and he went to Girton College, Cambridge to study social and political sciences. The army would have paid, but he wanted to keep his options open. He was, he says, different – with that military habit of keeping everything neat, folded and ship-shape. He did rugby, boxing and student politics, as college president. When he graduated he nearly went back to the regiment – but politics seized him instead and he swerved off in another direction: he went to work in the House of Commons for Conservative shadow minister Caroline Spelman, then took a job at the think-tank Civitas.

So what did the army get out of this? He retained his commission, technically still a military man. His presence in the university was a positive, they reckoned, influencing other students. And he chose to give something back by joining the London Irish Rifles TA in 2007, retraining on a team commanders' course: now he's in charge of twenty-four Territorials. London Irish are South London and definitely not posh, he says. Poshest TA of all is the Honourable Artillery Company, founded by Henry VIII, inhabiting a magnificent ancient building, recruiting public-school boys from the City.

The army remains tightly structured by class. Fresh out of his (not very posh) private school, Second Lieutenant Quentin found himself commanding seasoned staff sergeants. Although they knew everything and he knew nothing, they called him sir. In Labour's tussles with the armed forces, class was spoken: the top brass still had those *Brief Encounter* accents unheard elsewhere in public life these days. In their complaints and political manoeuvring, Lord Guthrie of Craigiebank and former chiefs of the defence staff gave off a whiff of class disdain. Instinctive Tories, perhaps, they remained part of an English inner establishment that could never shake off the old conviction that Labour could never be entirely legitimate as a government.

Lance Corporal George Anderson, also setting off the next day, addressed the lieutenant as Mr Quentin or sir, although he was older and earned more, working for estate agents Kinleigh, Folkard and Hayward, and had been to a tonier public school, Ampleforth. He was also more experienced, having completed a six-month tour in Iraq in 2004. He was a lowly NCO because he did not want the extra work and responsibility.

Why the TA, putting life and limb at risk a second time? Afghanistan and Iraq are far away; Helmand and Basra will join other dusty places on war memorials: who remembers Chillianwallah now? 'I do think there is some altruism. I do believe in the long-term future of Afghanistan, but it's only part of the reason. You join because you want to go out on operations. Look, I went to Iraq and on my first day in Basra I was up in top cover and I could have had my head shot off, but I thought brilliant, this is brilliant. It cuts out the rubbish in your life. There I'd been in my office, listening to someone argue over £5000 when they were buying a £2 million property in Notting Hill, and you think what's the point? This makes you feel alive.' He had been in combat twelve times, saw three soldiers blown up, all surviving, one without an eye, was mortared at Basra airport and laughed as he recollected newly arrived journalists jumping out of their skins. Both men watch the news avidly every day, wondering if the latest soldier death is someone they know.

The lieutenant hoped to leave Afghanistan better for its people. 'The other day I was at the stall in Peckham and this man comes out of a shop and offers me any fruit I wanted, pulling me into his shop to give me things. He'd come over from Afghanistan a few years ago and he's just grateful for all we're doing for his country.' Iraq was quite different. Lance Corporal Anderson admitted: 'I wouldn't wear uniform in the street in London in those days. Wherever you went people argued – Bush and Blair lied, it's an illegal war. Personally, I think removing Saddam was no bad thing, but people would just fall silent if you said where you'd been.

'But now it's Afghanistan, people get emotional with you, and wish you luck.' He was headed for Mazar i Sharif, the lieutenant for Kandahar, where attacks are frequent. They have spent the last six months training full time, including a week learning basic phrases in Dari and Pashtun. When they arrive, they would train for two weeks at Camp Bastion in Helmand, where they know they will be mocked by the regulars. Then they head off to train and mentor Afghan NCOs.

Quentin said his family was apprehensive. 'There will be good communications out there and I can talk to them on Skype.' He paused and added, 'I can't alleviate my mother's fear, but she didn't say "Don't go." We had emotional farewells. It's a time to say things you might not ever say otherwise, things you should say, but you never quite get round to.'

Home and Abroad

By 2010, the army was full up. Was it the attraction of fighting a real war, or the effect of recession and unemployment? Either way, our small professional army feels far removed from ordinary life. Soldiers often come from army families, a separate cadre whose discipline and regimental loyalties are incomprehensible to their peers. Labour put them to work in conflicts far removed from the German garrisons and Ulster patrolling that had been the army's staples since the Falklands war. What was the point of maintaining a military machine, with its TA appendix, if it did not rumble into action? By and large, the criticism that came the government's way was functional. The chattering classes disputed the morality and geopolitical rationale of Iraq. The military class and its dependents were more concerned about planning and preparedness, a lack of armoured vehicles or helicopters.

Conclusion

Labour bequeathed a public realm that shone. They renovated, restocked and rebuilt schools, hospitals and clinics, arts and sports venues, parks and museums. J.K. Galbraith once talked about private affluence and public squalor; now there was plenty of the former, despite the recession, but much less of the latter. Public spaces no longer felt second-best or the shabby poor relations of commerce. Sober academics talked of a renaissance of England's northern cities, and you could say the same of Glasgow and Belfast. For years to come, civic buildings will stand as monuments to the Labour era.

They had to spring-clean the dilapidated state inherited from the Tories in 1997. At Wright Robinson School in Gorton and Lea Valley High School in Enfield we saw how proud modern surroundings had strengthened the determination of teachers and students alike. But school and hospital buildings were no guarantee of learning or healing. A bigger test is what happened in the lives and minds of citizens. Here, Labour's impact is much less obvious. The social state we are in now is not much different from 1997. The broad judgement has to be that not enough altered in the fabric of our country, given Labour's commitments on equality and fairness. The country remains strongly defined by class, regional disparity, inequality, and individual and business under-achievement.

As for the way we think and speak, Labour failed to challenge the predominant public discourse, which was negative and mean-spirited. Yet they did nudge the political centre of gravity leftwards – on public services, on income distribution and even on poverty. Labour set the tone adopted by the coalition government, at least initially. The Tories only returned to power – and then to share it with the Liberal Democrats – once they had learned to ape Labour on inequality and social justice, and to disguise their ideological wish to shrink the state.

The good Labour did and the bad they avoided make an impressive list. Public services measurably improved. Children got a better start in life; 600,000 fewer were living in poverty and a million pensioners enjoyed more comfortable times. Our interviewees lined up to give praise: for a sparkling new further education college, for Sure Start, community policing, community projects in Birmingham, advisers for young job-seekers or the resurrection of Chase Farm Hospital. Patients became more satisfied with their NHS treatment and waiting lists vanished. Most parents were pleased with their children's schools. In their very different ways, PC Dawn Harrison felt she was making a difference to children's lives in Gorton, and John Hogg to his students in Middlesbrough. Britain remained profoundly unequal, but the minimum wage and childcare helped millions of families do better, as many more single mothers went out to work. Without Labour's measures, inequality would have worsened.

You cannot, however, shake off an enervating sense of disappointment. This was a government without much sense of direction after 2001. On the biggest issues, notably climate change, its record is paltry. Labour failed on housing – failed to reset a badly functioning market or secure the building of enough new dwellings. They failed in their handling of the economy. This was a government that did not know enough: when company directors threatened to migrate if their tax was raised, ministers did not know to call their bluff; when bankers proclaimed the end of the world if investment and retail banking were split, ministers deferred.

The UK economy had long been over-dependent on finance.

Conclusion

But Labour's adulation of the City was extraordinary, especially in the light of its own history. Even after the crash in 2008, given a chance to start anew, ministers could not break their habit of bowing to City demands. Other countries took action; opinion polls showed that the British wanted a tougher response; yet Labour refused to countenance a tax on financial transactions or measures to shrink the banks to a safer size. Ministers gave no voice to public outrage at the immediate resurrection of the bonus culture. After the crash Labour's only policy was more of the same.

Brown had said: don't ask awkward questions about the City, and finance would pay enough tax to allow social spending to grow. Yet the tax proceeds were not enough; Brown's spending rushed ahead of revenues. Income tax needed to rise: it was the fairest way to pay for school and hospital improvements. That fiscal cowardice left a structural deficit that damaged Labour's reputation for sound economic management.

Polls naturally showed people more eager for services than for increased tax. Here should have been the stuff of political argument. Yet before the recession Labour never made the case, apart from raising National Insurance once. Nor did they even consider the property taxes needed to control the housing bubble. Nor higher inheritance tax to pay for social care.

In 2010 Labour were replaced by Old Etonians and Old Westminsters, many of them very well off. So much for changing Britain. No plates had shifted in the strata of Britain's social geology. Labour did not try to break the hold of the few on power, money and status. Ministers never said that the ill health, obesity, drunkenness, truancy, school failure, teenage motherhood and childhood unhappiness lumped together by the Tories as 'Broken Britain' were in fact the symptoms of Britain's abiding inequality.

Income and wealth remain less fairly shared in Britain than in other developed countries. Rates of social mobility are low. Labour's failure is all the greater because – to their credit – they commissioned the studies and reports that exposed the extent of social injustice. As the incomes of the top decile soared, ministers averted their gaze. Labour reluctantly raised the top rate of income tax to a modest 50 per cent, but only a month before leaving office, and then only on incomes over £150,000. Boardroom and City pay expanded unchecked despite the widespread revulsion expressed in polls and even in the right-wing media. The people were well ahead of their inert government.

Labour's latter years were tainted by disgust at parliament, MPs and parties. Opportunities to reform politics were missed before and after the expenses scandal. Labour's constitutional reforms lacked a proper theme. They failed to change how the Commons was elected despite conceding the case for proportional voting in Scotland, Wales, Northern Ireland and even London itself. Party funding was left in the pockets of multi-millionaire donors. The role and composition of the Lords was shelved.

Labour lacked a clear idea about the size and shape of the state. Government had to be powerful if it were to tax, spend and grapple with inequality. But that did not necessarily mean the state had to be repressive or crimp people's sense of freedom. Labour liberalism had its moments with freedom of information and, above all, the 1998 Human Rights Act. But their liberalism ebbed and flowed. Their working-class voters were not civil libertarians and New Labour feared being thought soft. It was no surprise, then, that Labour should emphasize control, on issues such as identity cards, detention, CCTV and imprisonment. The eruption of Islamist terrorism after 9/11 saw Labour's instincts play out in repeated legislation to imprison without trial. All governments struggle to balance freedom and security. A reactionary government would have abrogated international conventions and deported terrorist suspects; Labour came nowhere near this. Many ordinary people, Donna Charmaine Henry on the Clapham Park Estate one of them, believed CCTV improved their lives, and there was strong demand in crime-prone areas for more, not fewer, cameras. The charge against Labour is that their tough state approach was inconsistent. When it came to boardrooms and tax, the state crumpled. Welfare cheats were hounded, while massive avoidance in tax havens went unchecked. Anti-social behaviour on the streets was penalized while grand larceny in the City was ignored.

Labour were ambivalent about migration. Their invitation to new European entrants to come to the UK stemmed from Brown's infatuation with neoliberalism, allowing him to boast of low inflation from low wages. Labour made no attempt to explain or justify the new arrivals or target compensatory spending on the areas and people who were most affected. A complementary house-building policy might have mitigated the local impact of immigration; there was none. Instead, unwilled and unexplained, migration may have damaged middle and lower earners; a large and willing new workforce kept wages unnaturally low in boom years when they should have risen at the bottom as they did at the top.

Labour's intervention in Iraq destroyed their reputation and broke their spirit. Yet if you leave out the particulars of this disastrous episode – Blair's character, the pusillanimity of Labour MPs, the dodgy dossier and the neoconservative regime in power in Washington – the Iraq war was British foreign policy business as usual. Soldiers were deployed because British policy was aimlessly committed to 'punching above our weight', as if that were a goal in itself. A desire for influence in the US and a continuing presence as a permanent member of the UN Security Council led to the Iraq war and over-commitment in Afghanistan. Labour were never likely to mount a root-and-branch review of the UK in the world; what is dismaying is how little they had to say – the Trident decision a reflex rather than the result of a process of thought. On Europe Labour barely bothered, during years when leadership in Brussels and the national capitals was in short supply.

Instead of a convincing story about Britain in the twenty-first century, we got Cool Britannia. But Labour's uncertainty about who we were and who we should be came from a basic and growing problem: how can governments lead when so many people are disaffected and apathetic? Many will not or cannot engage enough to understand even a minimum about public services or foreign policy, how the system runs and how it is paid for.

Conclusion

People persisted in believing untruths – such as that four out of ten people in Britain were foreign-born. Or that crime was rising when it was falling, and police numbers were falling when they were at a historic high. The gap between perception and policy was one of Labour's biggest problems, which they half realized but could not solve. Perhaps it is irresolvable.

Labour were desperate not to get caught out by opinion. Like teenagers transfixed by a video game, they tracked every poll and focus group. Labour could not make up their mind whether to represent the people or to inspire and lead them. After defeat in 1992, Labour's leaders had convinced themselves that the electorate was essentially conservative-minded. The electoral system made this partly true: winning the House of Commons could depend on as few as 200,000 unattached voters in marginal seats. Labour's in-house pollster, Philip Gould, kept reporting that these voters thought like *Daily Mail* readers. We talked to the Hatt family because they represented this line of thought; you could hear it echoing in the views of Andy Roberts, the Rotherham butcher, too. The Hatts were never persuadable; they were life-long working-class Tory voters. Labour could never satisfy them, however restrictive they might have been on immigration, how-ever many additional police officers they paid for. Labour should have reached out instead out to the many others who, across class and across the regions and countries of the UK, would sup-port progressive government. The other response ought to have been electoral reform, removing the unfair weight of this hand-ful of unrepresentative super-voters.

Labour convinced themselves that progressive policies could only be pursued by stealth and must be offset by populist Tory gestures on choice or 'reform'. In their second term the camou-flage became the purpose. Blair's political talents were spent on a 'choice' agenda pegged to a political calculation that was both wrong and unnecessary.

Labour forgot an old truth. People will rally round a battle flag; parties need a rousing cry. At the 2010 election the public sensed the sham manifestos on offer. Instead of a debate on tax versus spending cuts as the way to lower the deficit, they argued over trifling sums to be cut from 'bureaucracy'. None had plans to tackle inequality. None had much to say about the UK's role in the world. The parties barked out promises of tax cuts here and small bribes there, like stallholders in a bazaar – 'Your Family Better Off'.

Treated like minors, offered no hard choices, the electorate often responded to pollsters with infantile contradictions: they wanted lower taxes and better services, safer roads but fewer speed cameras, cheap food but kindness to farm animals, less obesity but less nanny state, children protected but free to live the *Boy's Own* tree-climbing risky adventures of yore. They wished politicians would stop bickering and yet they wished parties were not all the same.

Writers on government are often drawn to Lorenzetti's allegorical frescoes on the walls of the municipal palace in Siena: on one side a benign leader of a happy and prosperous land, on the other a country in wrack and ruin. Government is rarely a question of such black-and-white clarity, but if forced to choose, then the Labour years belong on the whole to the good government of that painting. Most Labour public policy was dedicated to improving the lives and lot of citizens. The Iraq war broke faith with those citizens, but it was not the defining event of Labour's years.

The charge is that they wasted the extraordinary opportunity of ten years of economic prosperity and secure parliamentary majorities under a leader of great political talent, facing only weak opposition. If ever there was a moment for boldness, courage and imagination it was between 1997 and the onset of the recession. Even after the crash, Labour had remarkable chances to redefine the national purpose and, despite more straitened circumstances, raise social ambitions and remedy inequality. Instead government ducked and dived, fearing the people instead of leading them. We remain perplexed at why a clever and well-intentioned group of men and women achieved so much less than they might have done. Why were their ambitions so limited? Labour governments are destined to disappoint their followers because the centre left sets the bar higher and hopes are inflated. Sometimes Blair did

Conclusion

express the full weight of his party's aspiration, above all with that exceptional promise to abolish child poverty. It was realizable, but only with a gigantic political effort, which Labour never had the nerve to muster. That is why a score for Labour's performance of, say, six out of ten is not good enough. Look at the record and it is hard to suppress a rising sense of indignation: 'Why not much, much more?'

Index

Index

Index

Index

Index

Index

Index

Index

Index

Index